Advance Praise for *The Real Environmentalists*

"*The Real Environmentalists* is a powerful reminder that true change comes from entrepreneurs who solve problems, not from speeches or slogans. Jim Beach highlights real-world heroes building companies that clean up oceans, recycle resources, and create sustainable industries. This book is proof that capitalism, done right, can save the planet."
- *Adam Coffey - CEO, Author and Advisor to the Middle Market*

"I loved *The Real Environmentalists*. Jim Beach really nails the hypocrisy of people who spend all their time blathering about how much they care about the environment, while flying private among their many massive estates - what he calls performative environmentalism. He also talks about the entrepreneurs who are really making a difference in the environment, working to solve problems such as ship breaking and recycling, battery innovation, and sustainable packaging. It's a fascinating, informative, fun read."
- *Margot Machol Bisnow – Founder of Raising an Entrepreneur*

"I first connected with Jim Beach as a guest on his fantastic School for Startups Radio show. His interview style was sharp, driven by a genuine desire to help entrepreneurs succeed. He brings that same practical, no-nonsense approach to *The Real Environmentalists*. This isn't another doomsday manifesto; it's a celebration of the unsung heroes who are fixing the planet, one brilliant business at a time. A powerful and inspiring read!"
- *Raghav Gupta – Founder and CEO of Posha, Building Robot Chefs*

"In this provocative (and sometimes intentionally annoying) book, Jim Beach argues against 'performative environmentalism' in favor of a serious commitment to saving our endangered planet, for our children and grandchildren. He highlights the 'gritty,' hands-on work of a group of 'real environmentalist' entrepreneurs – scientists and businesspeople who are leveraging the inherent resources of capitalism to make products or offer services that deliver concrete, positive environmental change. I hope Beach inspires others to engage their creativity to develop more pragmatic, real-world solutions to pressing environmental problems."
- *Philip A. Glotzbach, Ph. D, President Emeritus of Skidmore College, and author of 'Embrace Your Freedom: Winning Strategies to Succeed in College and in Life.'*

"Meet the Real Environmentalists, a new perspective on sustainability that highlights entrepreneurs taking on the planet's toughest challenges directly. These stories demonstrate how vision, courage, and capitalism can drive genuine change. With determination, innovation, and fearless execution, Jim Beach shines a light on the visionaries redefining what it means to be an environmentalist. This is a powerful call to action—and a hopeful guide for anyone who thinks business can help save the world."
- *Scott "Intake" Kartvedt – Former Blue Angel Pilot and Author/Keynote Speaker*

"Ever since I met Jim Beach as a guest on his School for Startups Radio show, I have been impressed by his passion for genuine sustainability and smart business practices. It makes perfect sense that Jim would blend these concepts together with his engaging new book, *The Real Environmentalists*. His straight-shooting, empathetic-yet-practical approach to finding and embracing the positive aspects of doing good work to make the planet a better place is brought home by the way he expertly shines the spotlight on the true heroes of today… the real environmentalists. A great and inspirational read for any business leader, aspiring entrepreneur, or people who want to make the world a better place."
- **John Shegerian, CEO/Chairman, ERI & Host,** *The Impact Podcast with John Shegerian*

"*The Real Environmentalists* is a refreshing and much-needed perspective on sustainability. Jim Beach highlights entrepreneurs who are actually solving problems, not just talking about them. As a hospitality entrepreneur, I've seen firsthand how small, intentional choices, like sourcing from local farmers and using biodegradable straws to help protect sea life can make a meaningful impact. This book proves that capitalism and environmentalism are not enemies, but powerful partners in shaping a cleaner, smarter future."
- *Brian Parenteau – Miami Restaurateur*

"Jim does a wonderful job of differentiating the posers, from the true innovators in the climate crisis we face. The book serves as an inspiration."
- *Jeremy Cotter - CEO of YouRise and Co-Founder of AllTrails*

The Real Environmentalists:
How Wayne Elliott and Other Capitalists Will Save the World

By Jim Beach

Atlanta   Manila   Sofia

Copyright © 2025 by Jim Beach and Wayne Elliott. All rights reserved. Printed in the United States of America. Except as permitted under the United States Copyright Act of 1976, no part of this publication may be reproduced or distributed in any form or by any means, or stored in a database or retrieval system, without the prior written permission of the publisher.

ISBN (Paperback): 979-8-2187-4827-2
Kindle eBook ASIN: B0FHR436BQ

Library of Congress Cataloging – in - Publication Data

Names: Beach, Jim, author.
Titles: The Real Environmentalists: How Wayne Elliott and Other Capitalists Will Save the World
Description: Atlanta, Startup Publishers, [2025] Includes references and index.
Identifiers: ISBN, ASIN
Subjects: Environment, Entrepreneurship
Classification: GE170 .B43 2025; HD62.5 .B43 2025

Startup Publishers' books are available at special quantity discounts to use as premiums and sales promotions or for use in corporate training programs. To contact a representative, please visit the Contact Page at www.StartupPublishers.com.

If you are looking for a publisher, please contact us via the site.

Dedicated to **William R. Beach V and Tatum Beach**

Table of Contents

Foreword by Shawn D. Nelson, CEO of Lovesac (Nasdaq: Love)	viii
Acknowledgments	ix
Introduction	x
Chapter 1 – The Performance of Environmentalists	1
Top Ten Environmental Hypocrites - #10 Nancy Pelosi	17
Rules for Thee not Me	
Chapter 2 – Milk Shakes	20
Top Ten Environmental Hypocrites - #9 Richard Branson	24
Unfulfilled Promises	
Chapter 3 – What Happens to Old Ships?	27
Top Ten Environmental Hypocrites - #8 AOC	37
Private Jets	
Chapter 4 – First ISO- Certified	42
Top Ten Environmental Hypocrites - #7 Jeff Bezos	55
Yacht Hypocrisy	
Chapter 5 – Battery Recycling	58
Top Ten Environmental Hypocrites - #6 Bill Gates	73
Carbon Offsets	
Chapter 6 – Strauss: A Life Changing Discovery	81
Top Ten Environmental Hypocrites - #5 Harry & Meghan	97
Coffee stirrer and Performing Bees	
Chapter 7 – Cleaning the Mess	100
Top Ten Environmental Hypocrites - #4 Barack Obama	116
Oceans Rising	
Chapter 8 – Better Products for Tomorrow	119
Top Ten Environmental Hypocrites - #3 Elon Musk	142
Space Mess	
Chapter 9 – Academic Scandals	147
Top Ten Environmental Hypocrites - #2 Al Gore	166
Al Jazeera the Money	

Chapter 10 – Conclusion 171
    Top Ten Environmental Hypocrites - #1 Leonardo DiCaprio 176
    U.N. Performances

Appendix 1 – The Methodology Behind the Celebrity Hypocrites 179

Appendix 2 – List of For-profit Environment Businesses 181

Appendix 3 – Strauss Naturals 184

Foreword

by Shawn David Nelson, CEO of Lovesac (Nasdaq: Love)

When I launched Lovesac, I wasn't trying to save the planet. I was just trying to make the most comfortable thing you could sit on. Period.

But growth has a way of forcing you to pay attention.

The more we scaled, the more obvious it became that: we were part of an industry built on waste. Fast furniture. Cheap materials. Planned obsolescence baked right in. And that realization? It changed everything.

We made a hard left. We designed furniture that could evolve instead of expiring. Modular. Washable. Built to last decades, not months. It's not just "sustainability." It's about products that can actually sustain. We now make all our upholstery fabric from 100% recycled plastic bottles. We began using fabric made from recycled plastic bottles (over 400 million so far). But that's just scratching the surface.

That's why this book matters.

The Real Environmentalist isn't a tribute to idealists shouting from the sidelines. It's about those of us in the game, builders, entrepreneurs, operators, trying to solve giant, gnarly problems from within the machine.

It's about people like Wayne Elliott, cleaning up global shipping one steel hull at a time. People who aren't waiting for permission. People who believe, like I do, that capitalism isn't the enemy, it's one of the most powerful tools we've got.

You'll read stories in this book that will challenge what you think an environmentalist looks like. You won't find sainthood here. You'll find grit. Vision. Guts. Execution.

To me, that's the new face of sustainability. Not some side initiative or corporate veneer, but a strategic advantage. A reason to build better things and do it with purpose.

If you're picking up this book, it's probably because you care. About the planet. About people. About building something that actually matters.

Welcome. You're in the right place.

- Shawn David Nelson

Acknowledgements

The author would like to acknowledge several people that have made this book possible.

At Strauss Naturals, Wayne Elliott and Paola Ludwig are tremendously helpful. This book would not have been possible without their support and assistance. I learned about life from Wayne Elliott. I learned how my body really works, too. Most importantly, my body now works better because of the great products from Strauss Naturals at https://straussnaturals.com/

From the writer's desk, I must acknowledge and profusely thank Frank Vincent Olis and Ivan Dikov. Without their help and support with research, writing, and mental support, this book would still be a dream.

At home, I would like to thank my family and friends. Thanks Team Beach!

I would like to thank the amazing entrepreneurs included in the book; Wayne Elliott, Larry Wyman, Kevin Gast, Gator Halpern and Stephen Mayfield. These heroes are saving the world!

And finally, thank you for buying and reading this book! Please write a nice 5-star review and buy your friend a copy or two.

Thank you all.

Introduction

If you don't care about the history of this book, and just want to read the good stuff, you can skip this introduction.

Allow me to introduce myself and to provide you with the history of this book. And some disclaimers. My name is Jim Beach and I have a podcast/radio show, five days a week. Starting in 2012, I have done some 2600 radio shows and won the Small Business Administration Media Award awhile back. The show is on some 100 AmFm radio stations around the country, in some format (there is a long 54-minute show and a 90-second vignette show). The show is called School for Startups Radio, check it out.

Allow me to digress. I do that a lot, but this story is worth it. An Atlanta Journal Constitution newspaper reporter did an article about an entrepreneurship class I was teaching at Georgia State University. He liked my thesis and said it should be a book. We decided to write that book and submitted it to McGraw-Hill publishers, a great name in publishing, through a friend of the reporter. They liked it and offered a contract. We, of course, accepted. They did not like our preferred name and suggested that we change it to School for Startups.

Almost simultaneously, I received a cease-and-desist letter from the lawyers representing Entrepreneur Magazine. Our preferred name was The Entrepreneur School, and we were already building a website to promote it. Amazingly, Entrepreneur Magazine owns the trademark on the 400-year-old word entrepreneur! My lawyer informed me that Entrepreneur Magazine had a long and successful history of defending their trademark and that we were sure losers. So, I gladly accepted McGraw-Hill's recommendation, and we became School for Startups. The book sold very well and has some 130 five-star reviews on Amazon.

Isn't it crazy that a magazine supposedly devoted to helping people build businesses is suing people for using that word! A real, old word that was around long before them! If you search for "trademark enforcement entrepreneur magazine," there are several articles and stories. My favorite talks about the incredible irony of the whole thing.

Anyway, digression is over. For the show I interviewed a Canadian entrepreneur named Wayne Elliott. He was instrumental in three amazing Canadian businesses, and I was blown away by his career and commitment to the environment. He started and operated Canada's largest ship recycling yard, invested some $20 million of his own

money researching and perfecting alkaline battery recycling, and now owns and operates Canada's most successful natural health company. We became friends almost immediately and he soon agreed to be one of the sponsors for my radio show and podcast. When he was making his yearly drive from Toronto to southern Florida, more about that craziness later, he stopped in Atlanta, and we had a very nice meal at the OK Cafe.

I had pointed out several times that Wayne's life deserved a book. He acknowledged that he had been thinking about writing one himself for quite a while. One of the things we promote in this book is greater transparency, and to that end, we want to acknowledge this agreement.

As I started writing and thinking about the thesis, I realized that Wayne embodied a whole class of entrepreneurs, specifically environmental entrepreneurs, that are frequently excluded from discussions of the environmental ecosystem. When the media talks about the environment and the associated players, they are usually referring to the academics, the politicians, the scientists, and the "villains," known as the oil companies. As the media's preferred enviro-narrative ends with the destruction of our planet, the good news part of the story is frequently left out. In fact, there is great news! The missing player, the environmental entrepreneur, deserves inclusion in all media discussions and tremendous praise for their accomplishments.

I proposed to Wayne, and he graciously accepted that the book be about more than him, but should include other real environmentalists, the entrepreneurs that will save our planet. This book tells the story of Wayne and several amazing entrepreneurs like him that I believe will in fact save Earth. I believe that together they have a power that the academics, politicians and scientists lack. This is an incredibly optimistic story that needs to be told.

Chapter 1
The Performance of Environmentalists

I love the environment! The five heroes introduced in this book love the environment!

I love being outdoors with the sun beating down on my ever-growing forehead, the feeling that your skin is slightly burning and getting pink. I love short hikes with a kid or two, sharing stories of the past, talking about the future and making fun of each other. I love exploring a cave or waterfall, usually trying not to get wet but eventually falling or slipping in the cold water.

I have climbed Mount Fuji in Japan, gone scuba diving on the Great Barrier Reef, been skiing in the highest mountain in New Zealand, and gone sailing with the European Hobie Cat sailing champion in the Mediterranean Sea. When I was 18 years old, I sailed the north Atlantic Ocean aboard the *R/V Westward*, a 125-foot schooner, for a summer doing research on whales and fjords.

One of the greatest days of my life happened in Vermont. It was fall; the leaves were at the highest level of color with bright red and orange leaves mixed in with the last green ones. And it snowed. A light dusting, maybe half an inch, covered the ground and trees. I was hiking with two friends up the Snowbowl ski area outside a village called Middlebury. The closest commercial building, other than the ski lodge, was a beautiful country bed and breakfast. The inn[1] was used in the Bob Newhart TV show "Newhart." The show was famous for a trio of brothers, Larry, Darryl and Darryl.

About half-way up the Snowbowl ski mountain, there is a tiny lake, really a pond, called Lake Pleiad.[2] It is used to feed the snow blowers making artificial snow and is nestled into a small level area. During some of the hike, you can see the mountain, but most of the view is obscured by trees, now with the light dusting of snow. The trail rather abruptly ends at the pond so you cannot see the pond until you are seconds from it, the foliage is too dense. The geese were migrating that week and had landed in the pond to rest. Our noise, embarrassing now in retrospect, scared the flock and just as we burst into the opening at the shore, the entire flock took flight. Thousands of geese squawking, two thousands of wings

---

1 https://www.wayburyinn.com/
2 https://www.middleburysnowbowl.com/trail-map/

flapping, and the noise of their ascent and their honks. The power from the thunder of the wings pounded every inch of my body.

Now regretting the intrusion, we sat in a mostly covered spot and embraced the noise of the wind and falling snow. Soon, we were rewarded with the return of a goose, one sole flyer. It came over the pond, dove low, checked the pond out, and returned to the circling flock. Then, three geese came in for inspection and then returned to the group. Then five, then ten. Within a few minutes, the flock had landed back on the pond. We watched for another thirty minutes and left as quietly as we could. It was one of the most impactful moments of my life and one of the times I felt closest to nature and God. I love the environment!

Furthermore, I have children. I love them very much. I want them to have kids, and I want all of them to have a clean environment with safe water and air. I am even willing to give up some things to join in the fight to ensure that they have a safe environment to live in! Like straws! Yes, I will gladly play along and give up real straws! Straws aren't a masculine look anyway. I heard that billions of straws are floating in the Pacific Ocean, forming a trash ball the size of Texas! You can walk across it, and you can even see it from space!

Actually, the Great Pacific Garbage Patch does exist. At 620,000 square miles,[3] it is closer in size to Alaska's 656,424 square miles. (Texas is America's second largest state with 268,601 square miles.) 94% of the patch is microplastics, so you can't see it from space. In fact, you could sail through it and not notice it. *National Geographic* noted that, "of the 79,000 metric tons of plastic in the patch, most of it is abandoned fishing gear."[4] Interestingly, the greatest source of plastic waste is not the countries you would guess. The United States and Western European countries did not make the list. The three worst polluters are India with 9,275,777 tons/year, Nigeria with 3,532,479 tons/year and Indonesia with 3,352,229 tons/year.[5] We will discuss more about the plastic patch later.

Furthermore again, I believe in climate change. I believe it was changing before man existed and before man started burning fossil fuels. I believe that humans have had an impact on the environment and climate. I also believe that many activists, scientists and believers on both sides of the debate make crazy projections and announcements that ultimately hurt their cause. And, the heroes

---

3 https://en.wikipedia.org/wiki/Great_Pacific_garbage_patch
4 https://www.nationalgeographic.com/science/article/great-pacific-garbage-patch-plastics-environment
5 https://www.dailymail.co.uk/sciencetech/article-13811929/Top-10-countries-plastic-pollution-world.html The remaining top 10 are China, Pakistan, Bangladesh, Russia, Brazil, Thailand, and the Democratic Republic of the Congo.

in this book, the Real Environmentalists, believe in climate change, too. Why else, asks Simon Sinek[6], would they be doing the great things that they are?

Some readers of this book may already be upset because they know they have already spotted a fatal flaw, or several flaws, a huge contradiction in my thinking and writing! They think:

> *"If this little lake, the surrounding mountain and the migrating geese are so beautiful, why were some greedy businessmen allowed to build a commercial ski slope there? If you love this spot, shouldn't it remain unmolested and pristine? Wouldn't that be even prettier?*
>
> *And kids? More than one? How many? You need and deserve more than one?!"*

I certainly understand these arguments. These arguments have merit.

For inquiring minds, I have four children. I am more concerned that the World's population has or will soon fall below the replacement rate[7] than I am concerned about overpopulation and food shortages. A globally declining population will excite many environmentalists. "Man is the problem; man is ruining the Earth," they say. Maybe so, but a declining population is a big problem, too. Ask Japan or Russia[8]. But that is for another book.

The conflict studied in this book is the fact that while we love the environment, we love air conditioning and cars, too. I love the incredible technologies that entrepreneurs, scientists, and inventors have created! I am a sweaty guy, and I live in the South, so I love my air conditioning. I love the Boeing 747 plane that safely delivered me to Australia, Japan and Spain. I love driving an Audi Quattro along a winding mountain road.

I love the environment and so I love spending time there. That may mean riding a loud, gasoline consuming snowmobile through Yellowstone National Park. It does not bother me that I must take a loud, gasoline burning jet to get there. It does not bother me that I must take a loud, gasoline burning car or bus from the airport to my favorite hotel in West Yellowstone, the Three Bear Lodge. It does not bother me that a group of men cut down thousands of trees and built West Yellowstone and the Three Bear Lodge.[9] It does not bother me that the Three

---

6 https://www.youtube.com/watch?v=u4ZoJKF_VuA
7 https://www.healthdata.org/news-events/newsroom/news-releases/lancet-dramatic-declines-global-fertility-rates-set-transform
8 https://www.newsweek.com/map-shows-population-crisis-ageing-decline-countries-risk-1997539
9 https://threebearlodge.com/

Bear Lodge has heat that keeps me comfortable in the night. I remember one morning in the early 1980s when I awoke to Willard Scott on the Today show telling America that the coldest place in the country that morning was West Yellowstone, Montana, exactly where I was. But I was warm, thanks to the heater built into the Lodge. Was I wrong to enjoy the heat?

In the Cayman Islands, there is a tourist destination called Stingray City.[10] Local dive masters have trained hundreds of stingrays to hang out at one particular sandbar. The stingrays know that the easiest place to get fed and have an easy, protected life is to live at Stingray City. Every day, boatloads full of tourists travel to the sandbar to fear the stingrays. The dive masters provide basic education and eventually coax many of the tourists to touch and even kiss the stingrays. The sandbar is a mile or two from the closest shore, so there is no way to get there without a loud, gasoline burning boat or jet ski. I like going to Stingray City and have taken my family there several times. Is that wrong? And yes, all four kids kissed a stingray.

Do you still believe that I love the environment? Or have I crossed some line by exploiting these poor defenseless stingrays? Am I now part of the problem?

The island also offers an opportunity to swim with dolphins.[11] Of course, these dolphins are in captivity, living in large concrete tanks, just yards from the real ocean. They are safe from predators and have easy access to food and the best dolphin medical care available. (My father was a pathologist at the hospital closest to the local Six Flags. He was called in one night because one of the park's dolphins was sick. He knew dolphin nothing, but we got free tickets to the park for that year. The dolphin lived. No animals were harmed in the writing of this book.) Dolphin scientists tell us dolphins are very smart, maybe the smartest animal on Earth.[12] I bet the dolphins are smart enough that they wish they did not live in a concrete tank just 20 yards from the real ocean. Is the dolphin experience company wrong to operate this business?

Some people love to fish and hunt. Are they wrong? Is it different to hunt an animal for food versus mounting it on a wall? Can I hunt if I drive a Tesla? Does that balance out? Is a Tesla with a gun rack the greatest oxymoron of all time?

But I promise to do my part! Especially with the straws!

---

10 https://www.tripadvisor.com/Attraction_Review-g147365-d2198364-Reviews-Stingray_City-Grand_Cayman_Cayman_Islands.html
11 https://www.dolphindiscovery.com/grand-cayman/
12 https://www.americanoceans.org/facts/how-smart-are-dolphins/

Oh, and this is the MOST important consideration! Sorry for not bringing this up sooner, because it is so important. Which social media channel is best to post about my environmental super-awareness? Is Instagram or Tik Tok cooler for proving how many straws I never used?

Performative Environmentalism

We have stumbled upon Performative Environmentalism.

Performative Environmentalism refers to the conspicuous display of environmental concern without substantial or effective action to address real environmental issues. It involves symbolic gestures, such as public statements, social media posts, and participation in environmental events, which serve to prove your environmental consciousness.

People participating in Performative Environmentalism say things like;

> *"I drove a Tesla before it was cool. Now, 7 of my 11 cars are EV."*
>
> *"I am a better friend of the environment than you are!"*
>
> *"I buy enough carbon credits to offset my emissions and the emissions of my gardener, chef and maid."*
>
> *"My eco-footprint is decreasing 10% each year. My yacht captain put a new coating on the yacht that reduces its fuel use by 5%!"*
>
> *"I hire locals to plant a forest in South America to erase the eco-footprint of my private jet and super yacht."*
>
> *"Prince Harry, Leonardo DiCaprio and I are receiving awards at the next Environmental Summit. We are flying in using 3 separate private planes to get there! Al Gore is presenting the awards. He flew in on a private 747 provided by the Sultan of Qatar!"*

Very rarely does the media ask the question that seems obvious to most, "What did Prince Harry really do to receive an environmental award?" Did he spend 4 months cleaning debris off beaches in southern India? What example of genuine commitment to environmental stewardship did he exhibit?

Ooops, sorry, I was wrong. After writing the above paragraph, I stopped and did some DuckDuckGo research (better than Google, DDG does not track you!) and learned that Prince Harry really did make huge sacrifices! I apologize, my lord, I was wrong!

From *The Independent*,[13]

> *Prince Harry and Meghan Markle have been named as environmental "role models" for deciding to have no more than two children to reduce their impact on the planet.*
>
> *Population Matters, a UK-based charity that campaigns for a "sustainable human population" said it had chosen the couple to receive an award for their "enlightened" decision.*

From *BusinessInsider,*'[14]

> *Meghan Markle and Prince Harry win $695 award from environmental charity for limiting family to 2 children.*

From *SkyNews*,[15]

> *Prince Harry and Meghan Markle win award for saving the planet two kids at a time.*

Prince Harry went much further than I am willing to go to help the environment! I am willing to give up straws. He is willing to give up sex! I bet he is mad since I called him a lord and not a Duke.

In another act of performative caring, Swedish climate activist Greta Thunberg sailed on a yacht from Monaco to New York to set an example of how to live without emitting carbon. In reality, her trip will emit four times more emissions than flying would have because her crew is jetting back home afterward.[16] Her spokesperson acknowledged, "It would have been less greenhouse gas emissions if we had not made this departure." But the performance is more important than actually making the planet healthier, and so, on with the sailing trip.

---

13 https://www.independent.co.uk/life-style/royal-family/prince-harry-meghan-markle-children-b1881705.html
14 https://www.businessinsider.com/meghan-markle-prince-harry-environmental-award-two-kids-2021-7?op=1
15 https://www.skynews.com.au/world-news/prince-harry-and-meghan-markle-win-award-for-saving-the-planet-two-kids-at-a-time/news-story/37a693e63433b1a56788e96e040e33e5
16 https://www.forbes.com/sites/michaelshellenberger/2019/08/20/the-real-reason-they-behave-hypocritically-on-climate-change-is-because-they-want-to/

In our era of heightened environmental awareness and constant judging of others, individuals and organizations proclaim their dedication to preserving the planet.

Environmentalism has become a cultural and political force, influencing policies, businesses, and personal lifestyles. And it is so cool and looks really good in *People Magazine*.

Amidst this wave of eco-consciousness, a peculiar phenomenon emerged – the performance of environmentalism. Some individuals and entities advocate for environmental causes publicly but fail to translate their rhetoric into meaningful action while on their super yachts.

Performative Environmentalism manifests itself in many ways.

One way is Greenwashing. Greenwashing occurs when corporations and businesses embellish their environmental credentials to appeal to eco-conscious consumers. They may use misleading labels, vague sustainability claims, or token gestures, such as eco-friendly packaging, to mask their environmentally harmful practices.

Apple CEO Tim Cook X-ed (tweeted) in 2020:

> *"By 2030, Apple's entire business will be carbon neutral–from supply chain to the power you use in every device we make. The planet we share can't wait, and we want to be a ripple in the pond that creates a much larger change."*[17]

Will that happen? Probably not. But the statement lives on and will be quoted until they replace it with a new platitude. And most importantly, BUY A NEW iPHONE EVERY YEAR! Is there any hypocrisy claiming to be green while mining an estimated 30 chemical elements, like aluminum, copper, lithium, silver and gold? Researchers have "sounded the alarm bell over smartphones for contributing to the depletion of several already scarce elements."[18] Just make sure you buy a new one soon!

---

17 https://www.forbes.com/sites/forbesbusinesscouncil/2022/08/08/how-companies-can-avoid-greenwashing-and-make-a-real-difference-in-their-environmental-impact/#:~:text=Simply%20put%2C%20greenwashing%20is%20selling%20your%20brand%20as,or%20marketing%20themselves%20as%20%E2%80%9Cgreen%E2%80%9D%20when%20they%E2%80%99re%20not.

18 https://www.cnet.com/tech/mobile/the-metals-inside-your-iphone-are-more-precious-than-you-thought-heres-why/

The Earth Island Institute filed a lawsuit in June 2021 against Coca-Cola for false advertising, The company had been advertising itself as an eco-friendly and sustainable organization, even though it was the largest plastic polluter four years in a row.

DeBeers, the world's largest diamond producer, declared it will also be carbon neutral by 2030. Do we hold it against them that they pled guilty to failing to provide mercury monitoring data, threatening thousands?[19] How would the happy bride feel if she knew her average-sized engagement ring stone is the product of the removal and processing of 200 to 400 million times its volume of rock?

Volkswagen paid $35 billion in fines and settlements for lying about its cars' emissions. Toyota paid $180 million for lying about its cars' emissions. Asset management company DWS paid $25 million for lying about its environmental policies. Energy company Eni paid $6 million for claiming its biofuel was green. Walmart paid $5.5 million for lying about products made from bamboo. Goldman Sachs paid a $4 million fine for lying about its environmental policies. Keurig, your coffee company, paid a $2.2 million fine for lying about its recyclability.[20]

Performative Environmentalism manifests in another way called Slacktivism.

Social media is the breeding ground for Performative Environmentalism, where individuals participate in online activism without tangible contributions to environmental causes. Clicktivism, hashtag activism, and viral challenges often prioritize virtual engagement over real-world impact, fostering a culture of superficial activism. Slacktivism is a portmanteau of *slacker* and *activist* and is the practice of supporting a political or social cause by means such as social media or online petitions, characterized as involving very little effort or commitment.[21]

People participating in Slacktivism say things like;

---

19 https://www.cbc.ca/news/canada/sudbury/debeers-court-timmins-mercury-pollution-case-1.6091664#:~:text=De%20Beers%20Canada%20Inc.,Mine%20ceased%20operations%20in%202019.
20 https://earth911.com/how-and-buy/which-companies-have-paid-the-biggest-greenwashing-fines/
21 https://en.wikipedia.org/wiki/Slacktivism

> "I 'Like' everything the Sierra Club posts. Some of it I don't like, but I 'Like' it online because that is socially responsible."
>
> "I never read petitions, but if I see environment in the title, I sign it."
>
> "My Livestrong wristband shows how much I care!"
>
> "If I click 'Like,' somebody feeds a penguin!"
>
> "Share this post to help baby eagles fly!"

Perhaps the most visible example of slacktivism is the Boko Haram story. Boko Haram, an opposition terrorist group, kidnapped hundreds of schoolgirls in Nigeria. The hashtag #BringBackOurGirls began to trend globally on Twitter (also known stupidly as X). Within weeks, it had attracted 2.3 million retweets including one from Michelle Obama, holding a sign displaying the hashtag. The campaign was labeled slacktivism by some critics, particularly as the weeks and months passed with no progress being made in recovery of the kidnapped girls.

According to Mkeki Mutah, uncle of one of the kidnapped girls:

> *There is a saying: "Actions speak louder than words." Leaders from around the world came out and said they would assist to bring the girls back, but now we hear nothing. The question I wish to raise is: why? If they knew they would not do anything, they wouldn't have even made that promise at all. By just coming out to tell the world, I see that as a political game, which it shouldn't be so far as the girls are concerned.*[22]

Over 100 of the girls remain missing but the hashtag lives on.

The final way Performative Environmentalism manifests itself is Tokenism.

In the world of politics, token gestures towards environmentalism are common. Politicians may endorse symbolic environmental initiatives to appease constituents or gain favorable public perception, without genuine commitment to transformative policies or systemic change.

Australia is beefing up its carbon credit scheme and establishing a market to fund environmental restoration. These big policy changes seemed like colonial practices being imposed on First Nations Aborigine people and their country, yet again. Controversy prevailed. To assuage the upset, an Aboriginal art piece was

---

[22] https://web.archive.org/web/20160114033605/http://www.aljazeera.com/indepth/features/2014/10/abandonment-bring-back-our-girls-2014101494119446698.html

selected for the cover of a key policy document. The cover was the only expression of co-design and collaboration. It was the "eco-colonial elephant in the room."[23] Controversy continued and increased.

Performative environmentalism often detracts from substantive discussions on environmental challenges and solutions. Australian officials thought a document cover could change the conversation. The focus shifts from systemic issues, such as corporate pollution or government inaction, to superficial debates about individual lifestyle choices or symbolic gestures. Here in America, we argue about toilet flushes instead of the billions of gallons of water wasted on carpet production.[24] And, now AI. Texas wooed ChapGPT to Texas ignoring[25] the fact that the state can't even keep its lakes full. So instead of "Don't Mess with Texas," the new slogan might as well be: "Don't Flush in Texas—ChatGPT is Thirsty."

Overexposure to greenwashing breeds skepticism and cynicism among consumers and the general public. As genuine environmental efforts are overshadowed by empty rhetoric, trust in environmental initiatives and institutions diminishes, hindering progress towards sustainability. Politicians who prioritize performative environmentalism over substantive action risk implementing ineffective policies that fail to address the root causes of environmental degradation. Token gestures and incremental measures may provide the illusion of progress while perpetuating unsustainable practices.

New York Times and USA Today bestselling author S.E. Smith summarized in their article "Performative Environmentalism Won't Reverse Climate Change." "Boasting about one's 'greener-than-thou' credentials can be more harmful than doing nothing at all."[26] And the costliest lie people ever sell themselves is that it's possible to buy their way out of injustice.[27]

---

23 https://theconversation.com/a-stench-of-tokenism-how-environmental-reforms-ignore-first-nations-knowledge-198393
24 https://www.floortrendsmag.com/articles/91325-new-process-could-conserve-water-for-carpet-industry
25 https://cbsaustin.com/news/local/ai-boom-strains-texas-water-resources-as-data-centers-demand-more
26 https://udreview.com/opinion-why-performative-environmentalism-is-harmful/
27 https://www.studocu.com/en-us/document/westminster-high-school/integrated-math/smith-2020-performative-environmentalism-wont-reverse-climate-change-bitch-media/90794574

Ecoterrorism

The term "ecoterrorism" refers to the use of violence or criminal activity to further ecological or environmental goals. It is the ultimate expression of Performative Environmentalism.

> "You won't listen to my demands to eliminate all oil use, so I will throw paint on the Mona Lisa."
>
> "Your logging is so disgusting that I will spike the trees with metal so the saws buck and kill the logger."
>
> Or, "the use of oil is so dangerous that I will glue my hands to a busy highway so sick people can't get to the hospital."[28]

Although the concept of using extreme measures to protect the environment is relatively recent, its roots can be traced back to the late 20th century when environmental activism began to take on more radical forms. Key events such as the publication of Rachel Carson's "Silent Spring" in 1962, which highlighted the dangers of pesticides, and the first Earth Day in 1970, which galvanized public support for environmental causes, played a significant role in shaping the movement.

As the environmental movement grew, so did the range of tactics employed by its advocates. While many pursued changes through legal and political means, others became frustrated with the slow pace of progress and turned to more direct actions. This shift toward radicalism was influenced by the broader countercultural and anti-establishment sentiments of the time.

One of the earliest and most influential groups was Earth First!, founded in 1980 by Dave Foreman and others. Earth First! adopted a "no compromise" stance, advocating for direct action to protect the environment. Their tactics included tree spiking (driving metal spikes into trees to prevent logging), road blockades, and sabotage of construction equipment.[29]

The 1990s saw an escalation in the scale and impact of ecoterrorist activities. One of the most notorious incidents was the campaign against the Vail Ski Resort in Colorado. In 1998, the Earth Liberation Front (ELF), an offshoot of Earth First!, claimed responsibility for setting fires that caused $12 million in damages. The group targeted the resort because of its plans to expand into lynx habitat, a

---

28 https://www.dailymail.co.uk/news/article-12129019/Furious-driver-trying-hospital-mounts-pavement-avoid-Just-Stop-Oil-London-march.html
29 https://www.dailymail.co.uk/wires/ap/article-11248285/Eco-warrior-Earth-First-founder-Dave-Foreman-dies.html

decision they believed would further endanger the species. "The Oregonian" describes the action as "the most destructive act of eco-sabotage in U.S. history." Six men and five women associated with the group were arrested.[30]

The term "ecoterrorism" itself is controversial and often debated. Critics argue that it is used to delegitimize and criminalize genuine environmental activism. They contend that the label of terrorism should be reserved for acts that cause significant harm to human life, whereas many actions by radical environmental groups target property, paintings and infrastructure rather than people.

Supporters of the term argue that the use of violence and criminal activity to achieve environmental goals poses a serious threat to society and warrants a strong legal response. They point out that performative acts such as arson, bombings, and sabotage can cause substantial economic damage and endanger lives, even if unintentional.

The debate is further complicated by differing views on the morality and effectiveness of direct action. Some performative environmentalists believe that radical tactics are necessary to draw attention to urgent ecological issues and force change in the face of governmental and corporate inaction. Others argue that such tactics undermine the broader environmental movement by alienating public support and inviting legal crackdowns.

In recent years, the landscape of ecoterrorism has evolved. The rise of digital activism and social media has provided new tools for environmental advocates to organize and spread their message. Hacktivist groups like Anonymous have conducted cyberattacks on corporations and government entities involved in environmental harm, blurring the lines between traditional forms of ecoterrorism and digital disruption.[31]

Australian senator Tuesday Concetta Fierravanti-Wells, a senior member of the ruling conservative Liberal party and former government minister, said that eco-terrorists were responsible for the country's unprecedented 2020 bushfire crisis.[32] The fires destroyed about 60 million acres, an area the size of Portugal.

Ecoterrorist Nikolaos Karvounakis was radicalized on online forums and planted an explosive device in one of Edinburgh's tourist hotspots. He was acting on

---

30 https://www.oregonlive.com/news/erry-2018/08/3cc02205f06447/ecoterrorism-in-the-west-a-who.html
31 https://redentry.co/en/blog/anonymous-full-cyber-attack-history/
32 https://www.dailymail.co.uk/wires/afp/article-7994687/Australian-senator-claims-eco-terrorists-caused-bushfires.html

behalf of the International Terrorist Mafia, a Mexican eco-terror group, and received an eight-year and four-month prison term.[33]

In 2023, France shut down the environmental activist group Les Soulevements de la Terre (SLT) for provoking armed protests or violent actions. Interior Minister Gerald Darmanin referred several times to "eco-terrorism" in relation to SLT actions in recent months, saying some activists had shown "extreme violence against police forces."[34]

And in 2024, two activists from Just Stop Oil sprayed orange paint on the prehistoric Stonehenge stones.[35] That did it! I finally agreed to stop driving cars, flying and using AC. Now that Stonehenge is defaced, I see their point! They *are* right!

No, they are asses, performative environmental asses.

Governments are starting to fight back against the ecoterrorists. In July 2024, a UK court found five Just Stop Oil protestors guilty of "conspiring intentionally to cause a public nuisance."[36] They had been blocking traffic on the M25 highway, causing people to miss doctor visits and funerals. Four of the protesters were given four-year sentences and the organizer a five-year sentence. Controversially, this places even non-violent protesting on a similar footing as violent crimes like robbery or rape.

Climate change, biodiversity loss, and other pressing environmental issues continue to drive activism, and the potential for violent radicalization remains. Ecoterrorists continue despite the potential for jail and their clear failure to win people to their side. Are they justified? Does the end goal justify any means? Do their actions win eco-normal people over to their side?

---

33 https://www.dailymail.co.uk/wires/pa/article-10519113/Eco-terrorist-jailed-planting-explosive-device-tourist-hotspot.html
34 https://www.dailymail.co.uk/wires/reuters/article-12218511/France-shuts-climate-activist-group-saying-provoked-violence.html
35 https://www.dailymail.co.uk/wires/pa/article-13546861/Just-Stop-Oil-activists-spray-orange-paint-Stonehenge.html
36 https://www.cnn.com/2024/09/14/climate/uk-climate-protests-policing-laws-prison-intl/index.html

Thesis of This Book

Special Note about this book before we continue. Each chapter includes two bonuses! First, included in this book are details about the Ten Biggest Environmental Hypocrites! These people talk about their incredible efforts on behalf of the environment while running their sprinklers excessively during a drought.[37] I hope your favorite star is not on the list. Some of the best discussions of certain climate hot button issues occur in these bonus pages, so do not skip them!

Why include this list of hypocrites? Keep this one stat in mind, as it summarizes the hypocrisy argument, "the richest 1% of humanity is responsible for more carbon emissions than the poorest 66% .... enough to cause more than a million excess deaths due to heat."[38] And who does the most bitching? The rich complain about the poor and worry about the consequences of the poor getting air conditioning. Environmental concerns are very much a First World problem. Said again because it is so important, "The top 1% of emitters globally each had carbon footprints ... more than 1,000 times greater than those of the bottom 1% of emitters."[39] These hypocrites deserve to be singled out.

Second, each chapter includes some new ways to think about our body and its health. Why is this included in a book about the environment? It will make sense later, I promise. Now back to the thesis.

Many people believe that ecoterrorists are justified. They believe that the environmental threats we face are so great that dangerous performative environmentalism is demanded and moral. Their desired laws have not been passed, so they believe attempting to deface the Mona Lisa will draw attention to their issue. Environmentalists fail to see that these destructive actions turn more people against their cause. Most of the media stories that cover the environment are entirely performative. Stories about Leonardo DiCaprio

---

37 https://www.latimes.com/california/story/2022-08-22/kim-kardashian-kevin-hart-california-drought-water-waste Dwyane Wade and Gabrielle Union's L.A. home exceeded its monthly water allotment by more than 1,400%, or 90,000 gallons. That was an improvement over the previous month, when their property exceeded its budget by 489,000 gallons. Actor Kevin Hart exceeded his home's water budget by 117,000 gallons, or about 519%, records show. Kim Kardashian exceeded her monthly budget by about 232,000 gallons. Kourtney Kardashian exceeded her monthly budget by about 101,000 gallons. Sylvester Stallone (not you Rocky!) used about 533% more than his allocated budget — 230,000 excess gallons. That was an increase from 195,000 excess gallons in the previous month.
38 https://www.carbonbrief.org/daily-brief/richest-1-account-for-more-carbon-emissions-than-poorest-66-report-says/
39 https://www.iea.org/commentaries/the-world-s-top-1-of-emitters-produce-over-1000-times-more-co2-than-the-bottom-1

testifying in front of the UN are more frequent and gets more Likes than stories about new advancements in carbon technology. If we made a list of the most famous environmentalists, it would include people like John Kerry, Al Gore, Leonardo DiCaprio, and Greta Thunberg. What has this group done to decrease the carbon released by factories, invent new recycling technologies, or discover more efficient technologies?

They have performed. They are only creating hot air! The people that are actually solving the problem, actually discovering new technologies designed to clean the past and protect the future, are largely unknown.

The real environmentalists are an unconnected group of entrepreneurs working to solve environmental problems. They do not testify in front of the United Nations; they present to venture capitalists to raise growth capital. They do not get awards presented by Prince Harry; they spend 80 hours a week programming a computer to set the perfect zinc ratio to eliminate exhaust from jet engines. People Magazine does not write awards stories about them.

They are capitalists. They plan for profits, not government grants. They make money by selling cleaner, safer, more efficient solutions. They have a passion for the environment, but they still dream of getting rich.

Let's make it clear. The thesis of this book is that The Real Environmentalists are not the scientists, lawyers, activists, academics or politicians that talk about climate change, how horrible climate change is and how humans have caused it, but the capitalist entrepreneurs working to solve the very real environmental problems we face, regardless of who caused them.

This book will argue that many of the eco-players are wasting time with their role in the environmental fight. But this book is not fighting against climate change. It is happening. We will not argue about the causes or whether humans are responsible or not. We will argue that time, energy and resources are being wasted by the very people claiming to be doing the most. We will argue that the media should treat most academics, scientists, media and politicians as more concerned with performative acts than solving any issues. The heroes are the entrepreneurs that spend time solving environmental problems.

Some may argue that academics are part of the solution, too. They do make huge contributions. For example, University of Missouri scientists discovered a way to remove 98% of those micro-plastics from the Pacific Ocean.[40] The question remains who will pay for the new technology to be deployed? Entrepreneurs.

Some academics are a big part of the problem. They make crazy predictions that hurt their cause. They study things without any thought for practical uses.

This book will introduce some of the amazing environmental entrepreneurs. They are the people that will solve the world's environmental problems and will get super rich doing it. They are not about the performance of environmentalism; they are *actually* making a difference.

Let's start with a Canadian entrepreneur named Wayne Elliott.

---

40 https://showme.missouri.edu/2024/mizzou-scientists-achieve-more-than-98-efficiency-removing-nanoplastics-from-water/

Top Ten Environmental Hypocrites

#10 Nancy Pelosi

How Much Do They Talk? (0 = not at all to 10 = all day) = 3

Amount of Environmental Action? (0 = plants trees daily to 10 = giving speeches) = 3

Real Environmentalist Score = 6

Nancy Pelosi, the long-serving Democratic Congresswoman from California and former Speaker of the House, has been accused of many types of hypocrisy, obviously in some part due to her very high position. Nevertheless, she has been accused of financial hypocrisy[41], #MeToo hypocrisy[42], Presidential pardon hypocrisy[43], Union hypocrisy[44] (what is that?), several types of COVID hypocrisy (both mask[45] and beauty salon[46]), health care hypocrisy[47], and environmental hypocrisy. And of being an ice cream hypocrite[48], and that is the worst kind of hypocrite you can be! Nobody forgets $12 pints of Jeni's in a $24,000 fridge during a pandemic. That was truly a Marie Antoinette "let them eat cake" moment, except colder and creamier. And she met her end with the guillotine!

Nancy has championed numerous legislative efforts aimed at reducing carbon emissions, promoting renewable energy, and addressing climate change. However, like other high-profile politicians, she has faced accusations of environmental hypocrisy. These criticisms primarily stem from her personal

---

[41] https://www.discoverthenetworks.org/other/pelosis-massive-wealth-greed-hypocrisy/
[42] https://www.washingtonexaminer.com/opinion/1741251/nancy-pelosi-biden-endorsement-reeks-of-metoo-hypocrisy/
[43] https://www.foxnews.com/media/geraldo-rivera-torches-nancy-pelosi-hunter-biden
[44] https://archive.thinkprogress.org/right-wing-attack-on-pelosi-over-union-hypocrisy-systematically-debunked-adca4616e6fb/
[45] https://nypost.com/2021/08/23/pelosi-cos-hypocrisy-unmasked-and-on-full-display/
[46] https://thenewamerican.com/us/politics/salon-owner-who-revealed-pelosi-s-hypocrisy-closing-shop-because-of-threats/
[47] https://www.foxnews.com/transcript/nancy-pelosis-obamacare-hypocrisy
[48] https://www.washingtonexaminer.com/news/2604392/you-should-be-ashamed-critics-unleash-on-pelosi-for-showing-off-freezer-loaded-with-ice-cream/

lifestyle choices, financial interests, and certain legislative actions that appear to contradict her public environmental stance.

Her $24,000 refrigerator is actually a big deal. The cooling industry is incredibly polluting, accounting for around 10% of global CO_2 emissions, which is three times the amount produced by aviation and shipping combined.[49] Her fridge is four times a normally-sized one. It's basically the Hummer of refrigerators, and just as subtle.

One of the most frequently cited examples of performative hypocrisy involves her use of air travel, particularly private jets. According to the financial reports of Nancy Pelosi for Congress, her campaign spent just over $500,000 on private jets during a 14-month period.[50] Again, private aviation is one of the most environmentally destructive activities on the planet. One reporter concluded, "it's a knock on her … for constantly establishing standards for the rest of the country while justifying failing to live up to them themselves — and preaching all the while about their 'moral' commitments."[51] While some argue that her demanding schedule necessitates efficient travel, critics see it as an example of her not practicing the environmental conservation she preaches. The carbon offset program apparently consists of Nancy clapping extra hard at the State of the Union.

Nancy owns a vineyard near St. Helena in Napa Valley. The mayor reportedly warned her and issued warnings about toxic runoff regarding the landfill situated at the top of the hill for years. The landfill had the potential to pollute water and vineyard land in the valley below, in addition to causing health problems for people breathing contaminated air. The warnings were ignored for years. Workers at the Clover Flat Landfill claim they were exposed to methane and contaminated water. Fifteen workers are suing for $300 million in damages.[52] Nothing pairs better with a glass of Cabernet than the subtle notes of landfill runoff.

Pelosi's real estate holdings have also been a source of criticism. She and her husband, Paul, own, in addition to the vineyard and their San Francisco home with a really, really big refrigerator, multiple commercial properties. Critics argue that living in and maintaining such expansive estates undermines their credibility as advocates for reducing carbon footprints and conserving natural

---

49 https://www.bbc.com/future/article/20201204-climate-change-how-chemicals-in-your-fridge-warm-the-planet
50 https://ijr.com/nancy-pelosi-snared-climate-hypocrisy-financial-filings/
51 Ibid.
52 https://bottleraiders.com/article/nancy-pelosi-gavin-newsome-napa-vineyards-workers-lawsuit/

resources. In the 1990's when the Presidio, the military base at the base of the Golden Gate Bridge, was being demilitarized, there was a very intense debate about the properties' future. One group wanted commercialization while the environmentalists asked for no new building, only using existing barracks as low-income housing. Nancy sided with the developers. Close-by properties owned by her husband exploded in value.[53]

In 2023, Nancy attended an award ceremony at the formally named Kennedy Center. The Goldman Environmental Prize was being presented and she was a speaker. When she came on stage, CodePink protesters began shouting about the Russia-Ukraine war. One protester explained, "it's a huge hypocrisy to have Nancy Pelosi speak at an environmental ceremony. Pelosi voted for almost a trillion-dollar Pentagon budget. That money should go for climate justice. The people awarded today represent communities that have been devastated by our war machine."[54] The protesters also said that her war policy will lead to a nuclear solution as Russia tries to break the war stalemate. So, if Putin decides to drop the bomb, it is her fridge's fault. Clearly.

Pelosi always fights back. In 2020, she was caught going maskless during the pandemic at a hair salon. There is nothing worse than dying with your roots showing. When exposed, Nancy played a reverse Uno card and demanded that the stylist apologize to her.[55]

Nancy, meet hypocrisy. Hypocrisy, meet Nancy!

---

53 https://www.discoverthenetworks.org/other/pelosis-massive-wealth-greed-hypocrisy/
54 https://dissidentvoice.org/2023/04/nancy-pelosis-climate-climate-hypocrisy-called-out-at-goldman-environmental-prize-ceremony/
55 https://www.presstelegram.com/2020/09/13/nancy-pelosi-and-the-hypocrisy-of-the-elite-gloria-romero/

Chapter 2
14 Years Old and Milk Shakes

Wayne Elliott was born in 1954 in Hamilton, Ontario, Canada, into a family steeped in entrepreneurial grit. His grandparents opened a grocery store in 1926 in the front room of their apartment in Hamilton's north end. They weathered the Great Depression and World War II with resolve and hard work, values passed down through generations.

Wayne's father, Kenneth, embodied the spirit of a true entrepreneur. Despite leaving school in the 9th grade, he operated a shipbreaking yard and owned a Dairy Queen. His mother occasionally helped in the family business when needed. Wayne has one younger sister, Lori, who worked alongside him for three decades, managing the office with the same work ethic their father instilled in them. Lori has now retired. Wayne, however, sees no end to his career as business is both his passion and his pastime.

Kenneth was an idea man. Once a venture became routine, he lost interest and moved on. One of those ventures even led him into politics. He valued doing things right the first time.

By age 9, Wayne had his first paying customers. Kenneth arranged for him to cut six neighbors' lawns. He charged $2 to mow a lawn, shovel snow, or Simonize a car, which was serious money back then. The message was clear: quality work was expected. Wayne recalls, "Anything I did half-assed, it didn't matter if it was washing the dishes, cleaning up the kitchen, or cutting the lawn; if I didn't do a thorough job, I had to do it again. And I realized that I didn't have to be a genius. The best thing to do is just do it right the first time."

When Wayne was 14 years old, his father bought a Dairy Queen from Ron Joyce, who later became the owner of the Canada-ubiquitous Tim Hortons[56] chain. The DQ was a small location with a walk-up window and no seats inside. At the time, Ron Joyce was a policeman and wanted to sell the Dairy Queen to open the second Tim Hortons store with Tim Horton, the Canadian hockey legend. Tim Hortons is the Canadian version of Dunkin Donuts, but culturally more

---

56 https://www.timhortons.com/

important. Half of all Canadians were conceived after a date at a Hortons.[57] Joyce died not so long ago, a multi-billionaire.

Wayne was put to work immediately, though he wasn't thrilled about missing weekends at the quarry with his friends. Still, he drank an endless number of milkshakes, sometimes 30 a day, he claims. "If milkshakes were healthy, I could live on them," he said. He loved the job. Yet, as a young fellow, Wayne didn't like it that the busiest days were Saturday and Sunday. He knew his buddies would be at the quarry swimming and having fun, going to a party.

At 16, frustrated with being underpaid, Wayne leased the Dairy Queen from his father. The girls working there earned $1.05 an hour while he made just $5 for a 12-hour shift. By paying a flat monthly fee, he kept all the profits and finally had control. Some Sundays brought in $300 profit. He bought a car, earned real money, and tasted the thrill of entrepreneurship.

Wayne learned that all it took was cleanliness, good service, quality, and a decent location. "Keep the windows and bathrooms spotless. No ice cream on the floor. Good product, friendly service. That's the magic," he says.

Alongside the DQ, Wayne also worked at his father's shipyard for $1.20 an hour. But it was the Dairy Queen that lit the fire. He realized he liked being the boss and was driven to improve every part of the business.

At 18, Wayne lived with his grandfather for a year, a time made sweeter by his football team winning the national championship. He credits both his work ethic and frugality to his Irish roots and his family's "school of hard knocks." His grandfather had left school in the second grade to work. Wayne was taught never to borrow money and never to waste anything. These principles shaped him deeply.

Wayne was also an outstanding athlete in his youth. That was in addition to working at the ship salvage yard and at the Dairy Queen. It is a time he remembers fondly, especially since his football team won the Canadian national championship that year.[58] He could have played football and baseball at a professional level. A Canadian football team offered him the opportunity with the team as a punter, which didn't appeal to him ($8,000 to live in Winnipeg!). He loved the game but preferred not to sit on the bench and didn't want to only

---

[57] This is a lie. Hope you were being attention enough to see that without being told. The point is, don't trust anyone. Read with your brain engaged. But also, Hortons is a big deal and fills an important part in Canadian social life.

[58] This calls for a joke or dig about Canadian football. Out of immense resect for Wayne, not Canadian football, I will refrain. But feel free to make your own Canadian football joke. Still, it is a national championship, so very impressive!

kick for a team. He also had an offer from a professional baseball team, the New York Mets. As a 16-year-old, he had pitched 21 innings in one day and struck out 42 batters at the major hardball tournament in Canada. He was a left-handed pitcher with good breaking pitches, a rarity. A Mets scout said he was the best amateur pitcher Canada.

Yet, he turned them both down. Why?

He couldn't fly. He still can't.

"I'd have been a nervous wreck flying 100 times a year," he says. Wayne once drove 32 hours from Toronto to Brownsville, Texas, for two meetings. He has driven millions of miles to avoid flying thousands of miles.[59] He drives to Florida every summer and to a shipyard in Cape Breton Island, Nova Scotia, regularly. Both are 24-hour drives one way. Or two and a half hours by plane. He is not exaggerating his fear of flying.[60] He has flown dozens of flights, but still the anticipation bothers him.

Maybe a drink would help? A nice glass of bourbon or whisky has made many men brave enough to fight a duel, have their leg amputated without painkillers, or ask a woman to dance. Wayne, however, doesn't drink at all. The actual flight isn't the worst part for him; it's the buildup and anticipation that he finds most challenging. Instead of a drink, to cope, he tries to keep the thought of flying out of his mind until the day of the flight. He still hopes never to fly again.

Because of Wayne's exposure to shipyards and such, his environmental awareness began in childhood. He vividly remembers the thick black smoke from burning insulation off copper wire at scrapyards creating "a terrible taste in my throat I'll never forget." At the time, there were no environmental laws. Hamilton Harbor was a dumping ground for steel mills and chemical companies. Even today, fish in Lake Ontario are so contaminated that people are advised to eat only one per year. The Canadian government reported, the Harbor "is the largest contaminated sediment site on the Canadian side of the Great Lakes. About 60 hectares in total, it contains about 615,000 cubic meters of polycyclic aromatic hydrocarbons (PAHs) contaminated sediment—enough to fill a hockey rink nearly three times over. These carcinogenic toxins are the result of years of

---

59 "millions of miles to avoid flying thousands of miles." Again, seeing if you are paying attention. The destinations did not change...
60 https://my.clevelandclinic.org/health/diseases/22431-aerophobia-fear-of-flying

industrial pollution from multiple sources dating back to the 1800s."[61] Oh, and if your ONE FISH per year has 3 eyeballs, only eat half!

Wayne was disturbed by the blatant pollution. He remembers a Santa Claus parade interrupted by a giant black cloud from a local mill, a stark reminder of how toxic the air had become. From age five, he visited shipbreaking yards with his father, watching fires burn ship interiors and insulation with zero environmental concern or governmental oversight.

Even in the 1980s, safety was lax. In 1983, his crew dismantled T2 tankers filled with asbestos, working without masks. He believes that exposure contributed to his father's death decades later. Wayne remembers the two major nickel smelters in Ontario releasing sulfur dioxide for years.[62] When environmental concerns finally arose, regulators gave them ten years to comply. The government never graced smaller businesses like this.

Despite these frustrations, Wayne's values stuck. He still finds it unacceptable how slowly change came, and how money and politics delayed progress.

His adventurous youth wasn't without hardship. At age 20, after recycling their first submarine in Charleston, South Carolina (the USS Barracuda), his father Kenneth sent him to Tampico, Mexico, to salvage two sunken ships. He was horrified by the lack of refrigeration, the makeshift equipment, and the dangerous steel-cutting methods. After five months of low pay and illness, he returned home. Even when offered more money to go back, he refused. Around the same time, he turned down a high-paying oil rig crane job after learning it required regular helicopter flights. The fear of flying again cost him the opportunity.

Wayne's life has been full of adventure and lessons. Yet ironically, it wasn't the toxic fumes, the torching of tankers, or refusing a helmet on the football field that nearly killed him.

It was the milkshakes.

---

61 https://www.canada.ca/en/canada-water-agency/freshwater-ecosystem-initiatives/great-lakes/great-lakes-protection/areas-concern/hamilton-harbour/randle-reef.html
62 https://ero.ontario.ca/notice/019-1107

Top Ten Environmental Hypocrites

#9 Richard Branson

How Much Do They Talk? (0 = not at all to 10 = all day) = 2

Amount of Environmental Action? (0 = plants trees daily to 10 = giving speeches) = 6

Real Environmentalist Score = 8

Richard Branson, the founder of the Virgin Group, is a well-known entrepreneur worth $5 billion and a philanthropist who has championed various social and environmental causes, such as the Carbon War Room. He owns some 400 businesses including Virgin Atlantic airlines and Virgin Galactic. Time Magazine even named him a Hero of the Environment,[63] which is a little like giving a pyromaniac the Fire Safety Award.

The fact of the matter, however, is that both these businesses are environmental disasters. The United Nations aviation body forecasts that airplane emissions of CO_2 are 900 million metric tons a year but will triple by 2050.[64] A person traveling between London and New York causes the release of around 1.7 tons of CO_2, which is roughly the same emissions created by the average person in Morocco over the course of a year.[65] In 2024, Virgin Atlantic airlines was found guilty of lying in ads, claiming their flights were now "100% sustainable."[66] Translation: "Our planes are powered by unicorn tears and good vibes."

Not to mention that space travel, especially in its current form, involves substantial carbon emissions and environmental impact. The rockets used for commercial space flights burn large amounts of fuel, contributing to pollution both on Earth and in the upper atmosphere. When asked about the environmental cost of Virgin Galactic's trip to suborbital space, Branson claimed that is the equivalent to one round trip from London to New York and back. Does that make

---

[63] https://content.time.com/time/specials/2007/article/0,28804,1663317_1663322_1669934,00.html
[64] https://www.nytimes.com/2019/09/19/climate/air-travel-emissions.html
[65] https://www.independent.co.uk/space/richard-branson-virgin-galactic-climate-change-space-educated-b1884133.html
[66] https://www.yahoo.com/news/sir-richard-branson-virgin-atlantic-174356394.html

sense? A Virgin Galactic spokesperson reiterated the fact and said that its emissions were offset. When *The Independent* asked for more information about the flight's emissions, Virgin Galactic refused to provide any information. Professor Paul Peeters, a researcher of sustainable tourism and transport at Breda University of Applied Sciences in the Netherlands, said, "It doesn't make sense to me. We are really struggling to cope with climate change … so to cause more climate change just for a few minutes of fun, I find that a bit difficult."[67] Joyrides for billionaires are not exactly the "systemic solutions" the planet was hoping for.

Much to his credit, Branson also told *The Observer* that he felt he had a responsibility to do something for the climate, given that so much of his empire is built on carbon-intensive transport industries. "There is no question that Virgin is involved in a number of businesses that emit a lot of carbon, and that is one of the reasons why I have to work particularly hard," he said.[68] Nothing screams "responsibility" quite like hopping into a rocket to draw a giant carbon signature in the stratosphere.

In 2009, Richie committed to invest 100% of all future proceeds of the Virgin Group from their transportation businesses into tackling global warming. It was a $3 billion commitment over ten years.[69] Bill Clinton and Al Gore, other people who frequently fly private jets, where there to shake his hand at the announcement.

Naomi Klein is an award-winning journalist, syndicated columnist and international and New York Times bestselling author of nine critically acclaimed books. She wrote that, "seven years into the pledge, Branson has paid out only a small fraction of the promised money, well under $300 million."[70]

She continued, "Branson's various climate adventures may indeed prove to have all been a spectacle, a Virgin production, with everyone's favorite bearded billionaire playing the part of planetary savior to build his brand, land on late night TV, fend off regulators, and feel good about doing bad." Sounds like Naomi would agree with this book's critical comments about performative environmentalism. Naomi basically called him the Elon Musk of tie-dye.

---

67 Ibid.
68 https://www.theguardian.com/environment/2014/sep/13/richard-branson-failed-climate-change-pledge?ncid=edlinkushpmg00000313
69 https://www.wired.com/story/how-green-is-richard-branson/
70 https://www.theguardian.com/environment/2014/sep/13/richard-branson-failed-climate-change-pledge?ncid=edlinkushpmg00000313

Branson's personal lifestyle choices further complicate his environmental image. As a billionaire, his lifestyle includes owning multiple properties, luxury yachts, and private islands. Necker Island, his private island in the Caribbean, epitomizes this opulence. Maintaining such properties typically involves significant resource consumption and environmental impact. While Branson has made efforts to incorporate renewable energy and sustainable practices on Necker Island, the overall carbon footprint of his lifestyle remains substantial. Critics argue that living in such luxury while advocating for environmental conservation presents a clear example of hypocrisy. It's like lecturing people on portion control while polishing off a 12-scoop sundae from Nancy's fridge, but on your private island.

Another aspect of Branson's environmental advocacy that has faced scrutiny is his promotion of carbon offsetting. While carbon offsets can play a role in mitigating climate change by funding projects that reduce or capture emissions elsewhere, they are often criticized for allowing high emitters to continue their activities without making substantial changes to reduce their own emissions. Branson's use of carbon offsets for his businesses, including Virgin Atlantic, is seen by some as a way to avoid addressing the root causes of emissions. This approach can be perceived as a superficial solution that fails to drive the systemic changes needed to combat climate change effectively. Planting a few trees doesn't cancel out your space joyride, Richard. Unless those trees are on Mars.

In conclusion, the perception of Richard Branson as an environmental hypocrite arises from several factors, including his involvement in the aviation and space travel industries, personal lifestyle choices, promotion of carbon offsetting, and financial interests. Virgin Galactic may be reaching for the stars, but when it comes to climate credibility, Branson's rocket is still stuck on the launchpad.

Chapter 3
What Happens to an Old Ship?

Ship breaking, or ship recycling, is a hard, dirty business. It involves buying an old dying ship, towing it to a shipyard, and taking it apart piece by piece. Besides steel, it is also oils, gases, asbestos, lithium, lead, arsenic, mercury and many other valuable and frequently hazardous wastes[71] that must be extracted, consolidated, stored and disposed of. It's a job that's not easy at all.

Breaking is environmentally dirty. Yet, it is far superior to the alternative. Ships that are not recycled eventually sink to the bottom or rot on a shore. Either way, they leak chemicals, oils, and fuels. Most old ships have asbestos that has never been removed. This is work that must be done.

Sometimes, government agencies use end-of-life ships and sink them, creating new reefs. The sunken boats can become new ecological habitats for thousands of creatures and dive sites while doubling down as great tourist attractions. In 2011, the government of the Cayman Islands sank a 251-foot submarine rescue ship called the USS Kittiwake.[72] It took a year and several million dollars to get the ship ready for its sinking. However, these cases are a rarity. Most ships do not receive such a gracious conclusion. Ships must be recycled because the alternative is much worse, much dirtier. Wayne says he associates sunken ships with tragedy, often with great loss of life. It bothers him because they don't belong on the ocean or lake floor.

On November 22, 2022, there was a 7.0 magnitude earthquake near the Solomon Islands in the South Pacific. Soon, oil began lapping onto the island of Guadalcanal's northwestern shores. A Honolulu newspaper reported that "the problem is a big one for the Solomon Islands. The offshore area north of Guadalcanal is called Iron Bottom Sound, named after the 1,450 airplanes and 111 shipwrecks on its floor, more than half a mile down."[73] Each shipwreck is an environmental disaster that is already happening or about to happen. Navy ships sank with thousands of tons of oil and gas, an unknown quantity of bombs, and chemical weapons. An estimated 3,800 Navy ships sank in World War II. According to a 2013 report released by the National Oceanic and Atmospheric

---

71 https://www.imorules.com/GUID-25C58EB4-2C4C-42FC-BDC0-A346C7058123.html
72 https://www.cnn.com/travel/article/kittiwake-cayman-dive-site/index.html
73 https://www.civilbeat.org/2022/12/ticking-ecological-time-bomb-thousands-of-sunken-ships-from-wwii-are-rusting-at-the-bottom-of-the-pacific/

Administration (NOAA), "there are at least 87 sunken ships in U.S. waters that pose a serious environmental concern due to the oil leaks."[74]

Let's play a mental game for a second. Which is more likely to happen? A Pacific island sinking due to climate change or a Navy wreck rotting open, leaking two million gallons of dirty oil and killing the local fishing grounds? (While you think about it, remember that 26% of the entire country of The Netherlands has been a meter below sea level for hundreds of years.[75] Their country sinking is a scenario that the Dutch hardly ever worry about because they trust their water engineers completely.)

In January 2023, the world's merchant (non-government) fleet consisted of 105,500 vessels[76] of at least 100 gross tons. That weight usually equates to ships of about 65 feet minimum to 700 feet in length. Of those, over half are over 1,000 gross tons, meaning a ship about 500 to 600 feet long. Imagine the impact of 56,000 ships of 500 feet each containing oil, gas, asbestos and God only knows what else rotting off our shores!

In addition to the privately owned ships above, the Navies of the world have thousands of ships and submarines. These present an even greater environmental challenge. These ships are larger and many run on nuclear power. South Korea has 138 marine vessels. Indonesia has 243. Russia has 265. China has 425, and the US has even more.[77] The big concern is countries like Thailand and Iran. Will the Thai Navy properly recycle its 86 ships? Or Iran its 66? Or Bangladesh its 66? Or Algeria its 96? Or North Korea its 186 ships and subs? One can simply imagine how concerned Kim Jong Un must be about properly recycling his Navy.

Wayne says the environmental carnage, and serious injuries and loss of life in India (Alang Beach) was horrendous for decades, but owners can be paid for their ships, including waste. They so often steam the vessels there under their own power for their last voyage. They just drive the ships up as far as they would go on the beach, which usually means a couple of football fields offshore out in the water. That's where they start to dismantle them, in the ocean. In the old days, 400-500 guys would all get together when it was time to pull a ship, when they thought they had taken enough weight off it, they would wait for a high tide, they'd get a rope and pull. They used to say, "A ship a day, a death a day," but in truth, it was worse than that for a period of time. At one point, when Wayne's shipbreaking crew were costing $20 an hour plus fees, taxes, etc., the workers at

---

[74] https://www.treehugger.com/shipwrecks-could-sink-environment-4862932
[75] https://netherlandsinsiders.com/how-much-of-the-netherlands-is-below-sea-level/
[76] https://hbs.unctad.org/merchant-fleet/
[77] https://www.businessinsider.com/most-powerful-navies-in-world-in-2023-ranked-ships-submarines-2023-8?op=1#1-us-25

Alang Beach in India were paid 20 cents an hour. Nobody had safety gear, there were bare feet. "So, how could we ever compete with that?" Wayne asks.

The fact of the matter is that very little ship recycling occurs in countries with enforced environmental protection. Most of it occurs in countries with almost no ecological oversight. What do the performative environmentalists think of that? Are they upset that ships get broken up for the good stuff and then the bad stuff gets sunk? They aren't. This book will come back to the topic later.

To make matters worse, zero ship recycling is required. Sunk ships are allowed to rot and release their dangerous contents unchecked. Times hundreds of thousands. No international law or country law requires that end-of-life ships meet a graceful end. Nor is insurance required in international waters for dead ship tows. "So if you and your friends are cruising across the ocean one night, and he's got his boat on autopilot, and you should have light on, of course, but if this dead ship tow, which doesn't even have to be lit up, runs into you, you're all going to die there, but there is no insurance for that required. They tow these ships without it," Wayne points out.

That is why only an idiot would enter such a minefield. Or a hero.

A First Step: A Scrap Yard

That brings us back to Kenneth Elliott, Wayne's father. A hero. Let's discuss ship recycling which occurs in countries that do enforce environmental protections.

Kenneth started a ship recycling company for the Levy family in Hamilton, Ontario. The Levys were in the scrap metal business with a foundry making brass and bronze ingots. They had a secondary steel division. Mrs. Levy hired Kenneth to run a new shipbreaking yard. Even though he was self-taught, she was always supportive of Kenneth and always took his side, even in disagreements with her own sons. He ran the business until Mrs. Levy died in 1969.

Working at a Dairy Queen was one thing but ship recycling was a whole other story. Kenneth had Wayne work in the shipbreaking, too, and this was how the latter got his first taste of real, hard work. Lawyers and academics talk about how hard they work while sitting in air-conditioned rooms and burning 93 calories per hour.[78] Shipbreaking burns about 500 calories per hour.

Thus, as a young teen, Wayne's summertime experiences were real work, doing terrible stuff, like breaking concrete around the stern of the ships with a pick and

---

[78] https://captaincalculator.com/health/calorie/sitting/

a sledgehammer. He learned how to operate a steel torch when he was fourteen and a magnet crane when he was fifteen. Wayne fell in love with the ships, even the ones that were old junk. The beauty and mystery of the sea captured him even ashore. He said, "I thought they were pretty cool."

Wayne could have bought the Dairy Queen. Instead, he knew he wanted to work with ships, and metal, and eventually the environment.

In 1973, Wayne started his own scrap business. The business was simple but tough. He attended farm auctions to buy scrap. He offered to clean dumps or trash piles if he got to keep the metals. For the first two and a half years, he didn't have a crane or any other lifting device, so he had to load the truck by hand. Naturally, that was highly time-consuming, and sometimes it would be a challenge. He'd rig the lugger truck to lift heavy diesel engines, rearend, etc., into the lugger box, which itself was risky and unsafe.

Wayne went door to door, from farm to factory, to see if they would let him place a collection box on their premises. It wasn't marketing but rather lots of legwork and being resourceful. That led to him gaining knowledge. There were notices in newspapers for auctions. He would cut up old equipment and tractors. However, loading items by hand was a tangible limitation for his business.

After two years, Wayne was able to acquire a small crane. Today, his yard has a 300-ton capacity crane, a 250-ton crane and several 100-ton cranes. His first crane was a little 7-ton crane but that was like heaven to him. Any crane was better than lifting everything by hand to load it. His first debt was leasing his first truck.

One day, Wayne went to a farm auction to buy a bit of scrap. It was one of his first auctions. He won and went to pick up the scrap, which turned out to be an old truck, hiding in an old barn. He couldn't get the truck out as the door was blocked, and the driveway to that door was steeply inclined so he couldn't pull it out with his truck. Since he needed to cut the vehicle up anyway, he thought he might as well do it inside the barn and carry out the pieces. So, he broke out his blow torch and started to cut up the truck. And he set the barn on fire. He's still not sure how it happened. Suddenly, the barn floor was on fire. Old barns are tinder boxes of old dry wood and hay. The walls followed before he had time to get out. The roof caught as he barely escaped. In under 5 minutes, the barn was gone. And the truck was a burnt crisp.

Wayne caught one of the many breaks he would get during his career. Hard, honest work buys good karma, the kind of good karma he had that day.

As the fire turned into smoldering ashes, the farm owner's wife came out of the house and said, "I was wondering how we were gonna get rid of that barn." Wayne took a deep breath of gratitude.

Wayne would haul garbage to the dump for body shops and other companies with limited scrap. He would break up car batteries for the lead inside, which was challenging due to the sulfuric acid involved. Eventually, after a few years, he moved from operating out of his dad's farm to opening a licensed scrap yard, allowing him to buy scrap metal from street peddlers, including those doing it part-time or as a full-time job. Those were other collectors just like he had been. He had moved up the ladder a rung.

A couple of well-established older sellers in the scrap business would sell him batteries on credit, and he would pay them back when he sold the lead. Wayne got his first loan, a line of credit, for $5,000, which didn't go very far. He preferred not to owe people or the bank money, so he made innovative deals with steel mills and others in the steel and metal industry rather than going to a commercial bank.

Wayne's Own Shipbreaking Yard

Wayne Elliott started his own shipbreaking yard in 1983. His dad Kenneth was also involved, and finished Wayne's shipbreaking teaching that year, during the recycling of the Erindale. More than 50 years later, his company, Marine Recycling Corporation (MRC), has been Canada's largest shipbreaker for decades. "The first job at our shipyard on the canal with ULS was to remove a sunken bottom of a 600-foot-long by 60-foot-wide lakes freighter, full of silt. Couple of broken fingers and lots of sore backs, the sunken 2,500 tons was removed 50 tons at a time using a diver and jet rod," Wayne recalls.

MRC is headquartered in Port Colborne, Ontario, and operates an additional shipbreaking site in Edwardsville, Nova Scotia. In recent years, it also operated at a site in Campbell River, British Columbia, through a joint venture, and is considering setting up a new site in Port Mellon in the same province.

In a development testifying to the environmental focus that Wayne brought to the shipbreaking industry, in 2000, MRC became the first ISO-14001 certified ship recycler in the world. For a shipbreaking company like Marine Recycling Corporation getting certified under the 14001 Standard of the International Organization for Standardization means following strict procedures to safely dismantle ships, handle hazardous materials, and minimize damage to the surrounding land and water. It also means regular audits to ensure compliance with both the ISO standards and local environmental laws, and continuous improvement required in these ISO programs "right to a point where, in the audit, you would look at how a tow motor could travel less distance, thereby creating less emissions."

However, back in 1983, it was a tough beginning for Wayne. That was the year of the global recession largely caused by the OPEC oil embargoes. The economy was so bad that Transport Canada gave commercial vessel owners an extra year on their five-year certificates, meaning that ships that were ready for demolition were allowed to sail another year. Wayne's newly founded company had little work. Hence their plans to break ships at Moore McCleary came to an end, and it was back to Hamilton.

Yet, the next year, it won the contract to break the USS Barracuda,[79] a submarine in Charleston Harbor, South Carolina. "Won the contract" meant it offered to buy the wreck for more than anyone else. Wayne, his father Kenneth, and four other Canadians drove from Ontario to Charleston and they scrapped the submarine right in Charleston Harbor. It was the first shipbreaking project that his family did as company owners.

Wayne's company bought the sub for $70,000. In the shipbreaking industry, it is standard for a yard to buy a boat and then sell its scrap materials for recycling. They hoped to buy a ship for $70,000, spend $200,000, and sell the metal for more than $270,000. The price of scrap always determined profit or loss each year in commercial shipbreaking. Submarines have a great deal of nonferrous metals in them and giant lead acid batteries. There are many sub pieces that are worth more than just the steel or iron scrap: copper wiring and cables, bronze and brass fittings, nickel alloys, rare earth elements, gold-plated connectors, among others. Getting them out is hard work. Submarines are tricky because they are meant to dive fast, so if you cut into a pipe in the wrong place, it will sink. Wayne's dad did a lot of research and studied the plans, and they carefully dismantled the sub off a wooden dock. Wayne ran the crane, a brand-new 35-ton American Crawler that he leased.

The dismantling of the USS Barracuda in Charleston Harbor was the first and last project they did for the US Navy. Theoretically, the Navy could have been their best customer, and they spent more than 20 years trying to get more involved in the US program for its mothballed fleet. Finally, the company won

---

[79] https://naval-encyclopedia.com/cold-war/us/barracuda-class-submarines.php#google_vignette

two aircraft carrier contracts on the West Coast in 1998. However, shortly after that, then-Vice President Al Gore put a moratorium on shipbreaking. This effectively halted the recycling of government vessels in the USA to shipbreakers, a ban that remained in force for four years.

Wayne was due to sign a lease on a yard in Astoria, Oregon. The carriers were to be broken there. Yet, the day before he was supposed to sign, the vice president issued his moratorium.

When asked about Gore's decision, Wayne said, "You know, he wasn't wrong. There was a lot of pollution that had happened on both coasts. California, Oregon, and Washington State have not allowed ship recycling for more than 20 years because of environmental performance. It's a very messy business if you don't do it right."

There was one culprit, in particular, who gave the shipbreaking industry a bad name. He will remain nameless, but he liked to call himself the "godfather of US shipbreaking." In a sense, he was. He once had 17 Navy vessels for dismantling on the East Coast of the United States. They had lead in their ballasts as well as manganese bronze propellers. Breaking a cardinal rule of shipbreaking, Smith went after all those components that are more valuable than the steel. In the process, he spilled some chemicals and ended up killing a man in his North Carolina yard. The government eventually shut him down and the Navy towed those 17 vessels back to the Navy Yard, after millions in steel repairs for safe towing back to Philadelphia.

So, Wayne became ISO certified at about the same time when the nameless culprit was spilling chemicals. This book will come back to that.

Beyond all belief, he was allowed to bid in later auctions and won more ships for recycling from the US Navy. He ended up with a yard in Brownsville, Texas, while Wayne's company had trouble getting into Navy work. Even those two aircraft carriers were never officially awarded to MRC by the US government because of Vice President Gore's decision.

Nevertheless, most of Wayne's business consisted of Canadian and US-flagged vessels from the Great Lakes fleets. In 1983, Wayne moved his company to Port Colborne, Ontario, which is currently their main shipbreaking yard and a scrap yard, and the famous Raw Materials Corporation's headquarters and battery recycling plant. He operates another scrap yard in the Niagara region near Lake Ontario.

Ships operating in saltwater service typically have a lifespan of about 30 years. Ballast water pumped in and out of the tanks exposes the bare steel to oxygen and causes corrosion (called wastage or rust). In contrast, ships that only navigate freshwater lakes can last 100 years or more. The oldest ship that Wayne recycled was built in 1898, and, recently, they brought in a freighter that was built in 1941. It was towed by tugs down and across Lake Erie. Sort of sad, isn't it?

For a smaller vessel, it takes two to four months before the shipbreakers are ready to work on any steel. When a ship first arrives, they ensure to empty any fuels, oils, and oily water from the tanks, and detergent wash them to prevent any oil from hitting the ground or water. The process begins with removing non-hazardous trash, such as furnishings, carpets, wood, glass, mirrors, and toilets, followed by the removal of asbestos, which is often the most expensive part of the project. After these steps, they begin cutting and processing the scrap metal for the steel mill and metal refiners. A lot of work goes into reducing every ton of furnace-ready metal, i.e., say the light weight of a ship is 7,000 tons empty. Cut 4-foot by 2-foot (average 200 pounds per piece) means there are more than 60,000 pieces to recycle the ship. If an average torchman can cut 6 tons per day (12,000 pounds, 50-60 pieces), that's 1,500 mandays. With six ground-burners that's 187 days. With the more recent advent of large portable shears, the team can cut up to 200 tons every day.

Financing Growth

Wayne knows all the fleets in the Great Lakes, and those fleet owners are familiar with Marine Recycling Corporation. It has been the only full-time shipbreaker on the Great Lakes for the past 20 years, which allows it to hear about what is to be scrapped. When the government has a job for ship removal for the Coast Guard or other agencies, they put it out for bid. MRC would decide whether to bid depending on the size of the job. There is now an abandoned vessels program which includes even small vessels, but MRC primarily focuses on larger ships, tugboats, and barges, both afloat and wrecked under water, partially sunk and often severely damaged.

For the past 40 years, Wayne Elliott has mostly stayed away from bank money, even though it is the most popular option for growing a business. Once MRC became more successful, its banker asked its CFO several times if they wanted to borrow money. Even when they needed financing for a significant piece of equipment, they would opt to finance through a finance company, requiring a down payment of 20 to 25%. They secured the loan with only the equipment being purchased, ensuring that nothing else was charged to the bank or pledged to the lender. While they might pay a slightly higher interest rate, Wayne explained that the financing company was competitive and did not require the extensive security measures that banks did, such as a cosigner.

Wayne recounted a case from 40 years ago, in which the bank ended up calling their loans when he encountered an issue with a junior partner. Although the company had never missed a payment, the situation made the bank nervous, leading it to take that action. During that period in the early 1980s, it was challenging to change banks or obtain insurance. He mentioned that they obtained an injunction against the bank and ultimately paid them off over the next six months to a year. He concluded by stating that he never borrowed from a conventional lender again.

In Wayne's company, the funding was mostly done internally but he also made innovative deals and borrowed against ships from buyers who had a vested interest or mutual interest with MRC. If the company had a slow month, the buyer could have a slower repayment month, and if it had a good month, the buyer would have a faster repayment month. Wayne compared this arrangement to conventional banks, noting how banks were more like the mafia, wanting their money every month regardless of whether the borrower had a bad or tough month. For Wayne, it was much more palatable to do business this way, avoiding the conventional banks and their extensive paperwork, fees, and security requirements (they are in actual control).

This worked for Marine Recycling Corporation, always with no interest whatsoever. The buyers would make their profits as middlemen, but the same risks were present. If the company experienced a slow month, it wouldn't have payments until they shipped the scrap. Instead of paying the full price, the buyer would deduct a specific amount from their payments based on the number of tons shipped. For example, if MRC had shipped 2,000 tons for a total amount of $1 million, it would repay at a rate of $100 per ton. This system allowed them to keep track of everything easily and ensured they were never at risk of a bank getting jittery on them. Wayne has been using this method for about four decades, stating that whenever they needed money, they had not gone to a bank.

Today, steel is worth approximately $300 per ton. For example, a ship weighing 7,000 tons, considered mid-sized in the maritime world, approximately 700 feet in length, would yield just over $2 million in steel, market depending.

All metals (copper, aluminum, stainless steel, cast iron) are infinitely recyclable and can be re-melted thousands of times while maintaining their quality. Thus, recycling metal makes a lot of sense in several important ways. It conserves natural resources that are finite. It also saves energy as melting scrap metal in a furnace uses about 80% less energy than producing metal from virgin ores. That way it also reduces air and water pollution, including the carbon footprint from mining and manufacturing. Not to mention that recycling metal saves money, supports jobs, and powers vital economic sectors like automotive, infrastructure, steel making, and construction with cheaper materials.

As his business grew over the decades, Wayne Elliott ended up with a bigger line of credit. It is popular today in business for firms on Wall Street to use almost 100% of their clients' money, which he was not comfortable doing.

If he borrowed $1,000,000 for a ship or ships, he would guarantee the purchasers of the scrap metal they wanted and pay back the money as he was shipping the scrap metal. They would deduct a repayment of $60 to $100 per ton, vessel depending. There could be different terms of payment, but he did everything possible to avoid conventional lenders. When people borrow money from a bank, there is usually a General Security Agreement (GSA) that often requires a personal signature, meaning everything a person owns personally, including their house and certain bank accounts, is at stake until the loan is paid. There are risks associated with this arrangement, stating that if a borrower has a set amount of equipment or assets when obtaining the loan, everything the business acquires afterward automatically falls under the bank's general security agreement. This situation often leaves borrowers with little to no assets available for additional loans if needed. Wayne sought to avoid that and did so successfully.

Top Ten Environmental Hypocrites

#8 Alexandria Ocasio-Cortez (AOC)

How Much Do They Talk? (0 = not at all to 10 = all day) = 4

Amount of Environmental Action? (0 = plants trees daily to 10 = giving speeches) = 8

Real Environmentalist Score = 12

It is a well-established fact that politics is packed full of hypocrites, with politicians often epitomizing double standards by preaching one thing while doing completely the opposite (the old "Do as I say, not as I do" mantra). US Rep. Alexandria Ocasio-Cortez (AOC), the dagger of the radical left wing of the Democratic Party, seems to be no exception to this rule. Presently in her fourth term, having become the youngest women to be elected to Congress at age 29, Ocasio-Cortez has established herself as one of the most vocal and visible environmental advocates in American politics.

She is constantly pushing for transformative climate policy. However, numerous incidents involving her and her staff have led critics to question the coherence between her proclaimed environmental principles and her personal or campaign-related decisions. Conservative and liberal commentators alike have accused AOC of practicing "champagne socialism," enjoying the very lifestyle perks she publicly opposes. GOP figures and conservative media in particular have highlighted the irony of her travel choices, often ridiculing her for "fighting inequality one mimosa at a time." Critics (especially conservatives and centrist Democrats) deem her plans too radical or economically unrealistic.

Arguably one of the most prominent US political figures advocating for aggressive climate action, AOC is best known for her signature draft legislation, the so-called "Green New Deal" (GND) resolution, which she co-introduced in 2019 together with Senator Ed Markey.

The Green New Deal supposedly seeks to address what is described as the "twin crises" of climate change and socio-economic inequality. To achieve that goal, it proposes a 10-year mobilization[80] for net-zero greenhouse gas emissions, jobs guarantees in the green economy, and overhauling infrastructure for sustainability.

Nonetheless, AOC's GND resolution failed miserably, with the Senate voting 57-0 against advancing it, with 43 out of 47 Democratic senators voting "present" to avoid taking a formal stance.[81] In 2023, AOC and Markey reintroduced the Green New Deal resolution, still to no avail.

Despite this, Ocasio-Cortez has given multiple floor speeches, press conferences, and media interviews defending the GND, and calling climate change "our generation's World War II."[82]

Besides that, the New York congresswoman has used her seat on the House Oversight Committee to grill fossil fuel executives and challenge regulatory agencies. She has opposed pipeline projects and fossil fuel subsidies. She has demanded funding for green energy programs and "environmental justice" in underserved communities.

AOC and her staff don't miss a chance to target her millions of followers on social media platforms with messages of how wildfires, floods, and extreme weather are symptoms of climate inaction, how the global climate crisis is a matter of racial, social, and intergenerational justice, and how an urgent transition to a green economy is needed.

In one of the more entertaining controversies surrounding AOC that has sparked massive accusations of hypocrisy, in September 2021, the New York congresswoman thought it would be a great idea to attend the ritzy Met Gala in New York City wearing a white gown emblazoned with "Tax the Rich" on her bottom. By attending the Met Gala, where tickets range from $35,000 to over $200,000, AOC drew criticism for appearing to enjoy the elite's privileges while protesting them.[83] Conservative voices lambasted the move as hypocritical "virtue signaling" as she was partying with the rich while telling them to pay more.[84] Even pro-left media outlets such as *The Washington Post*[85] observed that wearing the slogan at such an exclusive gathering undercuts its sincerity. Fast-forward to July 2025, and the House Ethics Committee formally found that AOC

---

80 https://www.investopedia.com/the-green-new-deal-explained-4588463
81 https://www.congress.gov/bill/116th-congress/senate-joint-resolution/8/text
82 https://reason.com/2019/01/22/alexandria-ocasio-cortez-calls-climate-c/
83 https://www.foxnews.com/media/twitter-ocasio-cortez-met-gala-hypocrisy
84 https://www.forbes.com/sites/danidiplacido/2021/09/15/the-controversy-over-aocs-tax-the-rich-dress-explained/
85 https://www.washingtonpost.com/opinions/2021/09/14/where-aocs-tax-rich-dress-clashes-with-progressive-politics/

had violated rules by not paying the fair market value for the borrowed dress and accessories.[86] She initially paid $990.76, well below the market value. The committee required her to pay an additional $2,733.28 to the designer and donate $250 to the Costume Institute (to cover her date's dinner).[87]

Ludicrous as the "Tax the Rich" dress episode was, it made AOC simply a hypocrite, rather than an environmental hypocrite. Other high-profile incidents, however, have demonstrated that her environmental hypocrisy is unconditional.

Thus, in a very recent episode, in March 2025, AOC was photographed flying first-class on a JetBlue flight from New York to Las Vegas to attend a "Fighting Oligarchy" rally with fellow far-left legislator Bernie Sanders. Critics argue this choice contrasts with her strong stance on income inequality and climate action, citing the higher carbon emissions per passenger in first-class.[88]

On a similar note, reports indicated that AOC's 2018 campaign made 66 airline transactions but only 18 Amtrak train rides. Critics suggested this travel pattern undermined her Green New Deal message.[89]

In response to the criticism, AOC acknowledged, "I also fly & use A/C," arguing that this didn't negate support for systemic change through the Green New Deal, which aims for 100% renewable energy and improved infrastructure.

In another similar demonstration of environmental hypocrisy, Ocasio-Cortez and her staff have been found to rely heavily on ride-hail services near public transit. In 2019, campaign filings showed over 1,000 ride-hail transactions (Uber, Lyft, etc.) and nearly $30,000 spent on car/van rentals, despite her campaign office being just 138 feet, that is, a minute walk, from a subway station. Critics view this as contradicting her environmental priorities.[90]

AOC's response to this criticism has boiled down to noting that personal carbon neutrality is difficult in today's world[91] and that focus should instead be on

---

86 https://nypost.com/2025/07/25/us-news/aoc-broke-house-rules-to-attend-met-gala-with-beau-riley-roberts-told-to-pay-additional-2700-for-tax-the-rich-gown-other-accessories/
87 https://www.vanityfair.com/style/story/alexandria-ocasio-cortez-met-gala-dress-fine
88 https://nypost.com/2025/04/07/us-news/aoc-flies-first-class-to-bernie-sanders-fight-oligarchy-rally/
89 https://www.foxnews.com/politics/ocasio-cortez-responds-to-criticism-of-travel-methods-while-pushing-to-address-climate-change

90 https://www.iheart.com/content/2019-03-04-aocs-hypocrisy-exposed-amid-green-new-deal-plan/
91 https://www.gq.com/story/can-aoc-ride-in-a-car

systemic change and regulation of major polluters.[92] Clearly, the firebrand Democratic congresswoman does not believe in the only too logical "lead by example" rule.

In another of Ocasio-Cortez's environmental failures revealing not just hypocrisy but also ignorance, during a 2019 visit to Colorado, she publicly shared infrared footage she believed showed industrial emissions from a fracking site. In reality, the location had no fracking operations, and the heat signature was from synthetic drilling mud, not pollution.[93] Industry representatives and state regulators pointed out that AOC's conclusions were factually incorrect and criticized her for ignoring the facts.

A further case demonstrating the New York congresswoman's environmental hypocrisy occurred in August 2025 when she drew criticism after celebrating the installation of dozens of new trash cans along Roosevelt Avenue in Queens. Even though she touted the bins as a community win, residents and critics rebuked the move as superficial, arguing it ignored more pressing issues like prostitution, illegal vending, and gang activity in the neighborhood.[94] One Republican council candidate harshly quipped the trash-bin push was akin to "putting sprinkles on s**t," highlighting local frustration that systemic safety problems remained unaddressed even as sanitation bins were added.

To add further to her accomplished profile as an environmental hypocrite, AOC has been rather shameless in using ridiculously alarmist declarations to push her climate change agenda. In January 2019, she famously told an interviewer that "the world is gonna end in 12 years if we don't address climate change."[95] Given that this book is released in September 2025, half of that period is now gone, and, if Alexandria Ocasio-Cortez is correct, us humans, and all of Planet Earth really, have only less than 6 years left to live!

On a more serious note, while AOC's environmental rhetoric has been fiery and apocalyptic, her actions have been far from the necessary credibility to back up her radical stances. "Fighting the Oligarchy" while flying first class has

---

92 https://grist.org/ask-umbra-series/should-we-judge-alexandria-ocasio-cortez-by-her-carbon-footprint/
93 https://thenewamerican.com/us/environment/aoc-s-colorado-trip-reveals-hypocrisy-and-ignorance-of-climate-change-crowd/
94 https://nypost.com/2025/08/30/us-news/aoc-mocked-for-war-on-trash-on-seedy-roosevelt-avenue/
95 https://thehill.com/policy/energy-environment/426353-ocasio-cortez-the-world-will-end-in-12-years-if-we-dont-address/

deservedly earned her and Bernie Sanders the branding of "eco-warrior hypocrites."[96]

Being as vociferous as she is on the House floor, on mainstream and social media, Ocasio-Cortez has managed to turn her Green New Deal into a central issue in Democratic politics in a way few others have. Yet, analysts have been emphasizing that the Green New Deal's goals are logistically unrealistic and hypocritical. The plan calls for complete transition off fossil fuels in a decade while rejecting nuclear—the most emission-free, high-output energy source widely available today. The conservative Heritage Foundation referred to the resolution's exclusion of nuclear power as inefficient and counterproductive, calling it "the great hypocrisy" given AOC's existential climate framing.[97] Even the left-leaning *Politico* has called the GND an "impossible green dream."[98]

No less outrageous than the disconnect between her environmental advocacy and her own practices are AOC's reactions trying to justify it, which add further to her image as an environmental hypocrite. Her pushback boils down to conveniently framing environmentalism as a systemic issue, rather being prescriptive for individual perfection. She happily accepts personal contradictions while arguing for broader policy overhaul.

While she spearheads vocally the progressivist agenda on climate change, the environment, and so many other issues that are central to the left, Congresswoman Alexandria Ocasio-Cortez clearly deserves her spot among the Top Ten Biggest Environmental Hypocrites.

---

[96] https://radaronline.com/p/aoc-bernie-sanders-eco-hypocrites-private-jet-rally/
[97] https://www.heritage.org/node/11284667/print-display
[98] https://www.politico.com/magazine/story/2019/02/07/green-new-deal-224928/

Chapter 4

First ISO-certified

As Wayne Elliott's businesses expanded, he became increasingly aware of the impact they could have on the environment. This awareness motivated him to take responsibility and make sustainability a core part of his business strategy. The more successful his ventures became, the stronger his commitment grew to ensure they contributed positively to the environment and the communities.

"I am proud we're the oldest active shipbreaker in the world. Even though most of our shipbreaking has been here in Canada for the last 70 years, we are proud of our record. We were the first ISO-certified shipbreaker in the world, by quite a few years, too. We were certified in December 2000, ISO 14001, which is the environmental certification. All our companies have been certified since then. But the rules here are much, much stricter. Some of the rules are stricter here in Canada than they are in the United States, regarding asbestos abatement, for example," Wayne noted.

When asked if the certification was of their own accord or if they were made to do it, Wayne responded that they did it themselves. It took them two years, and it's not cheap because there are annual internal audits and annual audits from a certification company they have been with for 24 years. He explained, "We thought that it would be a requirement, and we wanted to jump the gun. It wasn't that we had a whole bunch of extra money to spend; we just believed in it. Being in the battery and shipbreaking businesses, we deal heavily with all the worst of heavy metals (lead, cadmium, mercury), polychlorinated biphenyls (PCBs), reactive metals, lithium, and so forth—all the heavy metals that are bad for our health."

Canada's Ministry of Environment enjoyed working with Wayne's businesses because they were the only ones in their sector that dealt with all this stuff. On the ships, they dealt with mercury, PCBs, asbestos, oil, and waste oil. PCBs are a group of man-made chemical compounds that were used in older paints, coatings, and electrical equipment due to their chemical stability and insulating properties. They are toxic, persistent environmental pollutants that can accumulate in living organisms and pose health risks, which is why their use has been banned or heavily restricted in many countries since the late 1970s.

Once, Wayne's Marine Recycling Corporation worked on two fish trawlers for the government that were abandoned in Newfoundland. Their refrigerator rooms were painted with paint that contained PCBs, so the whole bulkheads had to be taken out and shipped to a treatment facility in Western Canada, which is a long way from where they are in Eastern Canada.

Wayne continued, "We dealt with some of the nastiest stuff in our business, and so you have to do it properly. You have to protect your people. But I was involved, you know, as a young person, really. What they would do, instead of taking the internal furnishings out, like the wood, the decks, and the flooring, they would wait until the wind was blowing in the right direction. This was with the blessing of Wayne's father's friends, the deputy chief and the fire chief in Hamilton, Ontario. When the wind was blowing out towards the lake, they could light the front end of the ship on fire and burn out all the accommodations."

Wayne recalled seeing that more than once. Years later, in 1984, the local fire department, police authorities, and provincial government did a training in their shipyard where they lit the front of the ship on fire, the accommodations, and fought the fire. They filmed that for a training video on how to fight fires aboard ships. "It's a big thing – a ship is surrounded by water, but people die when there are fires aboard ships. So, it was very important that they did that," he said.

Wayne acknowledged that they had some polluting ways. He points out that in other parts of the world, like Asia, there are still all kinds of terrible things going on, where rules are not enforced and safety is a nightmare. He added, "It's harder to compete, but there's only one way to do that business. And that's as safely as you can do it, and that's what we try to do, every day and reward staff monthly for no lost time accidents (our record duration is 1,680 days)."

When asked which countries have the absolute worst conditions, he responded, "Bangladesh and India have the world's largest shipbreaking operations. I would say not to the same extent as others, but Turkey has its own issues. They beach some vessels bow first, leaving the largest concentration of waste, dangling at the after end, unsecured and tied to nothing, free to blow with the wind. There are fuel tanks, oil tanks, and machinery spaces in the stern. There are boilers and asbestos; the worst of the waste is in the stern end of a ship. The stern just floats around with the current, and they can get a hold of the bow of the ships, with about 25 of them over there at a time. In Turkey, one yard is certified and supplies the other yards with ships, and the steel mill loves the ship plate because it is 10-20 steel, free of tramp elements. In Turkey, the stern of the ship with the huge majority of the contamination and waste is the last to come out of the water. However, there's a risk involved. In a monsoon or hurricane, those ships could be all over the place, and the environmental impact would be severe. It's just not anywhere near the standards of Canada or the United States. It wouldn't be tolerated in North America or Europe."

He concluded, "I don't know of anywhere that's tougher than Canada in terms of safety and environmental regulations; they are very serious. The authorities in businesses like ours are crucial, so we've always had to ensure that we get along with them. It was a terrible thing to get on the bad side of those folks because they're getting paid anyway. And you're not while you're spending time with them or doing things that they insist you do to remedy a situation. The authorities generally know whether a company is truly diligent or not, by both the files and records inside and outside of the operation. Intent is a big part of all our laws and regulations."

Navigating Business Risks and Market Uncertainties

Wayne Elliott's experience of running successful companies while actively prioritizing environmental stewardship has taught him a lot when it comes to managing risk in business. That includes the importance of assessing whether a business could survive if things went wrong. There was a time when a steel mill Wayne supplied changed its payment terms without notice, which put his business at risk. He had the realization that if the mill failed, his business might not survive, either, so he gradually reduced his involvement. Although the mill eventually succeeded and continued operations, there was a need to carefully measure risk and not jeopardize one's entire livelihood, like signing away one's house as collateral. He had learned the lesson that it was important to balance passion with practicality in business. His grandparents feeding many at the north end of Hamilton often didn't know if they would have enough for supper for themselves. That was part of his upbringing.

Wayne had an experience from 40 years back when a bank advised him not to take such a major risk, but he did it anyway. In 2007-2008, there was another instance in which the price of scrap metal soared, leading to a situation where his company was spending a significant amount of money daily on purchasing scrap metal. Many scrap yards temporarily closed due to cash flow issues, but his business managed to stay afloat, even though it was a close call. He would never take that kind of risk again, especially after the ferrous scrap market crashed just ten days after he had confirmed all the sales. He had mortgaged his sister's and father's homes to stay open and continue buying scrap. He gained customers then, but it was a close call. That was the last time he had anything to do with borrowing like that.

The biggest challenges Wayne encountered came from dealing with large corporations like General Motors Corporation and the International Nickel

Company, which were always tough encounters. While he could recount numerous losses, particularly with ships, the real risk in his business came with every acquisition of a ship. The scrap market changes every 30 days, which means the value of the ships they acquire can fluctuate significantly over time. Sometimes it takes a year before some of the scrap gets shipped, making it a 100% gamble. That is a risky and frustrating aspect of the business that Wayne dislikes.

There are two sides to the shipbreaking business: commercial work and government contracts. For commercial fleets, like the four vessels MRC has in Lake Erie and Nova Scotia, they purchase the vessels outright, taking on all the associated risks. However, with government vessels, the winning bidder is usually paid to do the work. Government vessels, such as old warships and Coast Guard boats, often have hazardous materials like PCBs, asbestos, and filler materials, making them more costly to recycle.

The commercial vessels are still in demand because they can be sold to Turkey, where they are well-compensated. The main competition comes from these Turkish buyers, who can afford to pay more because steel mills in Turkey set scrap metal prices based on the purchase price of the vessels. This means the Turkish operators are almost always guaranteed a profit, working on a cost-plus basis. On the other hand, Wayne's business faces greater risks because it can't even secure 60-day orders from steel mills, making every acquisition a gamble.

The average cost of a ship varies widely depending on the type and size of the vessel. The general estimate, based on the average value of a large, full-sized ship in today's market—specifically a "full Seaway size" vessel, the so called Seawaymax vessels, which is 740 feet long and 78 feet wide would be around two and a half million dollars once it's cut up into four-foot by two-foot pieces or smaller and delivered to the steel mill.

The width is determined by the constraints of the St. Lawrence Seaway canals. There are eight locks starting in Port Colborne, which go from Lake Erie down to Lake Ontario. Each lock drops the boats about 35 feet, allowing them to pass from one lake to the other. This lock size determines the maximum dimensions of the ships that can traverse the Seaway.

The Panama Canal can accommodate every size ship in the world, including supertankers and Panamax-sized freighters. The width of a ship is determined by where the cargo is being hauled and the voyages being undertaken. In the Great Lakes, there is a 1,000-foot lock at the bottom of Lake Superior, which is 110 feet wide. This lock accommodates the thirteen "1,000-footers" that operate in the Great Lakes, measuring 1,000 feet long and 105 feet wide. However, these massive ships cannot enter Lake Ontario or pass through the St. Lawrence Seaway due to their size.

Wayne's company typically works on at least two, if not three, ships at a time due to the extensive preliminary work involved, such as oil removal, tank cleaning, asbestos handling, and the removal of non-metallic furnishings inside the ship's superstructure. This initial labor must be financed before any scrap metal is recovered.

As noted in the previous chapter, there are significant risks small and medium-sized businesses face when dealing with banks. General security agreements often give banks first position over a company's all assets, including new purchases. Additionally, banks often require personal guarantees from the business owners, putting their homes and savings at risk. That is why, for the past 40 years, Wayne has steered clear of bank financing, instead opting for more innovative financing solutions. This method has the advantage of aligning the financial outcomes for both parties; if his company has a bad month, so do the brokers. In contrast, banks demand repayment regardless of the company's performance. This goes back to a common saying in business: banks will give you an umbrella when the sun is shining, but when it starts to rain, they want to take it back. Thus, Wayne's experience has shown it is important not to live lavishly and ensure that enough money is left in the business to keep it running. With an overhead in excess of a million per week at one point, tougher times are tougher.

Doing business in Canada presents its own challenges, particularly due to the high tax burden. Companies pay 26% on profits left in the business, and personal income tax can be as high as 54% for those in the top tax bracket. After taxes, a business owner might be left with only 20% of their profit, and that's before paying additional sales taxes for goods and services. Canada's tax system is not as favorable for business growth compared to the United States, where municipalities can offer tax incentives and other forms of support to businesses. For example, a steel mill in Kentucky has received reduced electricity rates and tax cuts, advantages that would not be possible in Ontario, Canada, due to restrictions in the Ontario Municipal Act. This regulation cost Hamilton, Ontario, 1,000 full-time jobs and millions in land tax revenue for the past 30 years.

There are challenges to business growth, particularly the increase in overhead costs when expanding operations, such as acquiring a second truck. Growth requires careful financial management to ensure that the increased overhead is eventually covered and that the new assets contribute to profitability. In Canada's tax environment, these challenges are even more pronounced, making borrowing a common necessity for most businesses.

In 1981, Wayne Elliott had a certain experience with his bank. It was extremely difficult to change banks, secure financing, or obtain insurance on equipment. A judge had ordered the bank to remain Wayne's banker, but about a year later, Wayne decided to part ways with it. Anyone who holds security over your assets puts you at risk. The bank that had caused him trouble was later revealed to have been poorly managed. He was told by a bank superintendent that their approach was like "going duck hunting with rifles pointed in the air while looking at the water." The bank had indiscriminately called in loans, often from clients who had never missed a payment, while allowing others who should have been called to remain in business. This sort of mismanagement happens, especially when the interests of businesses and individuals do not align. Contrast this with Wayne's relationship with steel mills, where there was no conflict of interest, as both parties benefited from a successful transaction—if he had a slower month, so did the mills.

It is truly difficult to start a small business, especially when underfunded. Wayne didn't initially think about borrowing money and started by leasing an old truck before eventually purchasing a new truck to pick up scrap boxes, which put him into debt. Wayne's story shows how essential perseverance is in entrepreneurship. As long as someone enjoys, or at least doesn't hate, what they're doing, they should keep pushing forward. With hard work and careful learning from mistakes, success becomes achievable.

At times, MRC would have six vessels in their main yard on Lake Erie, at Port Colborne, and as many as four in their yard at Cape Breton, Nova Scotia. Executing projects on Canada's West Coast would see the company deal with as many as a dozen vessels at once. In some cases, they did not completely recycle those vessels but instead removed all flammables and liquids, such as oil and fuel, to lessen the danger to the environment until the government bid them out for recycling. Even so, if one counted across the country, Wayne's company would have as many as a dozen vessels in their recycling yards at the same time, an impressive accomplishment for an environmentally friendly business.

The People Behind the Hard Work: A Football Team Culture

Behind every successful venture is a team of dedicated individuals brought together by unique management, and Marine Recycling Corporation is no exception. Understanding the environment in which Wayne's workers thrived reveals the true foundation of his sustained success.

When questioned about the workforce, Wayne stressed that most of the work was dirty and involved extreme conditions, such as heat and cold. He confirmed that his employees were not unionized but his management maintained very good relationships with them. He described the company as a family-run business, likening it to a football team where everyone is important and appreciated, resulting in a happy work environment.

He noted that his family has had some long-standing employees, with the longest-serving employee starting with his father at the age of 15 and still working there at 75 years old.

MRC only had so many people trained in the shipbreaking business, so there were times when there was just a handful of men. In the main yard, there would usually be 25 or 30 full-time workers, and they also had some contractors. The MRC employees wouldn't do all the work themselves; they would contract out some of the oil work and tank cleaning, which Wayne considered the two major areas they hired out. The company had its own mechanics and welders, along with a lot of equipment, so it took a fair number of tradespeople. They jobbed out a fair bit of work as well, they had four mechanics, three millwrights, and two welders. While they handled most of the heavy equipment repairs themselves, they contracted out some of the specialist work. There could easily be 40 or 50 people on site, though usually not more than 25.

It has been crucial for Wayne's business to retain its trained staff as there aren't shipbreakers like there are car dealers or restaurant waiters. MRC had to find and train their workers themselves. Considering all the traveling involved in the shipbreaking business, it would be easy to make $100,000 a year. Wayne's employees tend to stay a long time, largely because of the pay and the specialized nature of the work. The company has done a lot of work with First Nations (the Native Indians in Canada) and had trained a number of First Nation individuals. It has had a growing number of First Nation workers, and this arrangement has worked out very well. Wayne is proud of MRC's alliance with First Nation bands in Canada, including formal partnerships.

The shipbreaking work is not the easiest or cleanest and not the kind of work everyone wants to do; it is hot in the summer, very cold in the winter. Nobody with a university degree would be looking to do what they do. Up on the North

Shore of Lake Erie, the weather could be extremely cold. There are some days when the yard would be shut down, particularly during a storm when ships have broken loose in the canal. On one such occasion, Wayne spent most of the night on the phone with the superintendent, and at 6:00 in the morning, from the deck of one of the ships 40 feet above the water while the wind was blowing at 40 kilometers per hour, with temperatures at −30 degrees. Such conditions could cut the skin, making it sometimes too cold or too windy to work. In the summer, however, MRC's yards wouldn't stop working for too long, even though the job could be hot and humid on the Great Lakes, with workers standing on steel in the sun using blowtorches.

Wayne has always been grateful for his employees who do a great job and are accustomed to the work. He really looks after his people, especially when they travel for wreck jobs, some of which might be in rather remote locations. Wayne hopes they will be doing work in Canada's Arctics in several ways involving recycling. Some jobs would require an hour-and-a-half helicopter ride from land, which was mostly ice. MRC estimated that the nearest hospital of any sort was hundreds of miles away. Some of the places where the company has worked are indeed remote, and MRC has had to make sure that its crew eat well and have good accommodation. It is important for everyone to be satisfied given the hard work involved.

On these outside jobs, Wayne's employees would generally work seven days a week, with no telling what hours they might put in. In one instance, they filmed a significant video of the bow of a ship lifted at 1:00 am in the morning, and it had worked out that way because they had to get it up onto the barge.

Wayne says he doesn't know many jobs that require people to work harder or in harsher conditions than his crews do. This creates another dynamic in the shipbreaking business: more than 95 out of 100 people don't want to do this kind of work no matter how much it helps save the environment.

Having the Luxury of a 'Queen's Charter'

Wayne's journey of grit and growth of his environmentally friendly business hasn't gone without its cast of characters—the ones whose boldness, flaws, and grit leave lasting impressions. In the world of heavy industry and scrapyards, these individuals often break the rules, bend reality, and somehow get the job done anyway. One such character was his father, Kenneth, whose stories echo with humor, audacity, and lessons learned on the fly.

One such story shared by Wayne goes back to the late 1970s, and involves Malahat, a mountain on Vancouver Island in British Columbia, on Canada's West Coast. At the time, he and his father were operating in a scrapyard located on the Inner Harbor in Victoria, the capital of British Columbia. Victoria was a beautiful place, popular with tourists, especially from Asia, and had become a favored retirement area.

Wayne had to load a railcar with scrap, after which a truck and float would arrive to transport a crane to a job site at a cement plant in Bamberton, which was across the Malahat mountain. When the truck and float, driven by a private operator named Butch, arrived, Wayne and his team loaded and secured the crane. His father planned to leave early the next morning. However, that day was Sunday, and the Lord's Day Act in British Columbia prohibited hauling cargo on Sundays. Despite this, Kenneth claimed they had a special permit, which Wayne knew was untrue, as his father wasn't known for following all regulations.

The next morning, they set off with the truck and crane, accompanied by him driving a propane-powered Ford Fairmont as an escort vehicle. As they slowly climbed the Malahat mountain, going only 3-4 miles per hour, a Royal Canadian Mounted Police (RCMP) officer passed them and stopped in front of the tractor-trailer. His father immediately pulled out from behind the float, cut in front of the police car, and confronted the officer. As the officer was getting out of his car, his father approached him and demanded to know what he was doing. The officer, surprised, asked if his father was involved with the cargo. The officer reminded his father that it was Sunday, and the Lord's Day Act prohibited hauling freight. In response, Kenneth boldly claimed they were operating under the "Queen's Charter" and threatened the officer, telling him to move his cruiser or face being reassigned to Wawa, Ontario, to count penguins, by Tuesday morning. The officer, visibly taken aback, glanced at the truck and crane, then reluctantly moved his cruiser and left. His father, unfazed by the encounter, returned to the car, chuckling about the fictional "Queen's Charter" escape.

The Queen's Charter was made up and meaningless. There was no such thing, and Wayne's father had fabricated the story on the spot. Yet, Kenneth's aggressive demeanor had been convincing enough to make the officer back down, even though Wawa, Ontario, didn't have any penguins (not unlike the entire Northern Hemisphere), and wasn't as far north as implied. Wayne stressed his father's audacity, describing him as quite the character and noting that this incident was one of his favorite stories about him. They continued their journey, unloaded the crane at the cement company, and began their job as planned on Monday morning. Wayne has enough stories about his father to write a book one day, as his father was truly a unique individual.

Bumping into Awareness Training

One factor that has significantly helped Wayne Elliott in his personal life as well as his business has been awareness training. He had an incident while rollerblading on the boardwalk in Hollywood, Florida, in which he accidentally bumped into a small person while skating. After skating for about 100 yards, he turned around to check on that person. It turned out to be a woman who had been in training for two years to become a self-discovery trainer. This unexpected encounter led Wayne to sign up for a workshop and later pursue personal training with one of the senior trainers.

Self-awareness is a unique experience that can be quite expensive but often reveals how little we know about ourselves. It's like peeling back the layers of an onion. Before this training, Wayne felt burdened by excuses and distractions that made it difficult for him to focus. The training helped him tremendously over the two years he participated in it, particularly to understand why he was so affected by the death of others. He often avoided funerals and discovered that the root of his deep-seated emotions stemmed from the death of his grandfather on the same day President Kennedy was assassinated. Wayne's parents discussed whether he was supposed to see his grandfather's body. He recalled how fear had prevented him from touching his deceased grandfather.

The training aimed to make participants aware of their identities. Wayne has a "warrior" identity, and he recognized that individuals could have other identities, such as a "victim" or "victimizer." The goal was to learn about these identities and to act and speak in ways that best served their interests and goals.

Unfortunately, Wayne had experiences in business in which his "warrior" identity led to poor decisions. In one instance, he ended up having significant problems with a company to which he proposed to supply their scrap metal. He was eventually told politely that his proposal was not feasible. Despite finding enough scrap metal on-site to sustain their needs for the quarter, he had made the mistake of saying there was "no silver platter" for him to take advantage of, which effectively ended that opportunity.

In any case, the self-awareness training was very valuable to Wayne. The only experience that had a more profound impact on his life was his relationship with Jim Strauss, who taught him about natural health and how everything in nature connects. The self-awareness training was challenging as it pushed him to confront his limiting beliefs, leading to noticeable changes in himself.

Wayne's mother and others recognized the transformation: he was different. He used to struggle to maintain focus during conversations, feeling a lack of control over his thoughts. Many people tend to dwell on the past, which can hinder their ability to stay present and focus on the current moment. It is important to be aware and present since most of life's experiences and opportunities lie ahead rather than behind. He is thankful to have undergone this training. He now feels more settled and capable of focusing on the present rather than being consumed by past and other distractions, playing like a movie in our head.

The most valuable lesson he learned was about present-moment awareness. This technique is simple and can be done quickly. It involves focusing all of one's attention on what they see, and it's best to look at open spaces rather than crowded or complex environments. One shouldn't fixate on specific colors or shapes but take in the overall surroundings. If thoughts intrude after a minute, let them pass and refocus on the sights.

This exercise extends to hearing and touch as well, encouraging individuals to be aware of sounds and physical sensations, for instance, the feeling of one's body in the chair and one's feet on the floor. It is about maintaining 100% attention to these sensations, allowing any passing thoughts to drift away without engaging with them.

This technique helps calm the mind, enabling individuals to make decisions without being overwhelmed by emotions. This practice allows someone to step outside their own head, viewing their feelings objectively. Focusing on being present has become automatic for Wayne, helping him quickly let go of negative emotions and focus on the matter at hand.

Since he adopted this technique, it has become easier for him to find solutions and think clearly, as emotions like anger or frustration can cloud judgment. It is important to not let past events interfere with present tasks. Wayne encourages everyone to try this simple exercise, which only takes a couple of minutes, and can help individuals stay focused and present, improving their decision-making ability. "I was very impressed with self-discovery techniques and workshops from Fort Lauderdale, Florida. Rob and Susan James created some very effective techniques, indeed," he said.

Doing More Than Many Environmentalists

As Wayne's business grew, it was doing more and more essential work by preventing ships from rotting on the coastline and managing the recycling process as environmentally as possible. For some reason, the shipbreaking industry is constantly facing public criticism, despite doing more for the environment than many environmentalists. His RMC (Raw Materials Corporation) invented what was considered the best demonstrated technology in the world for recycling alkaline batteries, and manufacturing a micronutrient additive widely used in the USA to grow corn.

The shipbreaking and ship recycling involve dealing with significant amounts of hazardous materials, including oil, fuels, asbestos, PCBs, mercury, and various other dangerous substances found in old marine vessels, especially warships. While these materials are inherently part of the ships, the key is to manage them properly. Every pound of asbestos ever handled by Wayne Elliott's family was sent to legal landfills and buried immediately, following strict protocols for hazardous materials.

Under Wayne's leadership, Marine Recycling Corporation implemented an expensive process for removing oil and fuels from ships. They began by vacuum-pumping all the oil and fuels, followed by recharging and washing the tanks, and draining the engines to ensure that not a drop of oil would hit the ground or water. This work was both expensive and time-consuming, often taking two to three months before the metal and waste work on a ship was completed. Ship recycling could never be a "white glove" business due to the sheer volume of waste, including internal furnishings, carpets, wallboards, mirrors, and toilets.

MRC's most recent innovation involved rolling ships out of the water onto dry ground. This method prevented ships from breaking loose in storms, as they were no longer tied up but instead securely positioned on the ground. This approach also ensured that nothing, not even a speck of rust, would enter the water. They not only cleaned but also graded and compacted the slipway, preparing it for the next ship to be rolled out on large, durable rubber devices.

Wayne's company also made significant advancements in terms of reducing air emissions by moving away from traditional torch cutting, which involved 20 people cutting ships into small pieces. Now, over 90% of the ship's structure was cut into steel mill-sized pieces using portable hydraulic shears, eliminating the need for torches and the resulting smoke.

MRC has been ISO 14001 certified for the past 25 years, which has required continuous environmental improvements. Each year, the company conducts internal audits before the annual recertification audit, which is a significant and costly endeavor. Despite the challenges, Wayne has pride in his company's achievements, noting that during recertification audits, it has become increasingly difficult for inspectors to find even minor variances, let alone major ones.

Even though true perfection might never be attainable, the program of continuous improvement had been a cornerstone of Wayne's operations for 25 years. Despite the inherent challenges of the industry, MRC has been committed to maintaining the highest environmental standards.

Corporate greed often prevents progress in environmental protection. Such behavior would never be acceptable in a courtroom, where financial motives wouldn't excuse environmental damage. For Wayne Elliott, that has never even been a question to begin with. His business keeps solving tremendous environmental challenges on daily basis – and not just in shipbreaking.

Top Ten Environmental Hypocrites

#7 Jeff Bezos

How Much Do They Talk? (0 = not at all to 10 = all day) = 10

Amount of Environmental Action? (0 = plants trees daily to 10 = giving speeches) = 8

Real Environmentalist Score = 18

The Clean Technica website wrote in June 2024, "Don't these 1% have a responsibility to cut emissions, not only in their business enterprises but in their personal carbon footprints? The most well-off do have the highest carbon lifestyles, after all. It seems that personal wealth does more than national wealth to explain the sources of emissions. So, climate progress means first curbing the carbon output of the wealthier among us. The richest 1% of the world's population produced as much carbon pollution in 2019 as the 5 billion people who made up the poorest two-thirds of humanity. Research shows that, for example, to even cut our carbon footprints in the US, its top emitters would have to cut pollution by 87% by 2030 while the bottom half could actually increase theirs by 3%."

They were thinking about Jeff Bezos when they wrote the above. He is #7 on our list of environmental hypocrites. Jeff is the founder of Amazon and Blue Origin and is currently ranked as the second richest person on Earth. Through his and Amazon's philanthropic initiatives and investments, Bezos has made significant contributions to various social and environmental causes. However, despite his efforts to promote sustainability, Bezos has faced accusations of environmental hypocrisy. He deserves it! These criticisms focus on the environmental impact of Amazon's operations, his personal lifestyle choices, and the activities of his space exploration company, Blue Origin.

One of the primary criticisms against Bezos revolves around Amazon's environmental impact. Amazon uses 3.4 quadrillion boxes per year. Every year, the entire Amazon forest is completely stripped to provide the boxes for Amazon. That is where the name came from. Each American receives and must dispose of 4,351 boxes from Amazon per year. As the largest e-commerce company globally, Amazon's operations have a substantial carbon footprint. The company relies heavily on a vast network of warehouses, transportation, and delivery services, all of which contribute to greenhouse gas emissions. The rapid delivery model that Amazon champions results in increased packaging waste and significant energy consumption. While Amazon has made strides in improving its environmental practices, such as committing to achieving net-zero carbon emissions by 2040 and investing in renewable energy, the scale of its operations continues to pose significant environmental challenges. Despite their efforts, the company was removed from a key list of climate-conscious companies in August 2023. But at least they are trying and set an aggressive goal, so he gets one point on the Reducing Their Footprint score card.

Bezos's personal lifestyle choices have also come under scrutiny. As one of the richest individuals in the world, he owns private jets, multiple properties and luxury yachts. These assets contribute to a substantial personal carbon footprint.

Surely, he needs private planes for security and convenience. So, let's forgive him for having one. He deserves it! What about the second? Maybe not. Maybe. Amazon is cool. And the third? No! That is excessive! He has two ultra-long-range Gulfstream G650ERs, registered as N271DV and N758PB. He recently added a Pilatus PC-24 to the fleet.

One house, two house, three? How many houses does he have? He recently purchased a $79 million spread on South Florida's Indian Creek Island, a seven-bedroom, 14-bathroom property spread across 19,064 square feet. Several months earlier, Bezos reportedly purchased a $68 million home located right next door, right next door! It's 9,259 square feet on 2.8 acres. He owns a property portfolio in Seattle worth a staggering $190 million, which includes five homes that went previously unreported. In April 2020, the online shopping magnate closed on a $16 million, three-bedroom condominium on the 20th floor of 212 Fifth Ave. He already dropped $80 million in June 2019 on the 21st, 22nd, 23rd and 24th floors. In November 2021, Bezos spent $78 million on a Hawaiian estate that stretches across 14 acres of pristine land. He paid $23 million in 2016 for the former Textile Museum in Washington's upscale Kalorama neighborhood. He also bought the 4,800-square-foot home across the street for $5 million in January 2020. Two years ago, Bezos purchased a $165 million mansion in Beverly Hills. And he has 30,000 acres in Texas for Blue Origin to blast rockets from. How many is that?

The Bezos yacht situation is the most indicative of his concern for the environment. He recently took delivery of the $500 million Koru superyacht. It emits an astounding 1,500 times more greenhouse gases than an average person. Despite being the largest sailing yacht in the world, the 417-feet long vessel will be responsible for more than 7,150 tons of CO_2 every year. But it gets worse!

The Koru has a support yacht that travels alongside to provide more stuff! The shadow vessel, Abeona, follows the mothership with every essential toy, tenders, speedboats, a submarine, and, of course, a helicopter.

Jeff Bezos' opulent wedding to Lauren Sanchez in June 2025 deserves a special mention in that regard. The Bezos-Sanchez wedding in Venice saw the arrival of a staggering 96 private jets. It is estimated to have produced 17.5 times more carbon emissions than a typical American wedding. That is estimated to be the equivalent to the average yearly emissions of 1,547 people, not to mention that the same estimate predicted at least two people would "die from heatwaves induced by the wedding carbon footprint."

Luckily, Bezos' Blue Origin space rocket company uses no energy and causes no pollution! Well, not really, but it is much cleaner than Elon Musk's SpaceX. Traditional rockets trigger chemical reactions that deplete the ozone layer. Richard Branson's VSS Unity rocket uses a mix of solid and liquid propellants. Elon Musk's SpaceX Falcon project relies on liquid oxygen and a rocket-grade kerosene called RP-1. Both deplete the ozone like a 1978 hairspray can. Blue Origin's rockets, however, are powered by a mix of liquid hydrogen and liquid oxygen. The propellants are much cleaner than conventional rocket fuel. Darin Toohey, an atmospheric scientist at the University of Colorado, said "that the main emissions from (Blue Origin's) New Shepard would be 'water and some minor combustion products, and virtually no CO2.'" Well done, Jeff! You get a point for that!

Chapter 5
Battery Recycling

Wayne Elliott began thinking about battery recycling as early as the 1970s. At the beginning, he and a friend used hatchets to break the tops off lead-acid car batteries. They would manually dismantle the batteries, often in rough conditions without the benefit of proper safety equipment or facilities, exposing themselves to the dangers of acid and heavy metals. They took the lead plates and transported them to Toronto to a smelter. After lots of extra work and travel, Wayne was able to sell the extracted metals for about $1,800 more than he had paid for the batteries. It was not a good long-term business, just too rough. After 10 tough money losing years, RMC stopped lead battery recycling and focused on other chemistries, primarily alkaline because; they make up 85% of all consumer batteries and nobody else wanted them.

He knew it doesn't take a genius to understand that batteries should not be placed in unprotected landfills, where they could contaminate soil and groundwater. While batteries make up less than one-tenth of 1% of municipal landfill materials, they could account for over 40% of the hazardous waste found in landfills.[99] Wayne felt that this issue should have been taken seriously much sooner by the public and the authorities.

Solving the Battery Problem

In 1985, he started Raw Materials Company Inc. (RMC)[100] to solve the battery problem. At that time no state, city, province or nation mandated alkaline battery collection or recycling. Since then, of course, the problem has gotten much worse. Each year, Americans throw away more than 3 billion batteries, totaling 180,000 tons of hazardous waste. The average American household buys as many as 90 alkaline batteries annually. A total of 86,000 tons of hazardous waste comes from single-use alkaline batteries. AA, C and D batteries make up 20% of all

---

99 https://www.financialexpress.com/business/express-mobility-improper-disposal-of-batteries-contributes-to-over-40-of-the-hazardous-chemicals-in-landfills-with-major-risks-of-groundwater-contamination-3700409/?utm_source=chatgpt.com
100 https://pitchbook.com/profiles/company/179956-90?utm_source=chatgpt.com#overview

hazardous household waste. Alkaline batteries are the double A, triple A batteries for remote, game controllers, flashlights, etc. You buy 90 a year.[101]

Less than 5% of these batteries are recycled in the US[102] If you search online for "battery recycling," the useful *Home Depot* site suggests, "Most places don't accept single-use alkaline batteries for recycling. You can't take single-use batteries to Call2Recycle drop-off sites at The Home Depot. In most places, you can put alkaline batteries, such as AA, AAA and D batteries, in the trash. They can be carried out to the curb with the rest of your household garbage. Many landfills will also accept trash bags that contain alkaline batteries."[103] That's right, just throw them away! Except in California, hide them in a milk carton and then throw that away!

Wayne was always thinking whether it was wise to stick with battery recycling for so long, but his deep belief in environmental stewardship kept him going. He was passionate about protecting the environment for future generations and was motivated by the impact they made in preventing consumer batteries from ending up in landfills. These batteries, used in remote controls, children's toys, and various electronic devices, could fill ten large freighters from the Great Lakes each year, and they had been ending up in unprotected landfills for decades. During his more than 35 years with RMC and two earlier efforts in 39 years, Wayne's RMC recycled over 500,000 tons of batteries, or enough to fill 20 full-sized lake freighters.

Remember the thesis of the book? Some people are really making a difference while some people are just putting on a performative act. Wayne Elliott started a business with no clear revenue and unknown, but very large, startup costs. His goal was to make money while solving some of the world's battery problems. More than just a business venture, it was a leap of faith rooted in real-world action—years of navigating regulations, designing custom recycling technology, hiring and training specialized staff, and dealing with the literally dirty work of environmental cleanup. He spent millions of dollars to make it happen. Who deserves more to be given an honorary United Nations title? Wayne Elliott or Leonardo DiCaprio? Who has spent more time, sweat, and energy cleaning ship oil tanks or fighting a lithium fire?

More importantly, if you recycle a ton of batteries and fail to post about it, fail to tweet about it, or fail to issue a press release, is it still a good thing? Is there value

---

101 https://healtheplanet.com/100-ways-to-heal-the-planet/batteries/
102 https://www.superfy.com/what-happens-to-recycled-batteries-the-ultimate-2023-guide/
103 https://www.homedepot.com/c/ab/how-to-dispose-of-batteries/9ba683603be9fa5395fab90124a115f1

in cleaning a shoreline if you get zero retweets or likes? How often do you think Wayne Elliott tweets?

In 2020, his company, RMC, helped break a record in Ontario, Canada, by recycling 50% of all consumer batteries sold in the region.[104] At their peak, they were recycling about 52%, equating to approximately 24 million pounds of consumer batteries per year,[105] that's about 12,000 tons. At the beginning, Raw Materials Company had long tables with conveyor belts built in. They designed and built the tables themselves. Employees would hand-sort the batteries as they moved down the tables, sorting on average 1,000 tons per month.

100% Battery Recycling

From his battery recycling business, Wayne lost money for 25 straight years. He knew this was a sign of resilience or foolishness, or both. He believed the environmental clock would advance much faster than it did. Governments would mandate alkaline recycling as soon as his technology was known. He started about fifteen or sixteen years too early, he says and wishes he had not wasted 10 years on lead batteries recycling.

That's when legislation in Ontario mandated that batteries must be collected to the best extent possible.[106] Ontario was the first Canadian province to make a battery collection law. RMC won the contract with the province and had responsibility for collecting spent batteries from 5,200 sites in Ontario. At their height, they collected 54% of the spent batteries sold.

RMC developed the best demonstrated technology in the world, with approximately 60% of the recycled battery material used as a micronutrient additive in fertilizers, particularly for corn used in ethanol production in the United States. Additionally, the steel fraction from the batteries was also recycled, achieving both the highest recycling rate in the world and a proprietary process invented in-house. Not an ounce of these batteries ever went to landfills.

Sixty percent of the battery (by weight) goes to the United States and is used as a micronutrient additive with fertilizer. Called "black mass," the iron, potassium, zinc, and magnesium mix is leached by a fertilizer company and added to their

---

104 https://environmentjournal.ca/canadians-recycled-a-record-amount-of-batteries-in-2020/
105 https://www.newswire.ca/news-releases/raw-materials-company-president-recognized-as-sustainability-leader-for-battery-recycling-at-clean50-summit-516086291.html?utm_source=chatgpt.com
106 https://ero.ontario.ca/notice/019-0048

products. Thirty pounds of their black mass covers an acre that will yield an extra twenty bushels of corn. That corn is juiced and turned into ethanol fuel. Wayne has sold black mass to the same family business for over 20 years. The families know each other well.

Wayne summarized, "[We] have done great business together in a strong spirit of cooperation and trust. They've made this work by turning tens of thousands of tons of what used to go in municipal landfill into a micronutrient additive for growing corn and other crops."

Additionally, steel jackets are 100% recycled. Steel jackets make up another 20 to 25% of the batteries' overall weight.

Finally, paper and plastic are shipped to and used by a waste-to-energy plant in Niagara Falls, New York, where they are converted into electricity through safe burning. RMC pays extra for this, but it gets them to 100% battery recycling. Batteries are thus completely recycled.

Disappointed in the United States

Wayne expected that the United States would follow suit and soon require battery collection and recycling as well. He was excited when California made its first attempt to do that in the mid-2010s but was disappointed when the law was not passed. He was excited and disappointed three more times.

Finally, on the fifth attempt in 2022, California passed battery recycling mandates.[107] Wayne Elliott was responsible to some degree for finally getting the law passed. A delegation of California lawmakers and bureaucrats traveled to Port Colborne, Ontario, to visit his operation. They had always been told there was no effective process for alkaline. They inspected everything and eventually left satisfied that everything was being safely recycled. Impressed by what they saw, they returned to California and successfully passed the legislation. Unfortunately, the law does not kick in until April 2027.[108]

As of late 2024, only eleven US states and DC have battery recycling laws.[109] This upset Wayne, and he wondered what is wrong with the other states! Then

---

[107] https://www.bdlaw.com/publications/california-passes-two-new-laws-to-overhaul-states-battery-extended-producer-responsibility-program-and-broadly-expand-states-e-waste-program/
[108] https://www.waste360.com/waste-legislation/12-states-setting-the-standard-for-battery-recycling-and-safety
[109] Ibid.

he shakes his head and walks away. The states that require recycling are California, Minnesota, New York, Washington, Vermont, New Jersey, Maryland, Maine, Florida, Colorado, and Iowa, alongside the District of Columbia.

Wayne's battery recycling business made money for 12 or 13 years. He sold the company but retained ownership of the site, leasing it to the company that bought the assets. The manufacturers had been extremely uncooperative, and Wayne felt lucky to get out of it. It was a shame what the manufacturers had gotten away with regarding battery recycling since a great majority of the batteries were going into unprotected municipal landfills via household garbage. There were over a quarter million tons of batteries a year going into landfills, which is a small percentage of landfill materials but responsible for over 80% of all heavy metals in landfills. This had motivated Wayne to enter the business, driven by concerns for his sons and hopes of having grandchildren. He lost money for many years.

50 Years Too Early

Wayne wasn't claiming to be smart, recalling that people said he was 50 years too early with his battery recycling idea. Raw Materials Company scuffled along with the businesses wanting to be green. The US Energy Department would come up and spend days with them, sending them two barrels of batteries with a total bill of only $1,000. RMC did hundreds of formal audits with Fortune 500 companies, government agencies, many for as little as $1,000 in gross revenue. It was a tough business.

The new operators are aggressively growing the business and have the financial backing to encourage battery manufacturers to fulfill their responsibilities. Wayne is excited about the opportunities if the government and the Courts side in favor of the environment.

During a television interview in which Wayne participated a long time ago, the interviewer asked him what was so hard about alkaline batteries. Wayne explained how the steel casing of the battery could rust, causing its contents to spill out. While acknowledging that there were some micronutrients in alkaline batteries, he stressed the presence of harmful substances like potassium hydroxide. He also underscored the dangers posed by mercury batteries, lithium batteries, and nickel-cadmium batteries, stating that the five heaviest and most dangerous metals were all related to battery recycling. Wayne challenged the reporter by asking if he would be willing to eat a battery, holding one up as a visual aid. The reporter declined as a clear indication of the risks involved.

Wayne didn't want his great-grandchildren to be affected by battery waste or for it to spoil the water table. He found it insane that batteries were still being disposed of in landfills and lamented the lack of legislative action on the issue. It took 20 years for legislation to finally emerge, after which his company, RMC, began to turn a profit.

Raw Materials Company operated successfully for another 13 years under Wayne's ownership but always believed it should have been making more money considering the dangerous materials they handled, particularly lithium, which he described as potentially the most dangerous due to its fire risk. Once RMC got involved with a government program, it achieved about 10 to 15% profit on sales, despite heavily investing in training and striving to maintain high standards.

Wayne was proud of what they had achieved, but also expressed a lingering sense of loss, saying his heart still bled for the deal they had closed. Raw Materials Company is now owned and backed by E360, a BlackRock company, the world's largest asset management firm, and he said he hoped they would take the operation further than he had been able to over the years.

When it came to battery recycling in the United States, Wayne voiced his long-standing frustration. He explained that Americans still largely throw batteries away rather than recycle them. He criticized the lack of infrastructure and stressed that those representing battery manufacturers had managed to discourage cities and states from pursuing recycling initiatives. California had just passed legislation on its fifth attempt, with Wayne questioning why it had taken so long for such an important environmental issue to be addressed.

Reflecting on California's population—nearly 40 million, about the same as all of Canada—Wayne was astounded by the sheer number of batteries in circulation. He noted how battery use had surged, with more battery-powered devices than ever before, including toys and games for children. Such devices were not prevalent during his childhood, highlighting how the demand for batteries has skyrocketed.

'Fly on the Back of an Elephant'

Each year, RMC recycles around 10,000-12,000 tons of batteries, a volume Wayne compared to "a fly on the back of an elephant," underscoring how much more needs to be done.

Wayne spoke with pride about their portable recycling system, which required no smokestack permits and could be set up almost anywhere. Developing it took years, during which Raw Materials Company made five major improvements to the original patent. He was especially proud of his chief engineer, who had been with him for 12 years and had previously worked in research at General Motors and was close to Wayne's family.

Shifting to electric vehicles, Wayne highlighted growing concerns around their batteries. He noted that a single electric transport truck battery could cost around $100,000. These large batteries, like smaller consumer versions in cameras and remote controls, are made up of cells linked in series. Wayne emphasized the risks associated with lithium batteries, recounting an incident where a tiny speck of pure lithium caused significant damage in the RMC laboratory. He described how a drop of sweat from a worker ignited the lithium, burning a six-foot diameter hole through 13 inches of concrete, underscoring the reactive nature of lithium.

Wayne expressed his regret about the safety risks posed by lithium in batteries, mentioning incidents of fires in devices and waste collection centers. He acknowledged the different chemistries involved in battery production but stressed that lithium is a common component. He lamented the excessive use of lithium, particularly in lithium-ion batteries that contain expensive cobalt.

Wayne agreed that the present situation could emerge as a significant opportunity for American companies, possibly hinting at BlackRock's interest in legislation that could facilitate battery recycling in the US. He recalled how much RMC had been anticipating legislation in California, and how pleased the company was when the delegation of 33 people, including a senator and a congressman, visited their operation. This visit was intended to verify the existence of a recycling process that could handle the growing battery waste, which led to the introduction of the California legislation supporting battery recycling.

Wayne highlighted the tremendous future opportunities in the recycling business but cautioned that entering the market requires substantial upfront investment, not to mention the hope for supportive legislation and collection processes. He recalled Raw Materials Company's experience in Ontario, where it managed the battery collection from 5,200 sites. Even so, he admitted uncertainty about how much they invested versus what they recovered from that endeavor. His company recycled about 12,000 tons of small consumer batteries annually for 15 years in Ontario before selling that business.

Throughout his career, Wayne Elliott has taken pride in the environmental benefits of his work. Despite the dirty and dangerous nature of his businesses, he finds satisfaction in knowing they recycle materials properly and help prevent pollution and conserving natural resources, such as iron, steel, aluminum, copper, nickel, and more.

The battery business was the most challenging endeavor Wayne had undertaken, spanning four decades. At its height, his Raw Materials Company Inc. managed to collect over 50% of the batteries sold in Ontario, which was a significant achievement. Despite such enlightened and critical efforts, the world continues to pollute the environment at an alarming rate due to corporate greed.

Wayne has this frustration with the large battery companies that, under the guise of promoting recycling, have actually done their best to demotivate progress in the 40 years he had been involved in the industry. Individuals would face severe consequences for such behavior, but corporations seemed to get away with it. Despite his lack of formal education in sciences and chemistry, Wayne's passion for the environment kept him engaged in the business. Very few people could say they lost money for 20 years in a row and still continued in the same business. However, once battery collection was legislated in Canada, his company had 13 consecutive profitable years.

As noted above, Wayne was especially proud of the technology RMC invented and built, which provided micronutrients for corn grown for ethanol in the United States. This technology, derived from alkaline batteries, has been highly successful in improving corn yields. Over the course of a couple of decades, under Wayne's leadership, the company continually bettered its battery recycling technology to near perfection. Despite the immense challenges, he is proud of the accomplishments in the battery recycling business, which is the most difficult yet rewarding work he has ever done.

As an environmentalist, ship recycler, battery recycler, scrap metal recycler and Canadian entrepreneur, Wayne has observed closely the developments in the United States, noting that there are fewer limits on corporate contributions to US political candidates, which has led to significant influence from industries like pharmaceuticals.

Tesla's Telling Troubles

There was shocking news in April 2024 when Tesla announced it would lay off some 14,000 workers, about 10% of its workforce.[110] This coincided with reports of Tesla's plummeting revenues,[111] with some reports[112] leaving one to wonder whether the company could go out of business. It is difficult not to question both Tesla's future, and the overall feasibility of electric vehicles (EVs). There are doubts about the world's readiness for EVs, the extensive infrastructure required for charging. Wayne noted that a Tesla car needed to be charged four times to get from where he was in Ontario to Louisville, Kentucky, for example. Long drives would become even more tedious with the added wait times for charging, which made EVs impractical for him.

Wayne also has concerns about the safety of using lithium batteries in cars given their reactivity and instability. Lithium is a reactive metal, and when a lithium battery is breached, it can explode and ignite a fire that worsens with water exposure, even just the moisture in the atmosphere. There are risks associated with using lithium batteries in vehicles that can crash, especially in wet conditions. Wayne points out recent reports about the increasing number of lithium battery-related fires, particularly in electric bicycles and other devices, which doubled between 2022 and 2024 in the UK.[113] The alternative battery technologies, such as nickel-metal hydride or nickel-cadmium batteries, had been considered, but their application is very much questionable because they have lower energy density, and would result in even shorter driving ranges. While Wayne understands that lithium's power has made it a likely choice, he still harbors misgivings about the long-term viability of EVs with lithium batteries, particularly in light of the Canadian government's plan to phase out gasoline-powered vehicles by 2030 or 2035. There seems to be trouble in the electric vehicle (EV) industry, particularly with the recycling of lithium batteries.

A pilot project, which might cost around $10 million, is typically done to test up to 10% of a plant's capacity before moving forward with full-scale production. Wayne draws on his experience with alkaline batteries, where his team opted to further their science by separating zinc and manganese, which opened more uses for the materials, including in the cosmetic industry. Despite the high cost of building a pilot plant, they decided against skipping this crucial step to avoid the risk of losing even more money if the full-scale plant didn't work as intended.

---

110 https://www.business-standard.com/world-news/tesla-lays-off-more-than-10-of-global-workforce-amid-dwindling-sales-124041600105_1.html
111 https://www.lemonde.fr/en/economy/article/2024/04/23/sales-falling-prices-cuts-tesla-s-revenues-plummeted-55-in-first-quarter_6669315_19.html
112 https://edition.cnn.com/2025/07/08/business/tesla-troubled-financial-outlook
113 https://www.fleetnews.co.uk/news/e-bikes-drive-lithium-ion-battery-fire-increase

Tesla, however, may have canceled their pilot program, and given the recent layoffs, it was unlikely it would proceed with a full-scale plant. It may be hoping that someone else would develop a more efficient method for recycling the batteries.

Moving On from Lead Batteries

Wayne's extensive experience with batteries began about 50 years ago when a veteran in the scrap business taught him about the lead inside car batteries, and how to extract and sell it. Throughout his career, he was working three different times in breaking lead batteries. The job is grueling due to the corrosive sulfuric acid that would destroy floors, equipment, and everything it touched. By 1998, Wayne decided to leave the lead business and shift his focus, driven by his belief that the environmental movement would progress more rapidly. He couldn't accept the idea of these dangerous "poison pills" being dumped into municipal landfills. He appeared on television to speak out about the risks posed by these batteries when they end up in unprotected landfills, seeping toxic chemicals like potassium hydroxide, nickel, zinc, lead, mercury, and cadmium into the groundwater. Mercury, cadmium, and lead are the three most dangerous metals to human health.[114] Wayne's concern for the environment has been inspiring him to really put in an effort to combat the problem. His inspiration stemmed from the troubling reality that the United States, for example, produces an estimated 180,000-200,000 tons of battery waste per year, while its total recycling annual capacity stands at only 35,000 tons.[115] Thus, more than 150,000 tons of batteries end up in municipal landfills every year in America alone, contributing to a significant environmental hazard.

Wayne is proud of the record-breaking collection efforts in Ontario, where his team managed to recycle 54% of all batteries sold in a single year, amounting to about 12,000 tons. To illustrate the magnitude of the issue, the 150,000 tons of batteries that end up in US landfills annually are the size of a large lake freighter, measuring 740 feet long and 75 to 78 feet wide. It would take five such ships, each filled with 30,000 tons of batteries, to match the volume of these "poison bullets" being buried in landfills every year.

After Wayne's Raw Materials Company ceased its operations related to lead in the late 1990s, his team shifted their focus entirely to other battery chemistries and the collection of these materials. At the time, there was no legislation

---

114 https://portlandclinicofnaturalhealth.com/the-big-four-toxic-metals-mercury-lead-cadmium-and-arsenic-exploring-their-health-impacts/
115 https://poweringautos.com/how-much-of-battery-recycled-in-us-each-year/

governing battery disposal and recycling in North America, neither in Canada, nor in the US. The province of Ontario, Canada, became the first to implement such legislation with its 2002 Waste Diversion Act.[116]

This legislation was significant because it allowed Wayne's company to receive fees from the producer responsibility organization representing all the major battery manufacturers who sold new batteries in stores. Initially, the program was managed by Stewardship Ontario for the first 12 years, and it was run quite effectively. However, due to their success in surpassing targets, the battery manufacturers' producer responsibility organization insisted that his team not acquire any new customers for two years. Wayne thought the organization's demand was completely evil since the battery recycling target should be 100%. He likened it to playing for a basketball team with a goal of winning only four out of 10 games—an approach he found unacceptable, especially given the potential environmental damage.

Corporate Greed Kicks In

Wayne's battery recycling effort faced tremendous challenges during the years between stopping lead recycling and welcoming the legislation encouraging corporations to have the various battery chemistries pay to have them handled and recycled properly. He went 20 years in a row with Raw Materials Company losing money. However, he had such a strong belief in what they were doing and truly thought that legislation mandating battery collection would be implemented faster in Canada and the United States.

Currently only four US states and the District of Columbia have legislated battery collection programs,[117] and California isn't starting until 2026, so there always seem to be delays. Wayne stresses that it is all about saving the corporate giants money, despite collecting recycling fees for each battery sold in Ontario. The recycling technology RMC developed exists and their plant in Port Colborne, Ontario, has proven it to be very efficient. Their recycling rate was about 84% of the battery, and if they counted the waste energy, it rose to over 92%, which was the highest in the world. It is at least double that of Europe, where they are still throwing batteries into a furnace just to recover the zinc, which constitutes 20% of the battery to start with. There is no industrial furnace, whether for gold, silver, platinum, or any metal, that recovers 100% of what is put in at the top end. There has never been a furnace in history that achieves this, as there are always slag

---

116 https://faolex.fao.org/docs/pdf/on115867.pdf
117 https://www.ppai.org/media-hub/is-federal-lithium-ion-battery-legislation-on-the-horizon/

and impurities. Thus, after processing, companies that use furnaces recover about 17% of the whole battery in the form of zinc metal, leaving 80% as hazardous waste.

When dwelling on corporate greed hurting the environment and people, for that matter, Wayne points out the situation in Palmerton, Pennsylvania, which has one of the largest piles of managed hazardous waste in the country. It is the site of a former zinc plant, now a mountain that stretches through two counties, which was added to the Superfund National Priorities List all the way back in 1983.[118] He notes that the company responsible for it would go bankrupt every few years, only for another Wall Street firm to come along and buy it. The pile has never been cleaned up, resulting in lead contamination in the streams and rivers, and children in the two counties exhibiting high blood lead levels. The situation is such a disgrace. They did build a new plant and move out of Palmerton, Pennsylvania, altogether, but the mountain of waste remains. The EPA could never get the company to clean it up or even start the cleanup process. In Wayne's view, this exemplifies typical Wall Street behavior, which is solely focused on making money, disregarding all else. For him, it is criminal to willfully pollute.

Wayne's Raw Materials Company operated under Stewardship Ontario for 13 years, after which the battery manufacturers' own program, Call2Recycle, took over. His view is that Call2Recycle, which is active in both the US and Canada, has done a horrible job in their 40 years, noting that it had only two states—Connecticut and Vermont—with legislation in place. It fought against legislation in California four times and succeeded in delaying it. The legislation was finally approved, only to be delayed for over three years before it could enter into force. Wayne is still startled how the law's implementation was delayed for three years instead of starting immediately. He thinks the battery manufacturers likely had significant political influence due to their thousands of employees, many of whom represent household names. These companies have all the excuses in the world for not taking action, and he criticized the recycling program for being disingenuous. The program boasted about recycling 8 million pounds of batteries in 2023[119] but there are hundreds of millions of pounds in the United States. The bulk of batteries disposed of in the United States still end up in landfills.

One of the problems is that it's unreasonable to expect the public to be responsible for sorting their batteries, especially given the mix of chemistries

---

118 https://response.restoration.noaa.gov/about/media/pennsylvania-mining-town-moves-beyond-toxic-history-denuded-mountains-and-contaminated-c
119 https://www.globenewswire.com/news-release/2024/03/04/2839644/0/en/Call2Recycle-Releases-2023-U-S-National-Battery-Collection-Recycling-Data.html?utm_source=chatgpt.com

found in collections. From RMC's over 5,000 collection sites in Ontario, these collections often include a mix of lithium, nickel-cadmium, nickel-metal hydride, lead, and alkaline batteries. Approximately 85% of all consumer batteries are alkaline, which is why Wayne chose to focus on them. The sheer tonnage and quantity of alkaline batteries made them a priority, as he preferred to transport full loads rather than a few barrels. At the same time, the corporate giants are primarily focused on recovering nickel, lithium, lead, and cadmium.

Wayne notes a situation involving faulty electric vehicle batteries where around thousands of these batteries were identified as defective. A Canadian company, Licycle, had guaranteed to recycle these batteries, promising to return the lithium and other components in a form that could be automatically reused in the production of new batteries. However, this outcome has not yet been achieved. Despite the company raising a billion dollars in the stock market, it has been unable to produce quality lithium that can be reused in the manufacturing of new batteries. Even after signing a contract with General Motors for faulty batteries, the company still hasn't succeeded in achieving this, and he expresses doubt that it is even possible. Lithium is particularly challenging to work with due to its reactive and dangerous nature, making it a difficult material to handle. Licycle went out of business.

Forced to Sell by Criminal Actions

Wayne stresses that his company RMC began to see profit after Ontario's battery recycling legislation was passed, and after it focused entirely on developing a highly effective process for recycling alkaline batteries. This success continued until the battery manufacturers' organization Call2Recycle took over responsibility for collection approximately four years ago. This organization breached their contract and suspended every large collector in Ontario for somewhat "nonsense reasons." As a result, RMC sued them, but the legal process in Canada could take up to 10 years, as those in the wrong often drag their feet to avoid consequences.

For Wayne this was a criminal act. The manufacturers collect a fee from every battery sold, with the intent of funding proper recycling. For example, if someone buys a four-pack of AA batteries in Canada, 24 cents of that purchase is allocated for recycling. However, the manufacturers are resisting the recycling of these batteries, effectively defrauding the public and willfully polluting the environment. If an individual engaged in such practices, they would likely face imprisonment, but these large companies continue to operate without facing any fines or penalties, despite government threats. Even if fines are eventually imposed, it would not make any difference, as the companies would treat it as a mere cost of doing business and would likely appeal, dragging the process out in the courts for years. While pollution grows.

Wayne and his company fought against the situation for almost two years without receiving any fees, resulting in significant financial losses. In the 2000s, no one could get away with such actions, considering it wasn't the 1950s where environmental damage was often ignored. However, the behavior of the responsible parties seemed to turn back the clock 70 years, and they are getting away with it. Given the financial strain, Wayne and his team decided to try and sell the business, despite having developed the best technology in the world for recycling alkaline batteries. RMC had successful dealings with major fertilizer companies in the United States who valued their material. However, the continued financial losses, amounting to millions of dollars due to unpaid recycling fees, made it unsustainable to continue. He and his team had hoped that the government would hold these companies accountable and ensure they received their fees, but unfortunately, that did not happen.

Thus, Wayne made a significant sale to a company owned by BlackRock, the world's largest asset management firm with around $10 trillion under management. BlackRock was a very reputable company with good people. Most of his company's assets, including the name, were sold to them. The transition process, which was highly complex due to the nature of the business, took almost a year. During this time, Wayne worked closely with BlackRock, who retained their employees and carried on the operations. He had hope that BlackRock would stay committed to the course. However, he was deeply troubled by the actions of the battery manufacturers, who had not made any progress and were offering only a quarter of what his company had been paid for 13 years, to collect, sort, transport and recycle alkalines. This amount didn't even cover the costs of collections, let alone the sorting and recycling processes. This situation is very criminal, if any regular person had been involved in such actions, they would likely be in prison by now. It is hard for Wayne to believe that such injustices were occurring and kept him up at night. He thinks there is some truth to the saying "ignorance is bliss," though that has not brought him any comfort. Ignorance is bliss!!

Wayne has deep concern about the future, particularly for his grandchildren, in the face of willful pollution and the theft from the public through the collection of recycling fees that are not used for their intended purpose. While both are crimes, it is the deliberate pollution that troubles him the most. Even though he is out of the battery business now, the staff and management have stayed on and continued the fight. They are still facing the issue of not being paid despite accumulating credits. Nevertheless, Wayne shares his hope that, with the new owners, the company he started 40 years ago, a reputable company, will be able to outlast the culprits and eventually succeed. Although his company handled 12,000 tons of batteries per year, a lot more than that was still going into the ground, and the broader impact he had hoped for, legislation across all 50 US states and all Canadian provinces, has not materialized yet. This is despite the obvious dangers these pollutants pose to future generations.

Top Ten Environmental Hypocrites

#6 Bill Gates

How Much Do They Talk? (0 = not at all to 10 = all day) = 10

Amount of Environmental Action? (0 = plants trees daily to 10 = giving speeches) = 8

Real Environmentalist Score = 18

Bill Gates, the co-founder of Microsoft and a leading philanthropist, has been a prominent advocate for addressing climate change and promoting sustainability. Through the Bill and Melinda Gates Foundation and other initiatives, Gates has invested heavily in renewable energy, climate research, and innovative technologies aimed at reducing carbon emissions. However, despite his significant contributions, Gates has faced massive accusations of environmental hypocrisy. These criticisms stem from his personal lifestyle choices, his investments, and the seeming disconnect between his advocacy and actions.

When you search on DuckDuckGo.com for a name and "environmental hypocrite," no name prompts more results than Bill Gates. He ranks so high on this list, reflecting the many others that have accused him of being a hypocrite. His performative nature is most on display when defending carbon credits.

Before delving into Bill Gates' environmental hypocrisies, let me mention "The Egyptian Book of the Dead." From about 1250 B.C., "The Egyptian Book of the Dead" helps the dead increase their chances of getting into paradise. It's a guidebook for navigating the next phase of existence. Part of the process is standing in judgment before gods Osiris and Thoth and the 42 Judges. The book helps you prepare a list of 42 sins that you did not commit to prove you are worthy of paradise. It's like that teenage game "Never Have I Ever" except for your soul.[120] In the game, players take turns announcing things they have never done. For example, one player could say, "I have never flown in a private jet." Players that have flown in a private jet must take a drink, fire 500 employees, or take off a piece of clothing, or whatever the stakes are. When standing before gods Osiris and Thoth and the 42 Judges, the recently dead announce the 42 sins

---

[120] https://parade.com/966617/parade/never-have-i-ever-questions/

they have never committed. For example, you, well, not you, you are reading and alive, but someone recently deceased could say, "I have never killed someone." Or, "I have never caused a nuclear accident killing millions of people." Things like that. If you get 42 of them, you get into paradise. Today, we call this The Negative Confession or The Declaration of Innocence.[121] Shakespeare summarized when he wrote, "The lady doth protest too much, methinks."[122]

In our society, when you declare your innocence, most people assume you are guilty. Using Bill Clinton's voice, read this: "I did not have sexual relations with that woman, Ms. Lewinsky." OK, back to your voice or you will get hoarse. Guilty, right!?

So, when Bill Gates (finally back to him!) says he never met with Jeffrey Epstein, that really means they had dinner several times, but never at the latter's sex island.[123]

And, when Bill Gates says, "I am not part of the problem," what he really means is, "I am the problem!" He even got mad, visibly irritated, when a reporter had the audacity to bring up private jet flights in an interview. [124] He owns only four business jets, Bill, the author of a book called "How to Avoid Climate Disaster," and took 392 flights on private jets in 2022 alone, an average of more than one per day.[125] And, he still had the cojones[126] to say, "I am not part of the problem." Wow! That is bold! Performatively bold!

Plus, Billy[127] owns a private aviation management firm and has invested billions of dollars in the world's largest business jet service provider. *The Wall Street Journal* wrote, "Gates is doubling down on private-jet travel … The billionaire's Cascade Investment LLC agreed Friday to team up with Blackstone Group Inc.[128] in a $4.7 billion deal for Signature Aviation PLC. The deal would

---

[121] https://www.worldhistory.org/The_Negative_Confession/
[122] Hamlet, Act III, Scene II
[123] https://checkyourfact.com/2020/06/26/fact-check-bill-gates-jeffrey-epsteins-private-island-17-times/ Sorry, being associated several times with Epstein is so gross, it had to be mentioned.
[124] https://nypost.com/2023/02/09/bill-gates-defends-private-jet-habit-despite-climate-activism/
[125] https://simpleflying.com/bill-gates-private-jet-collection/
[126] Cojones versus cajónes, a raging demand….
https://www.latinorebels.com/2015/09/15/cajones-or-cojones-step-up-your-spanish-slang-game-political-media/
[127] That's a typo, sorry, his name is Bill, not Billy. Typo.
[128] That's a name that makes me feel all warm and fuzzy. Ahhhhhhh, Blackstone Group … Let's say it together! Ahhhhhhh, Blackstone Group …

boost Cascade's stake in the world's largest operator of private-jet bases to 30%, from a previous 19%."[129]

Bill's environmental hypocrisies don't end there. He has a brand-new superyacht! The 373 feet long vessel has pop-up balconies, multiple libraries, fireplaces, a private elevator, and a hospital.[130] It runs on the tears of Microsoft employees, facilitated by collection tubes at every desk in Seattle. That's not true, are you paying attention? It does run on emission-free power from green hydrogen. Seriously.

All of that is okay, because he is not part of the problem. He does carbon offsets, so, all is good, no harm, no foul. Carbon credits are permits that allow the owner to emit a certain amount of carbon dioxide or other greenhouse gases (GHGs). One credit allows the emission of one ton of carbon dioxide or the equivalent of other greenhouse gases. Carbon credits are also known as carbon allowances.[131]

Carbon offsetting schemes claim to neutralize the effects of your CO2 emissions. One problem with carbon offsetting is that it won't do much to reduce the volume of emissions being generated. It absorbs carbon in the future.[132] The World Economic Forum concluded, "It's an approach that some say might even cause people to disassociate themselves from the issue and deflect attention from the immediate dangers posed by climate change."[133] Take a step back and ask if the whole idea makes sense: "I can hit you because later I say sorry," or "It's okay if we pollute this river, if we clean it up someday," or "I can fly private from one yacht to another yacht without consequence. I have a guy that cleans behind all my environmental destruction." It is performative bullshit. By continuing to use private jets, Gates undermines his credibility as an advocate for climate action and sets a poor example for others.

The Institute for Applied Ecology studied green projects in developing countries to earn carbon credits. "Overall, our results suggest that 85% of the projects covered in this analysis … have a low likelihood that emission reductions are additional and are not over-estimated," the Institute wrote. "Only 2% of the projects … have a high likelihood of ensuring that emission reductions are additional and are not over-estimated."[134]

---

129 https://www.wsj.com/articles/bill-gates-joins-private-equity-firms-in-4-7-billion-deal-for-private-jet-company-11612534767
130 https://luxurylaunches.com/transport/bill-gates-hydrogen-powered-megayacht-launched.php
131 https://www.investopedia.com/terms/c/carbon_credit.asp
132 https://www.weforum.org/agenda/2019/06/what-is-carbon-offsetting/
133 Ibid.
134 https://www.weforum.org/agenda/2019/06/what-is-carbon-offsetting/

In 2023, *The Guardian* reported that, "the forest carbon offsets approved by the world's leading certifier and used by Disney, Shell, Gucci and other big corporations are largely worthless and could make global heating worse." It continued, "More than 90% of their rainforest offset credits – among the most commonly used by companies – are likely to be 'phantom credits' and do not represent genuine carbon reductions."[135] The whole thing is a scam! Damn it! The whole environmental performative industry rests on credits working. Not only performatively but really working! How will Bill appear righteous now? He defends his plan, of course. The sweepers that come behind him are better than the sweepers that follow JLo, King Charles, or Meta Zuckerberg.

How did Zuckerberg not make this list of the top 10 environmental hypocrites? Just his "house" in Hawaii qualifies him to be on any list of stink. Huge parts are buried underground à la a James Bond villain. Elon was the leading contender for the next Bond villain, but Zuckerhouse puts him in first place. The bunker-house includes a 5,000-square-foot underground shelter, with its own energy and food supplies. There is a blast door too, of course.[136] When asked, ChatGPT suggested that "Benedict Cumberbatch's ability to portray genius-level intellect (as seen in 'Sherlock') combined with a cold, detached demeanor would make him a compelling Zuckerberg-like villain in a Bond film." Bryan Cranston was ChatGPT's suggestion to play Gates. Cranston is "known for his iconic role as Walter White in 'Breaking Bad,' Cranston has the range to portray a character who appears mild-mannered and unassuming on the surface but harbors a powerful, strategic mind and a darker side. His ability to switch between a charming persona and a more sinister one would suit a Bill Gates-inspired villain perfectly."[137] We digress.

Greenpeace concluded, "Carbon offsetting is truly a scammer's dream scheme. It's a bookkeeping trick intended to obscure climate wrecking-emissions. It's tree planting window dressing aimed at distracting from ecosystem destruction. It is the next big thing in greenwashing — and we must not be fooled. The climate crisis is real, and we all need real solutions. Meanwhile, the fraud of carbon offsetting is built upon many of the hallmarks of a classic con."[138]

---

135 https://www.theguardian.com/environment/2023/jan/18/revealed-forest-carbon-offsets-biggest-provider-worthless-verra-aoe
136 https://www.wired.com/story/mark-zuckerberg-inside-hawaii-compound/
137 ChatGPT
138 https://www.greenpeace.org/international/story/50689/carbon-offsets-net-zero-greenwashing-scam/

Their report takes it a step further:

> "Offsetting incentivizes the commodification of nature and allows powerful corporations to take over the lands of vulnerable communities, risking human rights abuses. Offset schemes often exclude local and Indigenous Peoples from land management practices that allow them to grow food and preserve biodiversity.
>
> Carbon offsets put a price on nature. We cannot allow the richest nations and corporations to commodify nature, and buy off lands in poorer countries for offsets, so they can keep polluting the atmosphere. Nature-based offsetting projects distort economies and take land and resources away from the local communities that need it most. Nature should remain off limits to corporate control for climate offsets."

In other words, even if it did work, it is morally wrong. Bill still disagrees. Despite being exposed to all of this, he defends *his* guy. "You have a guy? I have a guy! He can get tickets to anything!" During a CNBC interview and follow-up article, he said, "Well, I buy the gold standard of, funding Climeworks, to do direct air capture that far exceeds my family's carbon footprint."[139] The Microsoft co-founder doth protest too much, methinks.

Climeworks has offices in Switzerland and Germany and has clients such as Stripe and Microsoft. Their site says they "offer carbon removal as a service for businesses and individuals who want to fight climate change. With our service, you can take action on behalf of the planet by permanently removing the CO2 emissions you can't reduce."[140] Bill really does have a guy, and he really is claiming that his climate clean-up guy is better than all the others. So, he is not part of the problem!

That is so cool! It says it "uses a technology called 'direct air capture' to capture carbon dioxide directly from the air." The firm adds that combining the CO2 that's been removed with underground storage enables "the permanent removal of excess and legacy CO2 emissions, which can no longer contribute to climate change." There!! Problem solved!!!

Oh, wait, wait, stop!!! This is confusing! Problem solved? Some company called Climeworks can successfully, permanently remove the bad CO2? A for-profit

---

139 https://www.cnbc.com/2023/02/07/private-jet-use-and-climate-campaigning-not-hypocritical-bill-gates-.html
140 https://climeworks.com/carbon-removal-technology

company? A for-profit company has solved CO2? This is the thesis of this book, right? Crazy entrepreneurs solve issues, save the planet! Right?

There's more. "His whole family?" Bill Gates says he offsets for his whole family. What about other families? Couldn't he spend more and offset a lot of families and then issue over, right? This is confusing.

The CNBC article changes course with just a few paragraphs to go. It's like the author realized the same thing all you readers just did. Entrepreneurs have invented cool ways to reduce CO2. Bill Gates uses it and is bragging about it. But you normal people still need to fly less. Now excuse me, I am off on my private daily flight. The article continued, "Gates has previously spoken about using Climeworks to 'pay for direct air capture.' While the sector has high-profile backers, it faces challenges. The International Energy Agency, for instance, notes that capturing carbon dioxide from the air 'is more energy intensive and therefore expensive than capturing it from a point source.'"[141] That translates to "it works for us billionaires, but you need to have access to less oil."

Wow, can you say hypocritical!

In May 2024, Climeworks opened a new plant called Mammoth. It "suck(s) planet-heating pollution out of the atmosphere like a giant vacuum."[142] The captured carbon is then buried underground. Problem solved! Really. It seems like the tech works. Nothing published doubts that it works. So, why aren't we celebrating, making the Climeworks CEO the president of the world, and partying in the post-climate change world!? It works! Do more of it!

No. No. No. That's unacceptable. There are some problems. Cost and scale namely. Luckily, those two are linked. Make more (creating the needed scale) and costs go down (making it affordable). That's a basic law of economics. Critics say these issues make carbon capture and storage impractical.

They are lying. There is another much, much bigger reason that we environmentalists aren't partying. They got what they wanted; the climate change problem is solved. Why aren't they happy? Because they do not want to help the climate. WHAT??!!?!? What are you talking about?

Once the carbon is captured, it is pumped underground. The carbon is pushed into wells, old, depleted oil wells. The carbon displaces the small amounts of

---

141 https://www.cnbc.com/2023/02/07/private-jet-use-and-climate-campaigning-not-hypocritical-bill-gates-.html
142 https://www.cnn.com/2024/05/08/climate/direct-air-capture-plant-iceland-climate-intl/index.html

remnant oil and pushes it to the surface. The oil can now be captured. It's called enhanced oil recovery. Sounds great. More oil and less carbon. Perfect.

No, no, NO! Climate capture "allow(s) fossil fuel companies to extract even more from aging fields. This kind of process makes some critics concerned that carbon removal technologies could be used to prolong production of fossil fuels."[143] Ah, reality welcome to the discussion. The opponents fight carbon capture because it could solve climate change in a way that continues the use of gas and oil. That is unacceptable. Their real goal is the elimination of fossil fuels. Their goal is NOT climate related. If their goal was climate security, they would celebrate carbon capture. Wow, the hypocrisy!

Said again because this is so important, the goal of many climate activists is not to save the environment but to stop the oil economy.

Back to Mr. Gates. Bill is hugely supportive of carbon capture, so he deserves credit for this brave stance. Maybe he is afraid of the climate culture rampage. Maybe he is afraid of being carbon cancelled.

Climeworks was invited to be included in this book. They refused to be interviewed. Why? Well, James Bond villains are never interviewed pre-movie! We don't even know who the new Bond will be.[144] Seriously, why not brag about what you have achieved? Most likely, Climeworks' CEO and PR department realize that the more they talk about it, the more likely they are to be cancelled.

More about the James Bond angle: Gates has also invested in a company or two that seem very villainous. His investments in geoengineering draw particular attention. Geoengineering may offer potential solutions to climate change, but it also carries significant risks and uncertainties. For example, they could geoengineer us into a global winter. Didn't you see the movie "Geostorm"? It has a Rotten Tomato score of 18% but the story is somewhere between 110% and 200% likely to happen before 2030. Soon. Gates biokills us all but Bond saves the day!!

These types of investments take money away from "more serious" investments in proven, low-risk solutions like renewable energy and energy efficiency. This is a good example of being damned if you do and damned if you don't. Gates gets criticized no matter what he does.

---

143 Ibid.
144 https://www.newsweek.com/james-bond-26-everything-we-know-next-007-film-1891233

The perception of Bill Gates as an environmental hypocrite arises from several factors, including his use of private jets, ownership of large properties, promotion of carbon offsetting, and involvement in controversial research initiatives. He scores very highly on the list of performative environmental hypocrites..

Chapter 6
Strauss: A Life-Changing Discovery

Remember that heart attack Wayne Elliott had at the age of 35?

It occurred after he didn't play sports for 10 years and maintained poor eating habits. The recent tests, conducted after he had myocarditis in 2023, confirmed that he had indeed suffered a heart attack back then. He vividly described the experience, likening the pain to being struck by a sledgehammer in the chest. What he always referred to as "an attack" caused him to lose his sight temporarily and fall to the ground. Upon regaining his vision, he found himself on his hands and knees but experienced no pain and simply got up and carried on without seeing a doctor. "After my heart attack at age 35, I refused all treatments and surgery. I had restricted blood flow in my arteries, but also throughout my body. We can have restricted blood flow in all our vessels, including the tiniest capillaries going to our skin," Wayne said.

However, following this incident, he began experiencing angina symptoms, including pinches in his chest. His heart went out of rhythm, leading to an irregular heartbeat for six years, which he found particularly distressing as he felt every beat. This condition, known as supraventricular tachycardia, prompted him to finally see a doctor. Despite this, he did not take any medication. Following the heart attack, he started to experience symptoms like chest pains, leg cramps, night sweats, and shortness of breath. Wayne lived with these health issues for over six years, never considering a natural health remedy. Rather he made plans to die in his 40s.

A Lifesaver

Six-and-a-half years after the initial attack, a dear friend introduced him to Strauss Heartdrops, sharing a personal success story about avoiding bypass surgery after using the product. Wayne's friend had also suffered a heart attack and had found success with Strauss Heartdrops. At that time, Wayne hadn't researched natural remedies and had instead prepared to die young, getting his affairs in order and transferring assets to his sons. His condition was not a surprise for his relatives because of his family's history of heart issues, and it was exacerbated by his lifestyle choices, particularly his milkshake diet. Wayne explained, "At age 40, the luckiest day of my life was when I was introduced to Strauss Heartdrops by a close friend, who himself had avoided open-heart surgery, taking Strauss Heartdrops." Inspired by his friend's recovery, he ordered a bottle of Strauss Heartdrops the very day he learned about the product. He did not want to undergo heart surgery or take any pharmaceutical drugs. He was hopeful and began taking the Heartdrops twice a day.

It turned out he wasn't wrong. He later felt incredibly lucky to have discovered the Strauss Heartdrops, stating that this discovery both saved and changed his life. Wayne described his previous state as near depression and anxiety, admitting he was unsure of the extent of his struggles. For eleven consecutive weekends, he isolated himself in his bedroom, watching the History Channel and hoping no one would call or knock at the door.

After starting the Heartdrops, Wayne experienced remarkable changes. Within two weeks, he regained hearing in his left ear, an issue he had not realized had been due to plaque or cholesterol buildup. He pointed out, "The hearing returned to my left ear, and I actually stopped wearing eyeglasses for five years." Within six weeks, his bronchial and lung health improved significantly. As his health continued to strengthen, he felt like Superman within three months. His symptoms, including angina, night sweats, and leg cramps, disappeared within three months. His energy levels soared around the 10–12-week mark. The anxiety he had been suffering from quickly dissipated once he started feeling better. He became so energized that he almost stopped sleeping and launched a new business. He felt as if he was on fire with enthusiasm.

"After three months, my energy increased dramatically to the point where I foolishly slept even less than my usual four to five hours a night. It's hard to describe how invigorating it is as you increase your blood flow," Wayne emphasized.

He became thoroughly convinced about the tremendous benefits of natural health products. He was amazed at how the Strauss family had perfected their formula, and how unbelievably effective it was. He got a little ahead of himself when he was ready for a second bottle of Heartdrops. He didn't know Jim or Peter Strauss at the time, so he approached the manager and asked for a discount on 100 bottles for his own study. The manager agreed, and Wayne kept a couple of bottles for himself while giving the rest to others. He was amazed that everyone, even those without health issues, experienced benefits. His 19-year-old son, at the time, had more energy and never slept in again. He received tremendous results, particularly for diabetics, and found it incredible how much the treatment helped them.

Strauss Heartdrops not only truly saved Wayne but also led him to develop a close relationship with their creator, Jim Strauss, and his son, Peter Strauss.

Wayne revealed, "In my fifth month of taking Strauss Heartdrops, I traveled to British Columbia and met Jim and Peter Strauss. Jim rode the train back to Ontario with me and traveled doing lectures and radio shows. That was the beginning of my learning of natural health, nature and how nature has everything perfect. After that trip, Jim spent two months per year, one month at a time, with me in Ontario living with my family. My relationship with Jim Strauss over a six-year period was the most profound relationship of my life."

They developed a strong bond, and Wayne eventually became the first Ontario distributor for the Strauss products, later expanding to cover all of Canada. Together they conducted lectures and numerous radio shows to promote the benefits of Strauss Heartdrops. Their relationship was marked by travel, public appearances, and numerous conversations in the car, which Wayne considered the most rewarding experience of his life.

During his time with Jim Strauss, he learned a great deal about the human body and the interconnectedness of nature and health. Everything in the body connects in a similar way to how elements in nature are intertwined. He had never met anyone as knowledgeable as Jim, who, despite not being a doctor, was a Master Herbalist and held a PhD in chemical engineering.

Jim Strauss had initially practiced as an engineer but stepped back from that field after the growing popularity of aspirin in the 1940s-50s, believing that natural medicine would no longer be needed. Eventually, Jim ran Saskatchewan Hydro for several years. However, as he observed the pharmaceutical industry, he began to question its effectiveness, realizing that many people struggled to stop taking medications once they started. This realization partly contributed towards the revival of his focus on natural medicine, an endeavor that he and his family have been operating as a commercial venture ever since.

Wayne decided he wanted to be involved in their natural medicine mission because of how it changed his life. The rest was history. He felt so grateful for regaining his health and life that he decided he wouldn't make a profit from the endeavor. Any profits would be used to provide products for those in need, which he did for several years. About 20 years later, Wayne purchased half of the company, and Wayne took over management, describing it as the most rewarding thing he had ever been involved in.

He had the desire to "scream from the mountaintops" for people to experience healing as painlessly as he did. While he did see a doctor and was diagnosed with arrhythmia, he never took any drugs. During the six years leading up to discovering natural medicine, he had prepared himself for death and did not explore alternative treatments or research other options, as he had been unaware of the natural route.

Fate's Intervention

The roots of Strauss Naturals trace back to a pivotal moment in 1979 when Peter Strauss, then just 15, watched his father, Jim Strauss Sr., face a life-changing health crisis. A sudden heart attack left his father struggling to regain his strength, unable to walk even the short distance across their living room. Faced with this challenge, Jim turned to the knowledge passed down through generations—a tradition of healing with nature's remedies that his grandmother and great-grandmother had practiced in the old country. Determined to recover without relying on invasive procedures or pharmaceutical drugs, Jim decided to create a natural heart tincture. He sent young Peter to Vancouver to gather the specific herbs needed for his formulation. The result was the very first batch of the Heartdrops—a blend so effective that, within weeks, Jim's strength returned. He not only walked across the living room but soon walked around the neighborhood block. Just months later, he was back on the ski slopes, proving the power of nature's healing.

Peter Strauss pointed out, "Strauss Naturals and its traditional products are the result of eight generations of practice in development, production and application of herbal remedies. Most of our products have been in use for centuries, having been passed down through generations of the Strauss family. The chain was almost broken when my father took a career in heavy industry instead of applying the herbal training he received from his grandmother. However, fate intervened and at age 57, Dad had a serious heart attack. He couldn't walk, or sleep lying down, and was told he would die without surgery and drugs. Thankfully, he remembered a better option. When I was 15, Dad had me assemble, process, and modify a collection of herbs until he was satisfied with the taste. This formulation restored Dad's health in less than a year and convinced us that we had to return to our family tradition."

Inspired by his rapid recovery, Jim knew he couldn't keep this remedy to himself. Friends, family, and even customers from their canopy shop were astonished by his transformation and began asking for Heartdrops for their loved ones. Word spread quickly, and within a year, people from all over western Canada and the northwestern United States were visiting the Strauss home, seeking the natural remedy and the wisdom behind it.

Recognizing the growing demand and the opportunity to make a greater impact, Jim made a life-changing decision. He sold their successful canopy shop and committed himself fully to herbal medicine, inviting Peter to join him as an equal partner. Together, they launched Strauss Naturals from their home, sharing the power of herbal healing with a growing community. By 1982, the business had outgrown their home, prompting them to establish a small local shop. Jim began hosting seminars, first in their hometown and eventually throughout southern British Columbia and beyond, educating people about natural health remedies. They invited health stores to these events, providing an opportunity for attendees to learn and experience their products firsthand. This grassroots approach helped get Strauss Naturals products into health stores, expanding their reach and impact.

The demand for natural remedies grew beyond Heartdrops, and the Strauss family began creating a variety of tinctures and teas, all made with the same care and tradition. By 1989, their rented space could no longer keep up with their expansion, and they purchased their own shop, combining manufacturing and client consultations under one roof. In 2000, as the demand for their products continued to grow, Strauss Naturals made a bold move to a much larger location. With this expansion, they not only reached more communities but also established sales territories and international distribution, sharing the healing power of their products far and wide.

Peter Strauss stressed further, "Today, our remedies are distributed worldwide, having achieved global recognition primarily by word of mouth from satisfied customers. Strauss Heartdrops, our flagship product, is used by thousands of new customers each year and this number continues to grow. Along with this natural formula for the heart and circulatory system, Strauss Naturals manufactures 9 herbal remedies. A sincere effort and commitment are made to ensure that our customers return to and maintain their good health. Balance and proportion are key in producing remedies that are not only effective, but in many cases, fast acting. We have been helping people regain their health for decades and feel privileged to represent the result of generations of experience, and our family's unique understanding and approach to making herbal formulas."

The Most Profound Experience of Wayne's Life

Wayne Elliott views his relationship with Jim Strauss as the most profound experience of his life, adding that Strauss Naturals saved his life not once but twice. In 2023, Wayne contracted COVID-19 for the third time, which was followed by myocarditis. Yet, the strength of his heart due to Strauss Heartdrops contributed to his survival during that difficult 10-day period. He regarded Jim as an uncle, a second father, and a big brother, cherishing the great conversations they shared.

At one point, Wayne's dog was misdiagnosed by veterinarians, leading to severe health issues. Desperate, he called Jim Strauss for help, hoping to find a remedy for his beloved pet. Strauss confirmed they had kidney and liver treatments available. Wayne requested that the herbal medication be sent to him via courier immediately. In those days, the treatments came in the form of teas instead of liquids or capsules. He mixed the loose tea with some canned dog food, and within a few days, his dog was back to normal. He couldn't believe the turnaround and called Jim Strauss to share the news.

Ever since developing his close relationship with Jim, Wayne has been passionate about helping people. He emphasizes his love for assisting others, particularly in the realm of health, stating that it has been incredibly rewarding for him. It warmed his heart every time someone received a natural health product, and he would give a bottle to anyone in need, knowing they would feel better, just as he had.

Much to his regret, Wayne had to step away from this involvement with the Strauss family herbal business about 15 years ago due to other business commitments. He had dedicated too much time to Strauss, traveling and doing radio shows. He had even taken over for Jim in giving lectures and presentations, which, however, resulted in him not paying enough attention to his business when his sons were younger.

Wayne gave the business he ran for the Strauss family in Eastern Canada to his friend who managed Western Canada. He revealed that he never made any money from it but took it up because the products saved his life. Wayne emphasized that every nickel he made from the herbal medicine business, aside from wages for a few employees, was given away in products. He still gives away a lot to this day, finding it very rewarding and a means of expressing his gratitude for how herbal medicine saved him.

The 'Cadillac' of Natural Health Products

Another Strauss product helped Wayne with his irregular heartbeat, and their kidney formula managed his high blood pressure. For the past 29 years, Wayne's blood pressure has been a consistent 120/70. Wayne also changed his lifestyle choices, and, despite his fondness for milkshakes, limited himself to one or two a year as a treat, instead of the astonishing up to 20 shakes a day that he used to consume. Even though at the time he maintained an athletic appearance from working out daily, he realized that looking good on the outside didn't necessarily mean he was healthy on the inside.

Wayne admired Jim Strauss's deep understanding of nature and how everything connects. He highlighted, "Jim always said, 'If you are not made from it, it cannot heal you. You can't expect man-made chemical drugs to heal or fix you (they never claim to do either, hence most are a lifetime proposition to deal with symptoms). It is like taking your vehicle to the lumberyard to repair with plywood and 2 x 4's. You need cells from which you are made, to help heal you.' Every cell in me believes that to be nothing but the truth."

Wayne elaborated, "'Everything we need is provided by nature,' Jim Strauss would preach and there is no doubt in my mind it's true. Until our farm soil was depleted and no longer provided all the minerals, humates, etc., as nature intended, we grew healthy fruits and vegetables. Our food animals were fed natural grains or grasses. Then came GMO 'foods.' Seedless or with seeds you can't grow anything with, but to make you believe it's natural (oranges, bananas and corn, to name some multi-decade modified foods). It takes a seed to reproduce anything. A human, giraffe, pine tree, or anything else. Genetic modification produces produce with weaker immune systems than the original version before GMO. Then we eat the produce and our immune systems are not getting what they need and were meant to have. It gets worse. The chemicals used, largely due to the weak crops, are many: pesticides, insecticides, fungicides, herbicides, chemical fertilizers and preservatives. Produce is shipped literally around the world. Nature expected us to eat foods specifically grown in our region in the seasons they are grown. I started the Iron Earth Canada company, to provide a soil amendment product that grows everything better and stronger, larger or more bounty. Best of all, 100% natural with zero additives!"

Although Wayne sometimes wished Jim would refrain from certain statements in his lectures, he noted that every word Jim spoke turned out to be true in his experience. Wayne emphasized Jim's genuine care for people and his commitment to a satisfaction guarantee. He explained that Jim would never sell a product unless he believed it was truly needed. He held great respect for Jim, who perfected formulas that have been around for over 200 years, with his son,

Peter Strauss, becoming the eighth-generation herbalist in the family. Wayne stresses that the Strauss herbal medicine products are well-known in Canada and have been commercially available for about 45 years, earning the family company a reputation as the "Cadillac" of natural health products.

When he dwells on the challenges posed by the economic environment following COVID-19, inflation, and rising interest rates, Wayne notes that many people are struggling financially, making it difficult to spend money on health products. To address this, the company aims to go directly to the consumer, offering the best deals and special products. Wayne recognized that spending $50 or $100 on health products has become a luxury for many. Despite this, he emphasized the importance of health, asserting that it is ultimately our wealth, even as families face increasing costs for food, transportation, and raising children. He remarked that these are some of the toughest times people have faced in recent years.

Wayne pointed out, "I will never understate my gratitude for Strauss Heartdrops, saving me, changing my life, and giving me high energy 30 years ago. Yet, my greatest pleasure since assuming management of the Strauss Naturals Company over 5 years ago, was in this past year, when we brought back two incredible products for females. It took one year since the decision was made to get them to market. The company needed Health Canada approval, just to switch from capsules to liquids, itself taking 8-9 months."

He revealed further, "The WOMAN'S WONDER formula is for relief from cramps and bloating during the menstrual cycle. Taken only 3 days per month (if it is a regular period, the day before period starts. If it's not regular, day one is the day the period starts). In our experience, few teens or adult females need a second bottle of this formula. No more missed school, work, hot water bottles. Incredible formula to relieve that monthly, natural female body function. The MENOPAUSE formula is for all stages of meno including pre- and post-issues routinely suffered by so many of our fair ladies. Everyone notices a big difference in one week regarding hot flashes, night sweats, and mood swings. Continued use will provide continuous benefits. This is our most complex formula with 20 individual herbs. 100% satisfaction guarantee as always with Strauss or a full refund of your money. Another home run for Strauss with products best in class and 100% natural."

Wayne reaffirmed his heartfelt gratitude for finding the Strauss products, expressing his desire for everyone in need to have the same access to them to help with their health. He reflected on Jim Strauss's dream of making herbal medicine products available through Medicare. However, he lamented that the medical industry often overlooks effective, affordable solutions, resulting in lengthy wait times for healthcare in Canada. He pointed out the concerning situation regarding nurses in Canada, noting the government's recent approval of 37,000 foreign nurses to address the dire healthcare crisis.

Resolving the Cholesterol Struggle

Wayne had a struggle with his cholesterol. This was because of his old habit of drinking dozens of milkshakes a day, which combined dairy and sugar, a lethal combination. He indulged in a milkshake for the first time in a year recently, as a treat, consuming it in about 30 seconds, but now only allows himself such treats a couple of times a year. His excessive consumption of beef from a young age is another contributing factor.

The biggest myth in Western medicine today is the blood cholesterol myth. His doctor saw his cholesterol levels as perfect and had no issues. However, eight out of ten heart attack victims, or 80%, had low blood cholesterol. Those with high blood cholesterol may have perfectly functioning bodies. The blood system is the only transportation system in the body; everything travels through the blood, including oxygen, water, food, and waste.

Cholesterol becomes a problem only when it is stuck somewhere, restricting blood flow or causing a 100% blockage. Some individuals find out through angiograms that they have a completely blocked artery. When he took Strauss Heartdrops, Wayne conducted his own study. Although he usually visited the doctor every six or seven years for blood work due to his great health as an athlete, he began going every five or six months to monitor the Heartdrops' effectiveness. His blood cholesterol level almost tripled over the year, shocking his doctor, who exclaimed, "Oh my god, Wayne, if you don't do this…" Despite that, Wayne felt fantastic and even tried to get his doctor to take the drops because he didn't look well. Unfortunately, the doctor declined and eventually had a heart attack.

The doctor struggled to understand that high blood cholesterol could be acceptable. Wayne reiterated that eight out of ten heart attack victims had low blood cholesterol, which is stuck in veins, vessels, and arteries, even the tiniest vessels to the eyes, as he had experienced. The tripling of his blood cholesterol meant that the Heartdrops were working to dissolve plaque, which could only pass through the blood system. This waste is disposed of in the bathroom, but his doctor could not grasp that high blood cholesterol was not inherently problematic.

Statin drugs are the best-selling drugs in the world for cholesterol. The first statin drugs were banned after a few years due to severe side effects, such as muscle deterioration. Statin drugs appear to govern the liver's function, much like putting a governor on a car engine. While the liver's only job is producing cholesterol, it actually has over 200 functions. The statin drugs do not remove cholesterol; they merely slow the liver's production of it and its other functions.

Blood thinners are designed to make blood pass more easily through veins and vessels, but if the Creator intended for humans to have watery blood, then that would have been the design. So, this is Western medicine's answer to heart disease: to shatter the liver's function to produce less cholesterol. It's called the Cholesterol Myth because that's what it is—a myth.

Just after over a year of taking Strauss Heartdrops, Wayne's cholesterol returned to 3.0, which he considered perfect. The scoring system is different in the United States, but that was when he knew he was cleaned out. He acknowledged that it took him over a year to reach that point, as he had been quite plugged up. As his cholesterol levels returned to normal, he continued taking Strauss Heartdrops every day for the rest of his life. He has been taking them for almost 30 years and plans to continue because they have worked so effectively for him. They are painless and one cannot overdose on them.

The body knows how to process natural substances. One cannot harm themselves by eating apples, asparagus, lettuce or anything natural. If someone eats too much, they may need to use the bathroom, but they will not get sick because the body knows what to do. In contrast, the body does not know how to process man-made chemical substances because humans were not created with any equipment to do so. None of the pharmaceuticals claim to fix anything because they don't; they only address symptoms. If they actually fixed anything, doctors would tell patients, "Your blood pressure is normal. Now you can stop those pills." This has never happened in the history of the world and never will because pharmaceuticals are designed to treat symptoms.

Deserving of Nobel Prize for Medicine

Wayne was his own proof of the effectiveness of the Strauss formulas, having tried them himself, as well as on his parents, friends, family, and customers. Not one person in 30 years has complained or reported to him any serious side effects or damage related to the products. He noted that the Strauss company also offered satisfaction guarantees. If customers were not satisfied for any reason, they could get a full refund without having to explain.

There are two sources of high blood pressure: the heart and the kidneys. However, taking the Strauss Heartdrops did not lower Wayne's blood pressure, which was the first clue that his issues stemmed from his kidneys. Two natural therapists, an iridologist and a reflexologist, informed him that he had issues specifically with his left kidney. He then took the Strauss kidney formula for three months, and up until he developed myocarditis recently, his blood pressure was consistently 120 over 70, regardless of his stress levels or sleep patterns.

Wayne recalls, "Even though I felt like a new man with incredible energy taking the Strauss Heartdrops those first few months, when I met Jim Strauss, I told him I still had high blood pressure and an irregular heartbeat. Jim told me if the Heartdrops did not lower my blood pressure then my kidneys or one kidney had to be the issue, given that it is either the heart, or kidneys, or both, that cause high blood pressure without exception."

He adds, "Jim then told me of the Strauss cardio support formula, intended for the various tachycardias and to help the body repair damaged heart cells. Three months later, after taking both formulas, my blood pressure was 120/70 and my heartbeat was regular. I was so delighted and certain of the efficacy of Strauss formulas and decided I wanted to be involved, helping people get what I got."

After Wayne developed myocarditis, which is inflammation of the heart, in 2023, his blood pressure fluctuated, and his irregular heartbeat returned. Wayne chose not to take any pills or drugs during this time. Three of his staff members or adult children experienced myocarditis after receiving the COVID-19 vaccine: an 18-year-old young man, a 20-year-old young man, and a 30-year-old young lady. All were hospitalized in intensive care and were not on any common drugs, each taking different medications in three different hospitals. This led him to believe that myocarditis was fairly rare until the COVID-19 vaccine's introduction.

Wayne took Strauss Heartdrops, the cardio support formula and the kidney supplement to address his arrhythmia and irregular heartbeat, which he had previously managed for 30 years. He quickly returned to work after his myocarditis, whereas the young lady took 22 months to get back to work. He recovered thanks to the natural herbal formulas he took, expressing his passion for the Strauss formulas and their impressively positive impact on people's health.

The Strauss product line includes a bladder formula, a kidney formula, and a cardio formula for irregular heartbeat and repairing damaged heart cells. This product is very effective, highlighting a common ingredient—goldenseal root—which is known as one of nature's strongest antibiotic herbs. The bacteria can be a significant problem in the kidneys, bladder, and prostate, making these areas slow to accept help.

Wayne recounted, "Several years ago, a woman called into The Power Hour Radio Show that I had been doing weekly. She said that she had had a urinary tract infection for the past 25 years and that she had tried every pharmaceutical her doctor recommended and every over-the-counter formula that she found. When she heard me on the radio talk about the Strauss bladder formula and how it was effective to help the body treat UTIs, she said to herself, 'Well, this won't work either, but I'm committed to trying everything I can to get rid of this terrible infection I've been suffering for so long.' She called into the show and said that after one week on the Strauss bladder formula she knew there was a difference and made an appointment to see her doctor, which she did a week later. To her amazement, she no longer had a urinary tract infection and felt compelled to call into the show and let me know. A very important herb, golden-seal root, is nature's strongest antibiotic herb, and is included in Strauss bladder formula, kidney formula and prostate formula for men. It turns out that bacteria is a real culprit in these parts of our body and stubborn to be rid of. Bacteria also grow very quickly in these parts of our body, so it is important to be diligent and take the formulas as directed."

Wayne himself used to wake up five or six times a night to use the bathroom, which interrupted his sleep. After taking the Strauss formulas, he now only wakes up once a night. His mother experienced similar results before she passed away a few years ago.

The formulas are safe and effective, and they come with a guarantee of satisfaction. Very few people ask for their money back, as the products have been successful in seven countries and have a loyal following.

The Strauss formulas are highly regarded in Canadian health stores. People from the United States could visit the Strauss website, straussnaturals.com, where they can find information about each formula and place orders online. With satisfaction guaranteed, it is a safe choice for anyone wanting to try the formulas.

Wayne deems the blood system to be the most important bodily function, noting that humans have 50,000 kilometers of veins and vessels inside them. Every single cell in the body, from the hair on one's head to the toenails, requires blood. If blood supply is severely restricted or cut off to any cell, it can lead to various issues, affecting the whole body. The brain alone uses 20% of all the oxygen the body takes in, so insufficient oxygen intake could result in a brain attack or stroke.

Wayne believes that Jim Strauss deserves a Nobel Prize for Medicine for the Strauss Heartdrops, citing their effectiveness, simplicity, and safety.

In 2024, he traveled around 20,000 miles to 700 different health food retailers, talking about the Strauss products. This extensive travel was motivated by his strong belief in the Strauss herbal medicine. Wayne and his youngest son started in Ontario, which has over 1/3 of Canada's population, before heading west, traveling around the Great Lakes to Manitoba, Saskatchewan, Alberta, and British Columbia. The Strauss plant and office are located in British Columbia, where they also have many customers.

They had only visited about 10% of Canadian stores so far and found the experience very interesting. There are a lot of retailers that are having tough times. This situation was particularly exacerbated by the COVID-19 pandemic. Malls in Ontario were closed three times, and with inflation, rising grocery prices, and gasoline costs, many retailers were struggling.

Wayne emphasizes how Strauss guarantees customer satisfaction, which is a rarity in the natural health business, and how returns are minimal because the products work exceptionally well. He himself is the best advertisement for Strauss Naturals after recovering from the heart attack he experienced at the age of 35 and surviving his battle with myocarditis in 2023. It is remarkable for him that the Strauss products worked and that people don't have to take them for life, only until their health issues are resolved. Although a bottle or two is a great way to prevent trouble!

Wayne's parents also really benefited from the Strauss products. The Heartdrops improved his mother's circulation, while both the Heartdrops and the prostate formula helped his father avoid surgeries.

Wayne recalls, "My father had the angioplasty treatment at Boston Medical and was told that he needed bypass surgery. I convinced my dad to try the Strauss Heartdrops for three months before returning to Boston, knowing they would retest him, which they did. At that point the cardiologist at Boston canceled my dad's bypass surgery. My dad was thrilled to avoid the open-heart surgery. Two years later, my dad told me that Boston Medical said he needed a prostatectomy. He hadn't told me that he had been on pharmaceuticals for his prostate for almost 2 years to no avail. After his experience with the Strauss Heartdrops, my dad was willing to take the Strauss prostate formula for three months, before returning to Boston. When he returned three months later, the doctor canceled his prostatectomy, and my dad lived another 12 years and died with a healthy prostate."

So, Wayne really loves the products of Strauss Naturals, they mean the world to him, as they saved his life twice and extended the lives of his parents.

Restrictions on Natural Health Companies & Free Speech

There are approximately 1,700 pharmaceutical lobbyists in Washington, DC, that is 17 per every United States senator.[145] Wayne who hasn't taken so much as an aspirin in 30 years finds it troubling that pharmaceutical advertisements dominate the media, often listing side effects quickly and quietly. Meanwhile natural medicine, like the products from Strauss Naturals, which have no serious side effects at all, and are generally beneficial for detoxing the body, face severe limitations. Natural health companies are heavily restricted in what they can say about their products – they can barely say what their products are for – unlike big pharmaceutical companies that can make broad claims about their drugs. There are regulations and fees on natural health product manufacturers, which create additional burdens on the industry.

Against that backdrop, in a no less ridiculous development, Jim Strauss was charged with practicing medicine without a license and claiming a cure. In court, Jim Strauss made compelling arguments by comparing natural remedies, like citrus fruit curing scurvy, to pharmaceuticals, questioning when a natural product becomes a drug. Despite making valid points, Jim was found guilty. However, he was only fined $100 for each charge. Even so, a dignified Strauss refused to pay the fine, and when the judge threatened jail time, Jim stood his ground, leading the judge to dismiss the case.

This raises the broader issue of free speech in the United States and Canada, as exemplified by a story about a man who was sued by the Gay Pride movement for expressing his opinion against taxpayer funding for a pride parade. The case went all the way to Canada's Supreme Court where the justices ruled unanimously in favor of the Gay Pride movement. While there is freedom of speech in Canada, it is limited to not offending others. This is a troubling development that restricts what can be legally or safely discussed in the country, including topics like religion.

There was an incident where Wayne was attending a meeting at a steel mill with some younger colleagues. He wasn't an artist, but he asked if he could use the whiteboard to illustrate his point. While he saw it as a "whiteboard," one of the attendees corrected him that it was not a whiteboard but an "erasable marker board." The individual further explained that calling it a "whiteboard" was racist. He was momentarily stunned, as he had not intended to make any racist remarks. Attempting to defuse the situation, he argued that in order to be safe from racism

---

145 https://www.congress.gov/congressional-record/volume-168/issue-26/senate-section/article/S603-2

accusation, the manufacturing of white, black, brown, red, and yellow cars and clothes would likely have to stop as well.

Wayne has had this frustration with how people can no longer say anything without being criticized or, in extreme cases, facing legal consequences. Just like the above-mentioned case, in which an individual lost at three levels of the court system for merely speaking out against taxpayer funding for a particular parade. There was nothing hateful in what the individual said, he simply disagreed with the allocation of public funds. This situation can be compared to the natural health business, where the restrictions are so severe that producers like Strauss Naturals can't even suggest what their products might do for conditions like blood pressure. That's the strange and difficult times faced by those in the natural health industry.

'The Icing on the Cake'

As Wayne Elliott's health improved tremendously thanks to the Strauss Naturals products, he was ready to tackle greater and greater challenges as an environmental entrepreneur.

He stated, "Bless your heart with the Strauss Naturals triple crown of products unmatched anywhere. Strauss Heartdrops, cardio formula, kidney blood pressure formula – these are the first 3 Strauss formulas I took almost 30 years ago. I continue Strauss Heartdrops every day myself for all these years and the other two formulas for 2-3 months every 18 months or so, to help keep all well. I went downhill between 35 and 40, but for the 31 years since, I've worked double duty and, until last year, I was managing director of five companies in the environmental and recycling businesses. I am now mostly full time on my greatest passion: helping people get well."

Wayne continued, "I've been in some difficult business and mostly seemed to start 'from behind' in the shipbreaking, battery recycling, scrap metal and auto parts businesses. Battery recycling was the toughest to break even and that acid ate everything: floors, equipment, buildings. Until the government mandated spent battery collection and recycling, we lost money for 20 years. Our start in shipbreaking in Port Colborne, Ontario, required we remove a sunken 600- foot vessel on the site. After a lot of work and our share of broken fingers, we finally removed the hull, and we started in 1983 with several ships ahead to recycle. The scrap metal industry is a tough business with lots of multigeneration, wealthy, well-established businesses, tough to compete with. I have always felt good about the benefits to our environment arising from our companies' work. Yet, I've found the Strauss herbal formulas business the most rewarding. Both parents and I avoided open heart surgery. So did many friends, athletes and others. Every bottle sold lets me know another person is going to do better and quite frankly, that makes me feel good about me, to be some part of this business and these results."

"I've had a very good life. Worked more than enough but that's okay. Never once went hungry, and never once went without a warm place to sleep. I've had a charmed life indeed including some of 'the school of hard knocks.' Lessons well learned. However, the most profound experience of my life has been my relationship with Jim Strauss. Thanks to Jim and the genius behind his formulas, these past 30 years are the icing on the cake! Always grateful to Jim, and miss him dearly. RIP, old friend," Wayne concluded.

Top Ten Environmental Hypocrites
#5 Prince Harry and Meghan Markle

How Much Do They Talk? (0 = not at all to 10 = all day) = 10

Amount of Environmental Action? (0 = plants trees daily to 10 = giving speeches) = 8

Real Environmentalist Score = 18

Prince Harry and Meghan Markle have positioned themselves as advocates for various social causes, including mental health, racial equality, and environmental sustainability. However, their actions show their blatant hypocrisy.

Remember, as discussed in Chapter 1, their incredible commitment to the environment? They plan to limit themselves to two children, and after that, No Sex![146] Do you know the CO_2 emissions per orgasm?[147]

One of Harry's friends told the media that when the prince checks into a hotel, he requests that his accommodation avoids using unnecessary plastic during his stay. He specifically asked for no plastic coffee stirrer and no plastic bag for his dry cleaning.[148] Ahhhhh, the duke sacrifices!

Much of the couple's environmental effort seems very performative. For example, an Instagram post highlighted that their wedding flowers were "sustainable" pollinators that promote healthy bee populations.[149]

---

146 The first part is true. They committed to having only two kids. They have made no public commitments regarding their sex life, but if their Q score keeps going down, they will. Harry's popularity is down 35 points since marrying Meghan.

147 Well, after typing that phrase, I had to Google it and find out! According to https://www.sciencefocus.com/ , a human breathes out around 500 liters of CO_2 per year. That's about 1kg in mass. For the world's population of around 8.2 billion, that's 8.2 million tons each year. So, 10 minutes of sex (being generous to Harry) might add 5 extra liters of CO_2.

148 https://www.mirror.co.uk/news/uk-news/prince-harrys-vital-request-staying-16267232

149 https://www.instagram.com/p/BhBVLz3AvCS/?utm_source=ig_embed

The horrible environmental impact of private jets is mentioned in the pages discussing Leonardo DiCaprio's hypocrisy. Harry and Meghan's private planes are just as dirty. In 2019, they faced a backlash for taking four private jet flights in just 11 days, including a trip to Elton John's mansion in the south of France. Elton John defended them by stating that he had offset their carbon emissions, but this did little to quell public criticism. *Newsweek* reported that in the two prior years, the pair took 21 private flights.[150] Several of the flights were to and from important polo matches. "Important polo matches," that's a funny, oxymoronic phrase!

Activists have criticized carbon offsetting as an excuse to continue polluting, arguing that it does little to change behavior. More about the hypocrisy and uselessness of offsets later in the book.

In 2019, Harry announced that he was launching a travel company, called Travalyst, "to mobilize the travel industry as a catalyst for good, aiming to transform the future of travel for everyone." The goal was to put more of the tourist money spent in emerging economies back into the local community. Currently, only 5% of tourist money goes to local communities. Booking.com, SkyScanner, CTrip, TripAdvisor, Visa and Harry's own foundation came together to cultivate more interest and awareness in sustainable travel.[151] Great idea! What happened?

It's hard to tell. There are almost no articles in the news about them. There were articles about its creation and then about when Harry left. Yes, Harry left. CEO Sally Davey said, "Prince Harry is the founder of Travalyst and remains an invaluable part of this organization. His role has not changed in any way, and he is regularly involved in strategic discussions and decisions alongside our partners and board."[152] However, his name keeps being placed in less prominent places on the site. He has stopped talking about it and is no longer on the board. At least he tried!

Another aspect of Harry and Meghan's lifestyle that draws scrutiny is their housing choices. The couple's move to a luxurious mansion in Montecito, California, has been highlighted as contradictory to their environmental stance. While their home reportedly features eco-friendly amenities such as solar panels and energy-efficient systems, the sheer size and opulence of the property seem

---

[150] https://www.newsweek.com/prince-harry-meghan-markle-hypocritical-21-private-jets-since-2019-climate-change-environment-1633426
[151] https://www.yahoo.com/entertainment/prince-harry-finally-breaks-silence-155756597.html
[152] https://www.iol.co.za/travel/travel-news/what-ever-happened-to-travalyst-and-is-prince-harry-still-involved-9ecb5e10-91f9-4e8b-8326-c9e96a5b2633

at odds with the principles of sustainability and minimalism they promote. Critics argue that living in such a large, energy-intensive property undermines the couple's credibility as environmental advocates.

The manner in which Prince Harry and Meghan Markle handle their public engagements and charitable initiatives also raises questions. Their high-profile and often glamorous appearances can overshadow the causes they are promoting. For instance, their appearance at the 2021 Global Citizen Live event in New York City, aimed at promoting vaccine equity and addressing climate change, drew attention not only for the causes they supported but also for Meghan's clothes and high-profile presence. Critics argue that their focus on maintaining a glamorous image detracts from the seriousness of the issues they advocate for, creating a perception that their activism is more performative than substantive. For their August 2024 trip to Columbia, her four-day wardrobe cost $100,000.[153] *Newsweek*, *People*, *Harper's Bazaar*, *Marie Claire*, *Vogue* and many other outlets did full spreads on each outfit.

In conclusion, the perception of Harry and Meghan Markle as environmental hypocrites is well earned.

---

[153] https://www.dailymail.co.uk/femail/article-13756675/meghan-markle-90000-clothes-jewellery-colombia-tour-harry.html

Chapter 7
Cleaning the Mess

Wayne Elliott is not alone. He is not the only incredible entrepreneur who has been working on solving part of the problem. When you realize that thousands of companies and technologies are being explored, there is a tremendous reason to be greatly encouraged. We are not going to drown from raising sea levels. Increased hurricane activity will not destroy every world city. Crop yields will be fine. Entrepreneurs will solve all these problems.

Remember how markets work. This makes it easier to sleep after watching the newest Hollywood disaster movie. If we are running out of water, the price of water will go up. The worse the situation, the higher the prices will go. Entrepreneurs will see the prices going up and think, "Hey, I can make money by selling water. Maybe if I tinker with that invention some more, it will work better." They will find a way to make water cheaper while still making money themselves. Soon, they will be rich, but the price of water will have gone down. Consumers win. Entrepreneurs win. Markets proven yet again.[154]

It may be easier to see it in a smaller scenario. Assume Hurricane Wayne hits Florida and destroys many homes and businesses. The demand for plywood, pumps, and water skyrockets. Mean people from Atlanta see the storm, buy a trailer full of plywood and drive to Miami to sell it. They charge 250% of the price they paid for the wood. It sells immediately. A local news reporter hears about this and reports about the horrible price gouging. The mayor signs an ordinance forbidding storm profiteering and announces that he is protecting the citizens from the horrible price gougers. Meanwhile in Atlanta, people hear about the mayor's ordinance and cancel their plans for another load of wood to take to Florida. Suddenly, the arrival of supplies in Miami stops, and the storm-ravaged houses sit unrepaired. Markets proven yet again.

There are two groups of environmental entrepreneurs. Some focus on cleaning the mess that we have made. Others focus on making the future cleaner with less mess creation. This chapter deals with the former, and the next chapter deals with the latter.

---

154 https://www.youtube.com/watch?v=M2B-wpEj-9k

Larry Wyman: Saving the Ocean

Larry Wyman has had an exceptionally successful career. Larry's journey began in the legal field but transitioned to a different path. After leaving his legal career behind, he entered the commercial real estate sector. During the 1980s and 1990s, he had a significant role in managing twelve major projects in New York City while working with HRO International. His professional endeavors also took him to Frankfurt and London. Eventually, Larry stepped down from his active role at HRO International and joined their advisory board. Despite this transition, he continued to engage in various projects.

Recently, Larry joined a promising new company named Okeanos. This organization is dedicated to combating the issue of plastic pollution in our oceans and rivers. Commenting on the topic about whether commercial real estate would ever recover from the COVID-19 pandemic, Larry notes a significant shift in workplace dynamics. The employees are increasingly reluctant to return to downtown offices, leading him to speculate that commercial real estate might be facing its demise.

For him, the situation might be overstated as a complete "death," but he conceded that the sector is likely "mortally wounded." The work being done at Okeanos is entirely unrelated to real estate, which he finds to be a positive aspect.

The Plastic Pollution Horror

One of the most urgent environmental concerns today is plastic pollution—highlighted by a massive accumulation of plastic waste in the Pacific Ocean, compared in size to the state of Rhode Island. This phenomenon is known as a "gyre," which is an area where ocean currents converge. These gyres collect a significant amount of floating plastic, which not only remains on the surface but also deteriorates and sinks deeper into the ocean, eventually entering the food chain. Approximately 1,000,000 tons of plastic are produced worldwide each day, with over 90% of it failing to be reused or recycled.[155] Instead, it is either incinerated, deposited in landfills, or dispersed into the environment.[156]

There's a grim forecast for the future, indicating that annual plastic production is expected to triple over the next decades – from 460 million tons in 2019 to 1,231

---

[155] https://bren.ucsb.edu/news/international-statistic-year-91-plastic-has-never-been-recycled
[156] https://apnews.com/article/climate-plastics-explainer-pollution-recycling-5dc4e1a1618a73930ba73db801bc0589

million tons in 2060.[157] This increase is driven by the oil industry's shift towards plastics as a substitute for declining fossil fuel demand. As a result, humanity is exacerbating its own pollution problem daily with rising plastic production, despite the pressing need for more sustainable energy solutions.

One of the alarming issues is plastic ending up in the human bloodstream. Plastic does indeed enter the bloodstream and there are multiple pathways through which this can happen. Plastic is made from petrochemicals and often contains various toxic additives. These harmful substances can leach into products stored in plastic containers. In other cases, plastic infiltrates the food chain, particularly in marine environments. As plastic degrades in the ocean, it breaks down into smaller and smaller pieces, eventually becoming microplastics. These microplastics are consumed by smaller marine organisms, which are then eaten by larger fish and animals, ultimately passing through the food chain to humans.

Microplastics have been detected in fetal tissue, which raises serious concerns about their impact on human health. There's a startling statistic that the average person consumes approximately the equivalent of a credit card's worth of plastic every week.[158] While the full extent of the health risks remains unknown, there is a growing suspicion that the ingestion of plastic is disrupting the endocrine system and contributing to the rise of cancers and other health issues caused by toxins that are still not fully understood.

Therefore, plastic pollution is not only an environmental disaster but also a direct threat to human health. Many everyday products contain plastic that often go unnoticed. Plastic, in and of itself, is not inherently bad. Plastic has several significant advantages—it extends the shelf life of food, reduces the weight of cars, and plays an essential role in protecting medical and pharmaceutical products. Its usefulness and versatility have made plastic ubiquitous in modern life.

The problem with plastic lies not in its functionality but in the fact that society has not yet found an effective way to dispose of it. There is a disheartening reality that a plastic item, such as a cup used for just 30 seconds, could persist in the environment for up to 400 years.[159] The key issue is that while plastic offers

---

157 https://www.oecd.org/en/about/news/press-releases/2022/06/global-plastic-waste-set-to-almost-triple-by-2060.html
158 https://wwf.org.au/news/2019/revealed-plastic-ingestion-by-people-could-be-equating-to-a-credit-card-a-week/
159 https://www.weforum.org/stories/2018/11/chart-of-the-day-this-is-how-long-everyday-plastic-items-last-in-the-ocean/

numerous benefits, its long-term environmental impact is severe, and humanity must find better ways to manage its disposal.

The Solution Beyond Recycling

Since there are currently no efficient methods for eliminating plastic waste, the most viable solution is to reduce its use. This requires finding alternative materials to replace some of the plastic in everyday products. At Okeanos, Larry Wyman and his team have discovered a way to do just that by substituting calcium carbonate, essentially finely pulverized stone, for a portion of the plastic used in packaging. By binding calcium carbonate with a small amount of plastic, they can reduce the plastic content in items like cups, boxes, and packaging by over 50%! Not only does this process significantly lower the carbon footprint associated with production, but it also allows for the creation of more sustainable products without increasing costs for consumers.

While plastic serves important functions, reducing its environmental harm through innovative solutions like those at Okeanos is essential for a sustainable future. One of the biggest questions in that area is whose fault it is that plastic pollution has spiraled out of control. Is the consumer to blame for not recycling effectively enough? Are recycling companies at fault for inadequate sorting processes? Or should the oil companies bear the most responsibility for producing plastics that don't biodegrade?

For Larry, the bulk of the responsibility rests with the manufacturers of plastic products. The problem originated from the very production of plastic, which was the "original sin." It's fundamentally unfair to place the burden of managing this material on consumers, especially when the disposal systems in place are woefully inadequate. People often feel good about putting their used plastic bottles or cups into recycling bins, and they are contributing to a solution. However, this sense of contribution is misleading.

Worldwide, the percentage of plastic that actually gets recycled is shockingly low, ranging from only 5 to 10 percent. According to the Organization for Economic Cooperation and Development, it stands at 6 percent. This means that the vast majority, 90 to 95 percent, of plastic intended for recycling ends up not being recycled at all. For Larry Wyman, the primary reason for this dismal statistic is the inherent complexity of recycling plastic. When different types of plastic materials are mixed together, they introduce various chemicals and properties that make it incredibly difficult to reprocess them into new products. In practice, this results in most plastic being impossible to recycle efficiently.

While recycling is often seen as a noble effort, it is far from a reliable solution to the plastic problem. The real issue lies with the manufacturers and the inherent challenges in dealing with plastic waste, underscoring the need for more effective strategies at the source of production.

The waste management trucks collect recyclables each week, only to seemingly throw all the carefully separated materials, plastics, cardboard, and more, into a single compartment. It appeared that the efforts to separate different types of waste are being undone as everything is "mushed together" in the truck. Consumer batteries, Wayne warned, have caught fire in these trucks. Larry notes that is the way during transit, but that the process is more complex. Once the recyclables arrive at a facility, they are sorted into various waste streams. Paper and cardboard are separated, while glass and aluminum are directed to different areas. Plastics, however, present a significant challenge.

There are seven types of plastic, and the small symbols with chasing arrows often seen on the back of plastic packages are meant to indicate the type of plastic, not its recyclability. Most people assume these symbols mean the item can be recycled, but the symbols are simply identifiers for the type of plastic, each represented by a number from one to seven. The difficulty lies in the fact that mixing two or more different types of plastic renders the material largely unusable. Different plastics have varying properties and characteristics, making them hard to repurpose. Sorting plastics is an expensive and complicated process, and even when they are sorted, the product is often of low quality.

This is an example of greenwashing, a situation in which consumers believe they are contributing to sustainability efforts by recycling, but in actuality, very little is being achieved. The heart of the problem is that the current recycling systems, while well-intentioned, are ineffective at making a real difference. As a result, the most viable solution is to simply reduce the amount of plastic we use. Hence, finding alternative materials to replace plastic, either partially or entirely, is the key to addressing the environmental crisis. By using less plastic, society can begin to mitigate the harmful effects that these materials have on both the environment and human health.

Two Visionary Founders

The story of Okeanos begins with two visionary founders, Florencio Cuétara and Dr. Russell Petrie, who shared a passion for both innovation and environmental sustainability. Florencio Cuétara comes from a long-established European family involved in the food business, particularly in food packaging for products like yogurt and candies. His family's ventures have played a significant role in the

European food industry for many years. Meanwhile, Dr. Russell Petrie, an orthopedic surgeon and a member of the medical team for the LA Chargers, had been working to improve surgical practices. Specifically, Dr. Petrie was interested in finding alternatives to the toxic plastics used in surgical anchors and artificial ligaments.

Their shared concern for the environment, particularly the ocean, stemmed from a personal connection to marine life—they are both avid divers. For Florencio, the turning point came during a swim in the Mediterranean Sea, where he stumbled upon a piece of plastic that bore his family's brand name. The sight of a cookie tray floating in the water, one that had likely been manufactured by his own business, shocked him into action. That was the moment he decided that there had to be a better way to reduce plastic waste.

Dr. Petrie, on the other hand, had been researching calcium as a potential replacement for plastics in medical applications. The two men joined forces, driven by their shared commitment to reducing the environmental impact of plastics. This collaboration led to the founding of Okeanos, where they began investigating how calcium carbonate, a mineral found in abundance, could be used as a substitute for plastic in various products.

By grinding calcium carbonate into tiny particles, the Okeanos team developed a method to bind the mineral with plastic, effectively reducing the amount of plastic needed in packaging materials. Their innovative approach not only lowers the carbon footprint of manufacturing but also offers a more sustainable alternative to traditional plastic products. Florencio and Russell's combined expertise in food packaging and medical technology enabled them to create a solution that has the potential to revolutionize the way plastics are used, providing a more environmentally friendly option for industries that have long relied on harmful materials. Through Okeanos, they are paving the way for a future where the impact of plastic waste on the environment can be significantly reduced.

Calcium carbonate is a common compound found in different natural forms (like lime, chalk, or limestone), and it's also used in products that people consume, especially antacids like Tums. It had often been used as a filler in packaging materials, similar to the way fillers are used in processed foods, because it was cheaper than petrochemicals. However, it was only ever used in concentrations of around 10-15%, as larger amounts either weakened the packaging or caused problems with the machinery used to make the products.

As they started their initially small enterprise, Florencio and Russell eventually connected with Mary Lehrter, a former engineer at Procter & Gamble. Lehrter developed a patented process that resolved both the processing and performance issues. She discovered a way to make calcium carbonate behave like a liquid during manufacturing, which allowed it to pass through machinery more smoothly. Additionally, she found a method to combine it with a small amount of plastic, enabling the production of packaging materials where calcium carbonate made up the majority, replacing the need for nearly all plastic.

Strategic Thinking to Help the Environment

Larry Wyman became Okeanos' Chief Strategy Officer, with his role centered around strategic thinking. While living in Miami Beach, he was a casual acquaintance of Florencio Cuétara, whom he met through their shared residence in the same apartment building. They developed a friendly relationship, and Florencio invited Larry to breakfast to discuss his new venture. Florencio, an expert in systems related to manufacturing and food safety, sought Larry's advice on broader business aspects such as fundraising, an area where he had significant experience from his real estate endeavors.

Initially, the venture was composed solely of Florencio and Dr. Russell Petrie, who were self-funding their startup. As they continued to explore the potential of their idea, it had commercial viability. The startup began to grow, incorporating additional team members such as Mary Lehrter, a scientist, along with administrative, sales, and marketing personnel. Due to the self-funding nature of the project, resources were limited.

By 2019, the organization was operating with a small team of four or five people. As the enterprise expanded, it became evident that they needed more substantial financing to continue their progress. Larry was brought on board to assist in raising capital and developing a more focused business plan. His role also included refining the company's messaging to better align with their objectives and enhance their overall strategy.

Okeanos is making rapid progress with commercialization, as its product has seen significant success and widespread application—it's now available on store shelves in various locations around the world. Major consumer products companies are actively testing it for diverse uses, ranging from detergent jugs and thin material wraps to agricultural films and cardboard substitutes.

The product's versatility allows it to be utilized in a wide array of applications. At present, there are approximately 30 separate tests occurring globally to explore its potential uses. One significant advantage of calcium carbonate is its abundance. It is found in numerous locations around the world, which means that their supply can be sourced locally, minimizing the need for extensive transportation and reducing costs.

The manufacturing process is streamlined and efficient. Just as one would expect similar results when using different brands of cake mix in the same oven, Okeanos' product integrates seamlessly into existing plastic manufacturing processes. Companies that previously used 100 percent plastic can now substitute a portion of it with calcium carbonate without altering their machinery.

The introduction of calcium carbonate into the market has proven to be cost-effective. In many cases, it is less expensive than the plastic it replaces. The innovation lies in its upstream approach: rather than requiring users to eliminate existing plastic products, the solution involves incorporating a more sustainable alternative from the outset. This method effectively reduces the demand for virgin plastic by substituting it with calcium carbonate, offering a practical and economical solution to the problem of plastic pollution.

Larry's wife has had mixed feelings about his increased busyness, especially given that he was supposed to be enjoying retirement in Florida. She is not particularly pleased with his constant preoccupation, partly because he is often unavailable to address her needs and partly because their conversations frequently revolve around his work.

At nearly 68 years old, his past career was in developing office buildings worldwide. While his work advanced the state of the art in construction, Larry feels it did not contribute significantly to solving global problems or leaving a lasting impact. In contrast, his current involvement in environmental sustainability feels profoundly meaningful. He views the opportunity to engage in a project with the potential to positively affect the world and address the pressing issue of plastic pollution as a rare and valuable gift at this stage in his life. This new purpose is so compelling that it has even replaced his previous enthusiasm for playing golf, marking the first time he has felt a strong desire to go into the office instead.

The opportunity to work on something potentially meaningful is a novel experience for Larry Wyman. He had a significant moment at the UN Climate Change Conference in Sharm El-Sheikh, Egypt, in November 2022, where Okeanos' new product was unveiled for the first time. The reaction was overwhelmingly positive, as the attendees were not familiar with the product or its potential as a solution to environmental issues. The experience of presenting on such a prominent stage and discussing the future of the world's environment was both exhilarating and humbling, contrasting sharply with Larry's previous work in office space development.

His past work includes several notable projects, particularly in New York City. Among them are Financial Square, a million-square-foot building located down Wall Street, and the Broad Financial Center. He also managed a significant renovation project at 380 Madison Avenue in Midtown Manhattan. Additionally, his firm completed more than 20 projects in Paris, which featured American suburban-style office buildings equipped with higher technology and greater efficiency than previously available in that market. Although these buildings may not be widely recognized globally, they are well regarded within the local real estate community.

To learn more about the Okeanos project and stay updated on its progress, go to the website https://madefromstone.com/. The site offers access to a monthly newsletter that provides updates on the project's development and adoption. Additionally, the site features a QR code system for products, allowing users to scan and view a comprehensive Life Cycle Analysis (LCA) of the environmental impact of the product compared to traditional options. Larry Wyman has invited people to engage with the project and promised that as the initiative gains visibility, the use of such technologies will likely become more common.

Kevin Gast: VVATER

Kevin Gast, the CEO of a new company called VVATER, is another inspiring environmental entrepreneur whose focus is on cleaning the mess that humans have made. VVATER is uniquely spelled as "V, V, A, T, E, R" to visually align the "Vs" into a large "W" symbolizing water. The company has developed a breakthrough water treatment technology and recently won the prestigious *Consumer Electronics Show (CES) 2025 Best in Innovation Award*. CES recognition is one of the most esteemed accolades for groundbreaking technology.

Before his role at VVATER, Kevin had a background in entrepreneurship, having engaged in several ventures before this latest endeavor. On his journey as an entrepreneur, he had extensive experience of over 20 years in various industries and technologies.

Alarming State

Several years ago, a critical global issue that needed urgent action caught Kevin's attention, access to clean drinking water. The ozone layer was once considered a major threat to humanity, yet the problem seemed to fade over time. While global warming remains a significant challenge, its most severe consequences may unfold over the next few centuries. In contrast, the lack of clean drinking water presents an immediate and dire crisis, as human survival depends on it within just a few days.

The state of the world's water sources is alarming, as they are increasingly contaminated with harmful substances, such as endocrine disruptors, pharmaceuticals, and antibiotics. These pollutants pose severe health risks, impacting people's daily lives in ways that are often overlooked. Based on the urgency of this crisis, Kevin Gast felt compelled to develop a solution, leading to the creation of VVATER.

As a global-minded entrepreneur, he sought to establish a company that could address water scarcity and contamination on a worldwide scale. The pronunciation of "water" varies by region—sounding different in Europe, for instance. With his diverse background, he described himself as South African by birthright, German by blood, and Texan at heart. He needed a company that could represent something global and solve a global problem.

VVATER's inspiring success stems from an innovative approach it takes in handling water treatment. The traditional methods of water treatment fall into four main categories: chemical treatment, filtration, membrane-based processes such as reverse osmosis, and biological treatment. These methods are commonly used in various settings, from household water filtration systems to large-scale wastewater and drinking water treatment facilities.

In recent years, a fifth method has emerged—electricity-based technologies. This category includes electrocoagulation and electrochemical processes, which use high energy in combination with chemicals, filters, membranes, or other technologies to enhance water purification. The primary goal of these treatments is to eliminate harmful microorganisms, such as protozoa, bacteria, and viruses that pose health risks. Additionally, water treatment involves adjusting the mineral content, such as reducing excess iron.

Despite the advancements in electricity-based water treatment, existing methods still required some form of filtration or membrane. Kevin's company conducted extensive research and development over several years, investing significant time and resources to develop new technology. This effort led to the creation of their Faraday Reactors which utilize a process known as Advanced Low Tension Electroporation Process (ALTEP).

Innovative Technology

The core principle of ALTEP is electroporation, a technique that disinfects water by using minimal energy and no additional substances. This process destroys microorganisms on a molecular level without generating harmful byproducts. Unlike traditional chemical-based water treatments, which rely on chlorine, fluoride, or other substances that may negatively impact health, this new method offers a cleaner, more efficient alternative.

The innovation has been widely recognized, with the media dubbing the company as the "Tesla of water treatment" due to its revolutionary use of electricity in water purification. This technology represents a major breakthrough in the industry, offering a sustainable and highly effective solution for water treatment without the drawbacks of traditional methods.

The technology had its limitations. The two biggest limitations were that it was not a desalination technology, meaning it could not remove salts from the water, and that it could not remove large solids. Specifically, anything above 20 microns could not be handled by their proprietary technology. However, conventional technologies could be used to address those issues.

VVATER's ALTEP technology is now primarily used in the real estate and aquatics industries. Many developers across the United States struggled with real estate development because local municipalities and counties could not provide sufficient wastewater treatment or drinking water facilities. The company provided a standalone system to handle both wastewater and drinking water. The technology was also used in aquatic facilities, such as Great Wolf Lodges and ARIA Resorts, where guests often experience skin irritation and a strong chlorine smell. The system improved the experience by addressing these issues.

The technology has also been used for on-site water reuse, particularly in places like Austin and San Francisco. In these areas, buildings over 250,000 square feet, whether commercial or industrial, were required to have an on-site treatment system. The company was also developing a residential consumer-based product, which aimed to replace water softeners, whole-house filtration systems, and reverse osmosis systems installed under kitchen sinks. This new system would be available at a fraction of the cost, require no maintenance, and eliminate the need for filter replacements while providing much cleaner water.

Clean water is essential, and modern water sources contain microplastics and "forever chemicals" (PFAs), which are present in products like shampoos, mascaras, and cookware. VVATER's technology can destroy PFAs, providing safer water. Plans include introducing their own natural spring drinking water, similar to brands like Evian or Fiji Water, but free of microorganisms and contaminants. The system would also infuse the water with hydrogen and hydronium ions, which are beneficial to health. Additionally, the company is considering launching a cold plunge system, which offers significant health benefits.

The ALTEP technology could be used across various industries and sectors. However, due to high demand, the company was rolling out the technology in phases, as there was already a long waiting list. Despite this, the technology has the potential to be applied commercially worldwide, solving multiple water treatment challenges on a global scale.

Many people do not fully grasp the severity of global water contamination. To paraphrase Benjamin Franklin, people only recognize the value of water once the supply runs dry. Water scarcity is becoming a widespread crisis, with approximately 1.8 billion people worldwide facing absolute water scarcity. In the United States alone, more than 50 percent of the population has experienced drought over the past two decades. Water is not an infinite resource, particularly drinking water, making water recycling an inevitable necessity in the future. Without implementing such solutions, water shortages will continue to escalate.

Direct potable reuse (DPR) is one method already being used in Texas and California. This process involves treating wastewater at a facility to ensure it meets specific safety and quality standards set by regulatory bodies such as the EPA, CDC, and the TCEQ. Once the water is properly treated, it can be discharged back into rivers, canals, or wells. But many wastewater treatment facilities in the US fail to meet regulatory standards. Instead of upgrading their systems, these facilities often choose to pay fines, as the penalties are relatively minor. As a result, contaminated water containing pharmaceuticals, antibiotics, and other harmful substances is frequently released into waterways, negatively impacting communities downstream.

This issue requires a two-fold approach. First, wastewater needs to be properly treated and converted into potable drinking water. Second, ensuring clean water discharge into rivers and other water sources is essential for reducing contamination. By implementing these solutions, water shortages in regions like Las Vegas and Arizona can be mitigated, while also improving overall water quality and environmental sustainability.

Diverse Business Experience

As an entrepreneur, Kevin Gast has diverse experiences in the pharmaceutical industry, hotel property development, and lodge management in South Africa. He came from a family-run business background, describing himself as a "salt of the earth" South African. He gained business experience in Africa, Austria, and Europe, beginning his journey with the family business started by his grandfather. His father took over the business in the early 1980s, and he later assumed control in the early 2000s. The conglomerate encompassed multiple industries, including pharmaceuticals, hotel businesses, construction, and civil engineering.

Throughout his career, Kevin has experienced both failures and successes. He started as a laborer on-site, mixing concrete and building houses with bricks, gradually working his way up through different fields. His extensive background includes expertise in civil engineering, mechanical engineering, and electrical engineering. He is passionate about solving problems, especially when they hold significant importance.

Kevin noted his family-owned game lodge in South Africa, called Swahili Private Game Lodge. He explained that it is similar to a ranch in Texas but includes hotel facilities. Tourists visiting South Africa for safaris often stay at such game lodges, and Swahili is a five-star facility that caters to international guests.

Kevin shared that spending time at the game lodge is a personal retreat for him. While some people relax by playing golf or engaging in other activities, he finds peace in nature. Being in the wilderness helps him clear his mind and focus better on business. Swahili Private Game Lodge serves as both a luxury destination and a personal escape, allowing him to reconnect with nature and refresh his mindset.

After conducting business in numerous countries, Kevin decided to tackle a larger issue—water scarcity and water cleanliness. The best way to address this global problem was from the United States. Originally from Pretoria, South Africa, like his compatriot Elon Musk, he had been traveling to and from the US for the past 20 years, gaining experience and building a strong network.

He ultimately chose Austin, Texas, as his home, making the move in November 2020. He has admiration for the city's hills, culture, climate, and community. Having spent significant time in various states over the years, he found himself drawn to Texas and its resilient spirit.

There was a survey that asked people from different states where they would move if their home state were to "blow up." The responses varied, with individuals from places like California and New York choosing different states. However, Texans were the only ones who stated that they would "go down with the ship." With this sentiment, Kevin Gast has deep appreciation for Texas despite not being American by birth. He is really highly patriotic, perhaps even more so than many natives, and his commitment to the United States and Texas is unwavering.

Kevin's passion for the community and dedication to improving people's well-being solidified his decision to settle in Austin. He wanted to see people succeed and remain healthy, and for him, Texas represented the perfect place to pursue those goals.

VVATER's Path Forward

VVATER's technology was initially incubated within a larger conglomerate where significant time and resources were dedicated to research and development. The team, which included himself, his father, two other engineers, and a broader network of professionals, conducted extensive work in the field. Throughout their efforts, they completed over 14,000 projects, experimenting with various water treatment technologies, wastewater management, drinking water solutions, construction, civil engineering, geosynthetics, and more. However, they eventually realized that the traditional methods they were using were unsustainable, prompting them to seek a better approach.

During this extensive R&D phase, the team experienced a technological breakthrough. Such discoveries often take time to fully understand and appreciate. Initially, they did not grasp the full potential of their innovation until they had tested and refined it. A turning point came when they were tasked with building a five-acre artificial beach in South Africa for a multi-billion-dollar development called Stein City. The project required a sustainable water source, but there was insufficient water available to maintain it. In response, he and his team implemented a solution that converted black water into clean, swimmable water, creating a fully functional and enjoyable recreational facility.

Seeing the success of this project, the team recognized the broader potential of their innovation. They then decided to separate the entire venture, including intellectual property, contracts, and all associated elements, into a dedicated company, which is now known as VVATER. With the company officially formed, they turned their focus to raising capital.

Kevin was fortunate to secure early-stage investment from Tim Draper, a world-renowned billionaire and venture capital pioneer. Draper, one of the first investors in SpaceX and Tesla, made a substantial investment in VVATER during its initial stages. Following this success, the company completed another funding round, which closed recently and is set to be officially announced soon. This round brought in an additional three billionaires, bringing the total number of billionaire investors on VVATER's cap table to four.

With strong financial backing, a well-structured pipeline, and a clear vision, VVATER has now moved beyond technological and commercialization risks. The company is currently in a pure growth phase, focused on scaling and expanding its impact in the water industry. In a remarkable success, in August 2025, VVATER was awarded a multi-million-dollar contract for the Direct Potable Reuse (DPR) & Water Reuse project for the $1.5 billion development in South Austin.[160]

Kevin Gast agrees that environmental challenges need to be recognized by everyone. Although he does not consider himself the world's biggest environmentalist, he deeply cares about the environment, particularly because he has three teenage daughters. The biggest challenges include the fundamental necessity of clean water: without it, survival is impossible, and everything else becomes irrelevant. Realizing this, Kevin spent the past 20 years breaking down clean water problems to their core elements.

With the recent changes occurring in the United States, deregulation is a key factor in enabling entrepreneurs and professionals to drive meaningful change. Many individuals across various fields, entrepreneurs, professionals, and academics, are actively trying to create solutions, but excessive regulation remains a significant barrier.

Drawing from his own experience working with regulatory bodies, Kevin observed that these institutions are not designed for innovation or change. Some states, counties, and municipalities still operate under outdated legislation from the 1970s, which mandates antiquated water treatment methods, such as adding chlorine to disinfect water without considering more advanced and effective solutions. He described this approach as outdated and ineffective.

Despite these challenges, Kevin Gast has strong optimism about the future. With the upcoming regulatory changes and advancements in innovation, the world will be able to tackle major environmental problems in a more efficient and effective manner.

---

[160] https://www.barchart.com/story/news/34224899/vvater-awarded-multi-million-dollar-water-reuse-project-for-a-1-5b-multi-use-real-estate-development-in-south-austin

Top Ten Environmental Hypocrites

#4 Barack Obama

How Much Do They Talk? (0 = not at all to 10 = all day) = 10

Amount of Environmental Action? (0 = plants trees daily to 10 = giving speeches) = 8

Real Environmentalist Score = 18

Barack Obama, the 44th President of the United States, has been an influential advocate for addressing climate change and promoting sustainable practices. His administration implemented numerous policies aimed at reducing greenhouse gas emissions, promoting renewable energy, and protecting natural resources.

His greatest environmental accomplishment was the signing of the Paris Climate Agreement. President Obama called the Agreement, "the best possible shot to save the one planet we've got."[161] When Donald Trump was elected, he "made the decision to withdraw from the Paris Agreement because of the unfair economic burden imposed on American workers, businesses, and taxpayer."[162] On his first day in office, President Biden signed an instrument to bring the United States back into the Paris Agreement.[163] Then, on January 20, 2025, the first day in office after becoming reelected to the White House, President Trump signed an executive order to withdraw the US from the Paris Agreement for the second time.[164]

One definition of hypocrisy is feigning to be what one is not. The Paris Agreement qualifies. Countries set their own start and goal points. India announced before the Agreement was signed that its goal for net zero compliance was 2070 and outside of Paris Agreement rules. India's coal requirement "is set to increase by 50% in the next decade, going by official estimates. Nandini Das, a climate and energy economist at Climate Analytics, says India is sending out mixed signals as it is 'rapidly expanding its renewable capacity, but at the same

---

[161] https://www.obama.org/stories/paris-climate-agreement/
[162] https://2017-2021.state.gov/on-the-u-s-withdrawal-from-the-paris-agreement/
[163] https://www.state.gov/the-united-states-officially-rejoins-the-paris-agreement/
[164] https://www.theguardian.com/us-news/2025/jan/20/trump-executive-order-paris-climate-agreement

time increasing coal consumption.'"[165] In 2022, China built approximately 66 new coal power plants, and in 2023, it built 78. The media was excited when they only built 37 in the first half of 2024.[166] In short, the Agreement does not "address the 'free-rider problem,' which stems from the fact that countries would enjoy the benefits of global efforts to limit emissions regardless of their contributions. This creates a temptation to ride on the emissions cuts of other nations, and can doom the overall effort: If everyone shirks, the global cuts never materialize."[167]

The most successful previous global environmental agreement was the Montreal Protocol of 1987, and it had great success limiting chlorofluorocarbons (CFCs). The Protocol had sticks and carrots. The Obama Administration demand carrots only, so no punishments for non-compliance. Diplomats "would also have needed a stick to punish India if it didn't agree, as they did with the trade barrier in the Montreal Protocol."[168] In other words, the Paris Agreement was designed to fail. So many backdoors and carveouts exist that the whole Agreement is a farce. How much of a farce?

If it were straight up, most countries should have achieved their goals, with India and China being the big failures. In actuality, they were the only two countries to meet their goals![169]

Since leaving office, Barack Obama has faced accusations of environmental hypocrisy, primarily due to his personal lifestyle choices and post-presidential activities. These criticisms highlight a perceived inconsistency between his public advocacy and private actions. The only logical conclusion? The Agreement was Obama performative bullshit. It was done for appearance only with no true belief it would make a difference.

Does Obama believe in climate change? Oceans raising? Or does he really believe that "this was the moment when the rise of the oceans began to slow and our planet began to heal"?[170] Look at his two vacation homes post-presidency. He has the Martha's Vineyard mansion that Homes and Gardens magazine says, "stands out as one of the most impressive properties we've ever seen."[171] The house is oceanfront at about three feet above sea-level. He also bought the

---

165 https://www.bbc.com/news/world-asia-india-58922398
166 https://www.mirror.co.uk/money/china-cuts-new-coal-power-33500909
167 https://insideclimatenews.org/news/28072021/pairs-agreement-success-failure/
168 Ibid.
169 https://www.pbs.org/newshour/science/only-2-countries-are-meeting-their-climate-pledges-heres-how-the-10-worst-could-improve
170 Barack Obama upon winning the Democratic nomination for presidency, June 03, 2008.
171 https://www.homesandgardens.com/news/president-obama-new-house-marthas-vineyard

Magnum P.I. "Robin's Nest" house from the 1980s Tom Selleck TV show. It was built in 1933, was architecturally significant, and included 8,500 square feet. He tore the house down and built a larger mansion and, most importantly, secured a special permit to maintain a seawall. According to scientists, "it has become clear that in fact seawalls are contraindicated in relation to preserving Hawaii's natural coastlines. Such structures do not protect the shoreline, however, and in fact directly result in existing beach loss by interrupting the ocean's natural flow."[172] The Obamas hypocritically fought the State of Hawaii to retain a beach-destroying wall. Their house is just feet above sea level. If he truly believes in the oceans rising, would he invest tens of millions in areas soon to be flooded? Large homes typically require more energy for heating, cooling, and maintenance, contributing to a higher carbon footprint.

Barack Obama's excessive use of private jets, visiting private yachts, his large carbon billowing parties, the requirement that as many as fourteen Secret Service agents travel with him, and his multi-million-dollar deal with Netflix all have raised eyebrows. Netflix causes substantial energy consumption and carbon emissions associated with digital streaming services. The construction of his presidential center in Chicago has drawn criticism from environmentalists about its environmental impact on the historic parkland.[173] It seems like money comes first to the former president.

---

172 https://beatofhawaii.com/magnum-pi-home-set-to-become-obama-hawaii-retreat/
173 https://www.ipi.org/ipi_issues/detail/the-battle-over-the-obama-presidential-center

Chapter 8
Better Products for Tomorrow

As mentioned in the previous chapter, there are two groups of environmental entrepreneurs. In the last chapter, the focus was on entrepreneurs cleaning the mess that already exists. This chapter deals with entrepreneurs that are making the future cleaner. This is happening at many levels. Some solutions are designed to change things in entire industries. Some businesses are built to make one product niche clear. When these are added together, it becomes clear that the world will survive in an increasingly clean and safe environment.

Dr. Stephen Mayfield: Biodegradable Plastics

Dr. Stephen Mayfield is tackling one of the world's very biggest problems and is trying to reshape one of the largest industries on Earth. He is fighting the big blob of microplastics in the Pacific Ocean. He is the author of the book, *Our Energy Future: Introduction to Renewable Energy and Biofuels.* His research career focuses on the molecular genetics of green algae, and on making bio-products using algae as a production platform, especially biopolymers. He received BS degrees in Biochemistry and Plant Biology from Cal Poly State University in San Luis Obispo, and a PhD in Molecular Genetics from UC Berkeley. Following a post-doctoral fellowship at the University of Geneva in Switzerland, he returned to California as an assistant professor at the Scripps Research Institute. He remained there for 22 years and became the Dean of Biology. In 2009, he became a Distinguished Professor of Biology and the Director of the California Center for Algae Biotechnology at the University of California, San Diego.[174]

Unexpected Turn: The Power of Entrepreneurship

Like many entrepreneurs, Steve's career path took an unexpected turn.[175] In the early 2000s, he was focused on basic scientific research at the Scripps Research Institute, particularly in gene regulation. He was following a structured career

---

[174] https://www.algenesislabs.com/steve-mayfield-phd
[175] This information comes from an interview with Dr. Mayfield on School for Startups Radio in September 2024

plan, publishing papers, and securing funding for his work. Then, something unexpected happened that shifted his trajectory.

He and his team successfully created a human monoclonal antibody, which worked exceptionally well. They demonstrated that the antibody folded correctly and bound as expected, which caught the attention of the pharmaceutical industry. A major pharmaceutical company approached him in 2002 with interest in his work on microalgae. The company suggested that he attempt to create monoclonal antibodies using algae, as these antibodies were expensive to produce traditionally. They believed that if produced in algae, the cost could be significantly reduced. Although he was surprised by the suggestion, he recognized the opportunity. He was an assistant professor at the time, and the offer of funding was too good to pass up. The company even offered a budget and the hiring of a technician to help conduct the research.

In 2004, his team published a paper demonstrating that a human monoclonal antibody could be successfully produced in green algae. They calculated the production cost to be just pennies per gram, which was revolutionary at the time because monoclonal antibodies were extremely expensive to manufacture.

For those of you that don't know, monoclonal antibodies are identical antibodies cloned from a single type, unlike polyclonal antibodies, which are a mix of various types found in the blood responding to different antigens such as viruses or bacterial infections. While polyclonal antibodies are beneficial for the body, they cannot be used as a targeted drug. In contrast, monoclonal antibodies can become precise therapeutic drugs. Many advanced cancer drugs advertised on television with a couple riding a horse in the surf are, in fact, monoclonal antibodies. These are highly specific and can bind to unique targets such as viruses or cancer cells, making them valuable in modern medicine. Many pharmaceutical companies were eager to find cheaper production methods. Dr. Mayfield's team's breakthrough showed this was possible using algae.

This moment was an epiphany for Steve. While he had been doing similar science all along, creating a tangible product made his work more relatable to the public. People outside of the academic world could now understand and appreciate his efforts.

The results were strong enough to be published in a prominent journal, the *Proceedings of the National Academy of Sciences*. This was a significant accomplishment in the academic world, but the breakthrough received unexpected attention from outside the scientific community. *The Los Angeles Times* reached out, expressing interest in covering the story. They sent a photographer to capture Dr. Mayfield holding petri dishes filled with algae, and within a week, his face was on the cover of the business section of the newspaper.

He had never considered issuing a press release about his research before, but he agreed. A few days later, the article appeared in the paper.

The turning point for him came when his mother called him after seeing his photo on the front page of the business section. She said, "Oh my gosh, I finally understand what you do." Although he had worked in science for 15 years and had frequently tried to explain his work to his parents, it wasn't until they saw a real-world application that they fully grasped its significance. For him, this was a defining moment.

In this moment, he understood the power of entrepreneurship. By translating scientific research into real-world products, he could not only advance his field but also connect with people in a meaningful way. It was this realization that set him on a path toward becoming a successful scientist-entrepreneur.

Basic research is the foundation of many companies and innovations. Whether it's self-driving cars or cancer treatments, they all stem from science, be it artificial intelligence or molecular biology. He returned to his lab and told his team that while they continue to do basic research, they would now also focus on its practical applications. This shift would help people understand and value their work, and in hindsight, he recognized that this decision was right.

The Road to Biodegradable Polymers

The company became Rincon Pharmaceuticals. This experience was the starting point for his entrepreneurial journey, though it didn't bring him significant financial gains. Despite the success of their technology, where they created several monoclonal antibodies and established programs with major pharmaceutical companies like Biogen, IDEC, and Pfizer, Rincon Pharmaceuticals faced challenges. The company didn't fail due to scientific shortcomings, but rather because of the economic realities of the pharmaceutical industry. Within the field of medicine, the cost of producing the protein (the "cost of goods") is often insignificant, making up only around 4-5% of the total expense of a drug. The remaining 95% goes toward advertising, clinical trials, and other associated costs. As a result, the cost-saving benefits of producing proteins cheaper in algae, while scientifically impressive, were not enough to sway risk-averse pharmaceutical companies.

Consequently, that program eventually faded away, and Stephen Mayfield didn't reap large financial rewards from the endeavor. However, the experience gave him valuable insight into the relationship between science and entrepreneurship. While he had always valued basic scientific research and publishing papers, this venture made him realize that what truly changes the world are products that can meet real-world needs.

By 2012, Steve shifted his focus, driven by the question of what products scientists can create that the world genuinely needs. This shift marked a new phase in his career, where he began to concentrate on the practical applications of his scientific work, blending research with a mission to develop solutions that could have a meaningful impact. This is the model that most scientists should follow!

His journey with Algenesis began after years of experience in the biofuel and biotechnology industries. In 2008, he founded Sapphire Energy, a biofuel company, and managed to raise an astonishing $300 million, a sum he described as "stupid money." Let's read that again. $300 million! The funding wasn't a testament to him alone, but rather a reflection of the biofuel boom at the time, a trend similar to the present-day excitement surrounding artificial intelligence. Investors were eager to throw money into biofuels, convinced it was a breakthrough that would change the world. And while the technology itself worked, producing biofuels from algae wasn't economically viable.[176]

By 2013, Steve had another epiphany: despite the large market for fuel, it's a $7 trillion industry, the cost of fuel is extremely low, around 40 to 50 cents per pound. The logic behind using advanced algae technology to produce oil, only to burn it as fuel, didn't make sense from an economic perspective. Instead, he pivoted and focused on products that could be sold to the highest bidder rather than the lowest. This realization led him to move away from biofuels and explore other valuable uses for algae.

His first step was to enter the food industry, leading to the formation of Triton Health and Nutrition. The company was later acquired by a Chinese firm in 2019. Afterward, he shifted his focus to polymers. Polymers were ten times more valuable than fuel, making them a far more attractive product. The logic was simple: if the effort required to produce polymers was the same as that for biofuels, why not create something that offers a much higher return.

---

176 https://extendedstudies.ucsd.edu/news-and-events/division-of-extended-studies-blog/february-2016/50-voices-of-the-future-stephen-mayfield-on-algae-biotechnology

This strategic pivot marked the beginning of Algenesis, a company focused on using algae to produce valuable materials like polymers, which have far-reaching applications and greater economic potential. By focusing on high-value products, he continued to push the boundaries of what algae can achieve, moving beyond fuel to more sustainable and lucrative ventures.

Supplanting Traditional Plastics

Algenesis concentrated on producing materials that address the growing issue of plastic pollution, particularly microplastics. Rather than creating a product that consumes microplastics, as some might assume, Algenesis produces the polymers that serve as the foundation for various types of plastics. Specifically, they manufacture monomers that are used to create polyurethanes, a versatile polymer that has a wide range of applications. Polyurethanes are found in everyday items such as the soles of shoes, car seats, tires, paints, and sealants. The reason for their widespread use is their unique properties: they are both waterproof and elastic, making them highly durable and flexible.

Polyurethanes were deliberately chosen because of their valuable characteristics and the potential to make them biodegradable. The world is facing an immense challenge with microplastic pollution right now. Steve and his team sought to create a polymer that could break down naturally over time. Biodegradable polymers are crucial in the fight against microplastic pollution, which is currently pervasive in oceans, air, and even within our bodies. Remember the big plastic blob in the Pacific Ocean? Microplastics.

By focusing on polyurethanes and their potential for biodegradability, Algenesis's goal is to make a significant impact in reducing the environmental damage caused by traditional plastics. Its work is showing innovation in materials science, particularly in creating products that can perform well while also being environmentally sustainable. In this way, Algenesis is not only contributing to the future of plastics but also addressing one of the most pressing environmental issues of our time.

There's a widespread presence of microplastics in our everyday lives. Plastic is everywhere, regardless of where one might be, whether in a car, kitchen, or at work. Nearly everything around, including shoes, shirts, hats, and various other items, is made of or contains plastic. These products shed microplastics into the environment daily.

There has been a rapid rise in plastics in modern life. Steve was born in the 1950s, a time when plastics were virtually non-existent. Back then, items were made from wood, glass, and metal. Plastics have only been a significant part of human life for the last 50 to 60 years, yet they are now an integral part of everything we use. This sudden ubiquity has serious consequences. Microplastics are now found in our drinking water, the air we breathe, and even in our blood. Alarmingly, recent research indicates that microplastics have made their way into the human brain, with an estimated 0.5% of our brain tissue now composed of plastics absorbed from the environment.[177]

Given that human beings have never encountered these materials throughout their evolution, the sudden and pervasive presence of microplastics is likely to cause unforeseen harm. The long-term health impacts of microplastics could surpass the damage caused by other well-known pollutants, such as cigarettes, smog, and toxins.

In response to this growing crisis, Steve and his team at Algenesis set out to create biodegradable plastics. While plastics are useful and have revolutionized many aspects of modern life, from food packaging to surfboards to footwear, the problem lies in their persistence in the environment. Traditional plastics break down into microplastics, which then linger for centuries. Algenesis, however, has developed polymers and plastics that are biodegradable, meaning they decompose naturally at the end of their lifecycle without leaving harmful microplastics behind.[178] Hero.

Steve's work with biodegradable plastics offers a promising solution to one of the most pressing environmental challenges of our time. These new materials maintain the functionality of traditional petroleum-based plastics while addressing the issue of plastic pollution, potentially reducing the long-term impact of microplastics on human health and the environment.

His company primarily sells its biodegradable materials to the shoe industry, particularly brands focused on outdoor products. The shoe and outdoor industries were among the first to recognize the potential of their materials and embrace them. The company sells monomers to factories that manufacture components used in shoes, including waterproof coatings for fabrics.

The potential applications for these biodegradable materials seem endless. The opportunities are vast but there are also challenges. As a startup with limited resources and bandwidth, Algenesis has to prioritize and focus on specific industries. This creates a balancing act between identifying which industries

---

[177] https://www.sciencealert.com/microplastics-detected-infiltrating-human-brains-for-the-first-time
[178] https://algaeplanet.com/stephen-mayfield-algae-storyteller/

would benefit most from their materials and convincing those industries to adopt them.

One surprising development for Steve's company was interest from the furniture industry. Some furniture manufacturers approached them, driven by increasing customer demand for sustainable, bio-based, and biodegradable materials. These customers were concerned about sitting on furniture that shed microplastics into their homes and sought alternatives. As a result, his team began collaborating with furniture manufacturers, with the hope that by the following year, chairs containing their biodegradable materials would be available on the market.

There are challenges and opportunities for innovative materials in various industries. As demand for environmentally friendly solutions grows, Algenesis continues to explore new markets while balancing the practical limitations of being a startup.

Steve's company hasn't received "obscene" funding. The situation back in 2007 was unique, right before the economic crash caused by the housing crisis, gas prices had doubled within a year. This dramatic increase reinforced people's belief that petroleum was a very finite resource, and its price could continue to rise indefinitely as oil was certainly post-peak. When this was combined with growing awareness of climate change and environmental concerns, there was a rush of investment in alternative energy and sustainability projects, including Steve's earlier ventures. Investors saw the potential in addressing these issues, leading to what he called "stupid money" being poured into the industry.

However, in the case of microplastics and polymers, people have not yet fully grasped the severity of the problem, nor have they recognized that his company offers a viable solution. Once the magnitude of the microplastics crisis became clear, significant investments followed. Within the next few years, there was growing realization of the crisis scope, and greater funding to solve these environmental challenges. While he referred to it again as "stupid money," the real issue lies in the lack of urgency. The data is already available, and action needs to be taken. While market trends and awareness influence funding, once the urgency of the microplastics issue is fully recognized, substantial resources will be allocated to address it.

The Journey to Adopt Biodegradable Plastics

Dr. Stephen Mayfield proposes mandating the use of biodegradable plastics by 2030. This mandate could revolutionize the industry and potentially lead to massive financial success for companies.

While members of the United States Congress recognize the severity of the plastic problem, they are unable to pass laws banning non-biodegradable plastics until there are viable alternatives in place. Lawmakers are hesitant to enforce regulations prohibiting traditional plastics unless there are scalable, functional replacements available. Therefore, the burden falls on companies like Algenesis to develop and scale bioplastics that can be used in everyday products. The goal is to prove that these sustainable materials can serve as a direct substitute for petroleum-based plastics without compromising functionality.

While there are biopolymers and biodegradable plastics capable of replacing existing plastics, the production and use of these materials are not yet widespread enough to support a comprehensive ban on traditional plastics. If non-biodegradable plastics were banned today, daily life would be significantly impacted. For example, common items like Starbucks to-go cups and other food containers would disappear from the market, leaving consumers without alternatives.

The journey to replace plastics is a process that requires time and effort. Nevertheless, Steve is optimistic. His company and others have already developed high-performance polymers capable of substituting conventional plastics without leaving behind harmful microplastics. The next step is to increase the production and integration of these biopolymers into various industries. Once it becomes evident that bioplastics can effectively replace traditional plastics on a large scale, lawmakers will have the confidence to pass regulations mandating their use.

During Steve's childhood in the 1960s, there was severe air pollution in Los Angeles. Despite knowing how to address the problem, by installing emission restrictors on cars, progress was hindered by those who profited from the status quo. Car manufacturers and oil companies were reluctant to adopt measures that would reduce their profits. They actively resisted change through misinformation and lobbying against new regulations.

Fortunately, in California, public demand for cleaner air led to legislative action. New laws mandated improvements in vehicle emissions, which ultimately resulted in significantly better air quality. This change in California eventually influenced global practices, demonstrating how local actions can have broad impacts.

Steve drew a parallel to the current situation with plastics. While solutions like bioplastics are ready and viable, existing plastic manufacturers are fiercely opposing these innovations to protect their economic interests. They spread negative information about bioplastics not due to environmental concerns but because these alternatives threaten their profits.

For sustainable solutions to prevail, it is crucial to challenge the status quo and support innovative alternatives. Steve hopes that with enough advocacy and public support, bioplastics will eventually overcome resistance and become widely adopted. While the transition may take time, proactive efforts can accelerate the adoption of effective solutions, potentially reducing the timeline from 20 years to five.

While it is true that these entrenched companies would eventually be interested in bioplastic technologies, they are currently not pursuing them. The primary reason for this reluctance is scale. The major plastic manufacturers are currently producing vast quantities of conventional petroleum-based plastics, in 2022, the world's plastic production reached 400.3 million tons, which equals 880 billion pounds.[179] In contrast, Stephen's startup is still in the early stages of production. His company can produce only a fraction of that amount, with plans to scale up gradually over the next few years.

Once his production reaches a significant scale, around 10 million pounds, large companies are likely to take notice. At that point, they may choose to acquire the startup or incorporate its technology into their own operations. However, as long as the startup is not yet producing at a scale that makes a substantial impact, these companies are hesitant to invest. They are currently making substantial profits from their existing technologies and are not willing to risk their economic stability on unproven alternatives. Proving the effectiveness of bioplastics at a large scale is crucial for convincing these companies to make the switch. The technology must not only look promising on paper but also demonstrate clear benefits in practical, large-scale applications.

---

179 https://www.actpac.eu/news/global-plastics-industry/

Bioplastic Shoes Are Here!

Steve has particularly high hopes for the prospects of bioplastics in the shoe industry. While his startup is in discussions with several major brands, these companies are still in the testing phase and are cautious. They are evaluating the bioplastic materials to ensure they meet their performance standards and consumer expectations. This testing process can take up to a year, as brands need to confirm that not only does the material perform well, but that consumers also accept and prefer it.

Currently, most of the support for bioplastic materials comes from smaller, emerging brands. These smaller companies have shown enthusiasm for incorporating bioplastics into their products, although many prefer to keep their collaborations under wrap until their products are officially launched. One such local company in San Diego is expected to release a new shoe line featuring bioplastics.[180] Steve is excited about this collaboration; the company is committed to making a positive impact with their innovative approach.

For those eager to support the advancement of bioplastics in footwear, please purchase from BLUEVIEW Footwear,[181] a brand his team has developed. BLUEVIEW offers sneakers made with bioplastic materials and are available for purchase on their website. By buying these shoes, consumers can directly contribute to the growth and visibility of bioplastic alternatives in the market. If BLUEVIEW Footwear gains enough traction, it could further influence major brands to adopt bioplastic solutions more rapidly.

BLUEVIEW Footwear uses an innovative bioplastic material Soleic, a biodegradable foam made from plants that is durable enough to be used in footwear. The brand has received positive feedback from customers who are praising the sneakers for their comfort, lightweight design, and overall quality. With sales of around 5,000 pairs already, it needs to significantly increase these numbers to capture the attention of major brands. If BLUEVIEW can achieve tens of thousands in sales, it will demonstrate to larger companies that there is substantial consumer demand for bioplastic alternatives.[182]

For those interested in following Stephen Mayfield's journey and learning more about Soleic, he recommended visiting the website SoleicMaterials.com.

---

[180] https://www.montereybayaquarium.org/stories/meet-sustainable-footwear-designer-dr-stephen-mayfield
[181] https://blueviewfootwear.com/
[182] https://today.ucsd.edu/story/sustainable-sneakers-uc-san-diego-scientists-create-the-worlds-first-biodegradable-shoe

Soleic, a blend of the words "sun," "sol," and "oleic" (oil), represents the material's origin and its environmentally friendly attributes.

Consumers take an active role in promoting sustainability by reaching out to their favorite brands. People express their desire for sustainable, biodegradable polymers in products by contacting brands through social media and their websites. If enough consumers demand these eco-friendly options, major companies will respond accordingly, as they are driven by consumer preferences.

When asked about the thesis of this book, Stephen replied, "I am convinced that science does not solve problems ... but products made from good science can!"[183]

Basic v. Applied Research

Around twenty-three years ago, Dr. Stephen Mayfield shifted the focus in his lab to practical uses. It was met with significant resistance. While half of his team embraced the new direction and were enthusiastic about developing products, the other half pushed back. One researcher, in particular, told him directly that if forced to pivot towards applied science, he would leave the lab! Steve would not force anyone to change, but he made it clear that the lab's mindset moving forward would include considering real-world applications of their research.

At the time, there was a clear divide between basic research and product-driven science. Many in academic settings viewed applied research as compromising scientific purity and as a pursuit of profit rather than knowledge. This perspective was misguided. He felt that scientists were overlooking the pressing societal challenges that their research could potentially address. He posed the question to his team: "If not us, who? If not now, when?" This became a guiding principle for his work.

Following his breakthrough publication that garnered media attention, he began receiving inquiries about licensing his algae-based monoclonal antibody production technology. Fortunately, a patent had already been filed, which paved the way for commercial interest. With venture capital backing, he launched his first company, Rincon Pharmaceuticals. Since then, he has founded four biotech companies in total.

Over time, resistance within the academic community towards monetizing research has largely disappeared. However, as recently as 2012, he gave a talk at UC San Diego, and received feedback from a dean that some faculty were

---

[183] From a 9/12/24 email to author.

offended by his shift toward problem-solving research! This criticism wasn't tied to age, discipline, or training, it was more about perspective. Some academics remained isolated in their scholarly pursuits, failing to acknowledge the broader crises facing the world. His own awareness was shaped by personal experiences as a surfer, fisherman, and hiker: he was painfully aware of the consequences of climate change, ocean degradation, overfishing, and plastic pollution. He had a strong sense of obligation to use his knowledge and tools to make a difference.

Looking back now, Steve is positive that he was absolutely right to adopt this mindset. With the current state of plastic pollution—its presence in human arteries, brain tissue, and potential links to heart disease and dementia—there is urgency of action. There are studies indicating that individuals with dementia have significantly more plastic in their brains than those without.[184] While this is a correlation, not causation, it reinforces his conviction that scientists have a duty to address these challenges. For him, "obligation" is indeed the appropriate word.

Biofuels from Algae

After founding his first pharmaceutical company, Steve was soon swept into the biofuels movement that surged around 2007. This was a time when oil prices soared, and the reality of climate change gained mainstream attention. In response, he founded a new company focused on producing biofuels from algae. The venture quickly attracted significant investment, and his pharmaceutical company was even acquired by the biofuels company to gain access to its foundational patents.

By 2013, however, he began to question the viability of algae-based biofuels. The problem wasn't the technology; by then, his team had established a 100-acre algae farm in New Mexico, producing 100 barrels of oil per day. They were refining the algae oil into diesel fuel, powering cars and even ships. Technically, it was a success. However, from a business perspective, Stephen saw a different reality.

The economics of the fuel industry simply didn't support algae-based alternatives. Fuel sold for 30 to 40 cents per kilogram, while food could sell for $2 per kilogram. Polymers commanded even more, at $4-$5 per kilogram. "Fuel is the cheapest thing we make. It is the cheapest commodity on the planet," Steve said. Given that, it made little sense to produce algae for fuel when the same

---

[184] https://journals.lww.com/neurotodayonline/fulltext/2025/05010/microplastics_accumulate_at_high_levels_in_the.1.aspx

algae could be used for higher-value products like food or polymers. "You don't sell to the lowest bidder," he emphasized. "You sell to the highest bidder."

Understanding these market dynamics, he made a pivot move to the leadership of Sapphire Energy, the company he had co-founded. He approached the CEO, CJ, an experienced executive from British Petroleum, and explained his reasoning for shifting focus from fuel to polymers and food. While CJ appreciated his passion and acknowledged the logic, she declined to change the company's direction. However, she encouraged him to pursue his vision independently and even offered support in doing so.

Taking that opportunity, Steve went on to found a food company in 2013 and a polymer company in 2016. His foresight proved sound. In 2015, oil prices plummeted from $100 to $30 per barrel in just six months, devastating the biofuels industry. His former company, along with others in the field, suffered as a result. Although biofuels have since regained some attention—particularly in sustainable aviation fuel—his food company thrived and was eventually sold in 2019.

In the oil industry, there is a saying: *"The best cure for high oil prices is high oil prices,"* and similarly, *"The best cure for low oil prices is low oil prices."* This means that price fluctuations are self-correcting over time—high prices suppress demand, while low prices boost it. However, this theory assumes flexible demand, which is rarely the case. People often don't have alternatives; they must drive their cars or fly, regardless of cost.

The instability of oil pricing depends on unpredictable factors such as wars and global supply shifts. This unpredictability wreaks havoc on some sectors while benefiting others, leading to an uneven and destabilizing effect on the economy. This volatility is a "wild ride" of capitalism—one that is, in fact, solvable. Yet, policymakers avoid addressing it, unwilling to interfere with what they call the "invisible hand of capitalism." In Steve's view, this invisible hand is not only clumsy but also destructive, causing collateral damage while failing to adapt to societal needs.

Research Salesmanship

Steve notes that the prioritization of practical issues in scientific research is not solely determined by individual scientists or academic institutions. Instead, it is largely influenced by funding agencies, whether federal entities like the National Institutes of Health (NIH) and National Science Foundation (NSF), state governments, or philanthropic organizations such as the Gates Foundation. These agencies decide what kinds of research are supported and pursued.

Once Steve began focusing on practical solutions, the US Department of Energy quickly backed his work. The reason is political and strategic. When government researchers or agencies request funding—say, $8 billion for energy research—it's much easier to make a compelling case to a senator or congressman if tangible results can be shown. Simply stating that the research is "basic" and doesn't produce anything concrete makes it a tough sell. In contrast, being able to demonstrate real outcomes, such as jet fuel made from research or biodegradable shoes, makes the argument far more persuasive. When lawmakers see visible and relatable results, like fuel that powers jets or innovations that reduce microplastics, they better understand the value of investing in science.

One of the failures within the scientific community is the lack of effective communication about the real-world relevance of their work. Scientists need to do more to show how their research solves everyday problems, which is ultimately what garners support and trust from both the public and policymakers.

Steve has known many Nobel laureates and, surprisingly, very few of them stood out as exceptionally intelligent in the traditional sense. What they all shared, however, was strong salesmanship. He argued that winning a Nobel Prize has as much to do with effectively promoting the significance of one's science as it does with the actual quality of the research. Because the selection process is human and subjective, it is like a beauty pageant.

Hurdles to Innovation that Solve Global Problems

The true measure of successful science lies in impact. Steve values research based on whether it has led to inventions or solutions that genuinely benefit people. By that standard, good science becomes clear—it's the kind that makes a meaningful difference in the real world.

He is one of the individuals who are the key to solving environmental challenges and sustaining life on Earth. For him, innovation exists and is capable of addressing major global problems. Unfortunately, there are two critical layers that complicate this optimistic outlook.

The first issue is the adoption of innovation. Electric cars, for example, illustrate how people often resist change, even when a better alternative is available. According to Dr. Mayfield, anyone who has driven an electric car for a week quickly realizes how superior it is compared to internal combustion engine vehicles, which are slow, heavy, and polluting. Despite these advantages, there remains substantial resistance to switching over. While people like the idea of progress, they dislike the discomfort of change. The simple act of plugging in a car instead of refueling it can feel disruptive to everyday habits, thus slowing down the adoption of new technology.

The second issue is geopolitical: the global competition for scientific and technological leadership. Steve has a deep concern about the direction the United States has taken, particularly over the past few months. If current trends continue, he warned, the US will fall far behind other countries such as China, Europe, and South America, nations that are actively investing in science and the jobs of the future.

He is concerned over the dramatic proposed budget cuts to the National Science Foundation (NSF), which will see its funding cut by 55%, from $9 billion to $4 billion.[185] He stressed the critical role of the NSF as the only federal agency supporting research in computer science and artificial intelligence. While other agencies like the NIH, Department of Energy, and Department of Agriculture have more specific domains, only the NSF covers the essential area of AI. Slashing its funding is self-sabotage—especially at a time when global competitors are ramping up investments in these fields.

Steve is also worried by what seems to be a growing anti-science sentiment in American politics. Watching the news, some senators and congressmen openly dismiss experts and scientists, labeling them as "elite" and untrustworthy. It is

---

185 https://www.govtech.com/education/higher-ed/university-researchers-alarmed-by-plan-to-slash-nsf-funding-by-55

baffling that after spending forty years developing expertise, people like Dr. Mayfield are being disregarded in favor of populist rhetoric. This devaluation of science and expertise is both dangerous and counterproductive, especially when scientific innovation has been the cornerstone of America's economic dominance.

People who dismiss science funding often lack understanding of how the process works and how competitive it truly is. Scientific research is far from a frivolous endeavor. When Steve submits a grant proposal, he is one of over a hundred applicants, competing for funding where only about 10% will succeed. This highly selective environment ensures that only the most relevant and impactful research receives support.

Part of Dr. Mayfield's responsibility as a scientist is not just to conduct high-quality research, but also to effectively communicate its importance. He uses his own work on algae as an example: many people might dismiss it as a waste of time—until they see how it directly led to the development of a shoe that eliminates microplastics. When the link between scientific research and real-world solutions becomes clear, public support often follows.

As a result, Steve stresses the systemic issue in the scientific community: the lack of training in public communication. During his time in graduate school, scientists were never taught how to convey their work to the media or the general public. Modern science education should include training in social media, public speaking, and digital communication tools such as podcasting. Being able to clearly articulate the relevance of scientific research—to politicians, journalists, neighbors, and friends—is essential. Unfortunately, the scientific community has historically been poor at this. Improving communication could significantly enhance public understanding and support for scientific endeavors – such as developing and adopting biodegradable plastics to save the environment.

Gator Halpern and Sam Teicher: Saving the Coral Reefs

Gator Halpern is a trailblazing environmental entrepreneur dedicated to the conservation and restoration of coral reefs. As the Co-founder of Coral Vita, along with Sam Teicher, he has made significant strides in combating the decline of these vital ecosystems, working to save the world's coral and promote sustainable practices. Their innovative approach to coral restoration has garnered them numerous prestigious accolades, including the Earthshot Prize[186] awarded by Prince William[187], and recognition as a United Nations Young Champion of the Earth.[188] Gator has also been featured in Forbes' "30 Under 30" and was named an Echoing Green Fellow, highlighting his impactful work in environmental sustainability.

Responding to the Coral Reef Crisis

Hailing from San Diego, California, Gator's distinctive name has always set him apart. Raised in a family with equally unique names, he embraced his identity while navigating the environmental challenges facing our planet. He is not only a leader in his field but also a proud father, recently welcoming his son, Arlo, into the world. His family has affectionately nicknamed the child "Mud Cat."

Through Coral Vita and his relentless advocacy for coral ecosystems, he inspires others in the fight against climate change and environmental degradation, proving that innovative solutions can emerge from passion and dedication.

Coral Vita is dedicated to the preservation and restoration of coral reefs, some of the Earth's most magnificent ecosystems. These vibrant reefs not only showcase breathtaking beauty for snorkelers and scuba divers but also serve vital ecological functions. Coral reefs support nearly one billion people worldwide, acting as natural barriers that protect coastlines from storm surges and providing a foundation for fisheries in tropical regions, which offer livelihoods and nutrition to countless communities. Additionally, coral reefs significantly boost local economies by attracting tourists eager to experience their wonders.

---

186 https://earthshotprize.org/winners-finalists/coral-vita/
187 https://earthshotprize.org/news/prince-william-visits-earthshot-prize-winner-as-2021-finalists-reveal-the-incredible-impact-of-the-prize/
188 https://www.unep.org/youngchampions/news/story/young-champion-earth-winner-latin-america-and-caribbean

Unfortunately, these invaluable ecosystems are under severe threat. Over the past few decades, half of the world's coral reefs have already perished[189], primarily due to climate change, along with other factors such as overfishing, pollution, and coastal development. If current trends continue, scientists predict that more than 90% of coral reefs could be lost by 2050[190], leading to an environmental catastrophe[191] that could disrupt up to 25% of all marine life and have dire socioeconomic consequences for industries reliant on these ecosystems.

In response to this crisis, Gator and his team at Coral Vita are pioneering reef restoration efforts aimed at revitalizing these ecosystems for future generations. Their approach parallels the principles of reforestation: by cultivating coral in innovative land-based farms, they can grow and nurture coral species before reintroducing them into the ocean. Using advanced techniques, the team scuba dives to plant these corals back onto degraded reefs, effectively reseeding and restoring the ecosystems. Through these efforts, they are not only addressing an urgent environmental issue but also fostering hope for the future of coral reefs and the countless lives they support.

Remember the USS Kittiwake, sunk in 2011 in the Caymans to form a reef? The submarine destroyer was intentionally submerged to create an artificial reef.[192] These days, Coral Vita would be involved in such initiatives. The barrier reefs surrounding the islands provide essential fisheries and act as a defense against storm surges. Unfortunately, many of the Caribbean's reefs, including those near the Cayman Islands, are facing alarming rates of decline, with estimates suggesting that up to 80% of these ecosystems are already dead.[193]

While sinking a vessel to create an artificial reef can provide some benefits, such as creating a diving attraction and offering habitat for certain marine species, it cannot replicate the complex and vibrant ecosystems of natural coral reefs. Artificial reefs do not possess the same capability to support the diverse marine life and ecological processes inherent to thriving coral systems. While such projects can create interesting diving locations, they fall short of sustaining the natural habitats essential for marine biodiversity.

---

189 https://www.nhm.ac.uk/discover/news/2021/september/over-half-of-coral-reef-cover-lost-since-1950.html
190 https://enviroliteracy.org/how-much-coral-will-be-gone-in-2050
191 https://theconversation.com/the-outlook-for-coral-reefs-remains-grim-unless-we-cut-emissions-fast-new-research-160251
192 https://caymantourism.co.uk/kittiwake-shipwreck
193 https://periodismoinvestigativo.com/2025/07/caribbean-coral-bleaching-crisis/

Replanting Coral Reefs

At Coral Vita, Gator Halpern's focus remains on restoring degraded reef sites and revitalizing natural ecosystems. There should be a collaboration with those involved in artificial reef projects and sea wall constructions, but Gator has reaffirmed that the primary mission of Coral Vita is to restore and maintain the health of natural coral reef ecosystems. By directly addressing the challenges facing these vital environments, Coral Vita aims to ensure their survival and growth in the Caribbean waters for generations to come.

Gator offered insights into his company innovative processes regarding the timeline for growing corals before they are ready to be replanted in the ocean. The duration corals spend in their land-based farms can range from six months to 18 months, depending on the species being cultivated and the desired size for outplanting.

One of the remarkable techniques employed at Coral Vita is known as micro-fragmentation, which significantly accelerates coral growth. This method enables corals to grow up to fifty times faster than their natural growth rates in the ocean. As a result, corals that are just one year old can reach sizes comparable to mature corals, which would typically take decades to achieve in the wild.

By leveraging these advanced techniques, Coral Vita is able to produce robust corals in a much shorter time frame, enhancing its efforts to restore and replenish coral reef ecosystems effectively. Gator's explanation underscores the potential for innovative aquaculture practices to contribute significantly to coral restoration initiatives, providing a promising outlook for the future of these vital marine habitats.

The size of the corals cultivated at Coral Vita varies depending on the species. There is a general estimate that a fully fused mature colony ready to be replanted onto the reef would typically be around the size of a softball.

These corals continue to grow once they are placed back in the ocean. The corals are indeed animals, despite often being associated with plants due to their symbiotic relationships. This relationship exists between corals and the algae that live within them, allowing the corals to perform photosynthesis.

In the evolutionary history of corals, they are part of the Phylum Cnidaria, which also includes jellyfish and other sea creatures. The corals build their skeletons out of calcium carbonate, limestone, over thousands to tens of thousands of years. This process has led to the formation of massive ecosystems, such as the Great Barrier Reef, which can be seen from space.

Once Coral Vita's cultivated corals reach the appropriate maturity size—around the size of a softball, as noted above—they are planted back into the reef. While they do not grow at the accelerated rates achieved in Coral Vita's controlled environment, they continue their natural growth patterns in the ocean. Over time, these corals can survive for hundreds, if not thousands, of years, gradually increasing in size each year. Gator's insights underscore the resilience and complexity of coral ecosystems, emphasizing the importance of their conservation and restoration efforts.

There is a question that inevitably pops up about the timeline for restoring coral reefs to their former glory: would it take thousands of years and does Coral Vita plan to accelerate the restoration process? The answer is that the fate of the world's coral reefs hinges significantly on humanity's response to climate change.

The urgency with which society addresses climate change, fossil fuel emissions, and the warming of oceans is critical. The oceans serve as a carbon sink, absorbing much of the carbon released into the atmosphere. However, this process also leads to increased ocean acidity and temperatures, both of which threaten coral ecosystems. The question of how quickly coral reefs can be restored fundamentally relates to humanity's ability to confront climate change decisively and avoid the catastrophic consequences that are becoming more frequent, such as the recent hurricanes devastating parts of the United States.

Gator points out that much of the efforts to tackle climate change should not be just about preventing loss, but also about enabling the restoration of coral reefs. There is a hopeful vision for the future that with the right investments in large-scale reef restoration projects over the next decade there is potential for thriving coral reefs to exist throughout the lifetime of Gator's newborn son. He has a desire for future generations, including his grandchildren, to experience the vibrant and majestic reefs that once flourished, like those seen by his grandfather. This vision underscores the urgent need for collective action and investment in both restoration and climate change mitigation efforts to ensure the survival of these vital ecosystems.

For-Profit Work Saving the Reefs

In addressing the financial aspects of his work with Coral Vita, Gator says there is a crucial need for funding coral reef restoration. There is expense of everyday necessities, such as diapers for his newborn son, Arlo, emphasizing that the operational costs for his organization must also be met.

Coral Vita is a for-profit commercial enterprise. While many nonprofit organizations engage in remarkable work in reef restoration, the funding available through philanthropic grants is insufficient to address the magnitude of the challenges facing coral ecosystems. At Coral Vita, the belief is that creating an industry around reef restoration is vital. By harnessing the power of capitalism, the company aims to demonstrate the significant value that healthy reefs provide, ultimately establishing an industry worth billions of dollars annually to support restoration efforts.

There are vast economic benefits provided by coral reefs. These ecosystems contribute trillions of dollars in services to communities and industries worldwide. As coral reefs continue to degrade, the economic value they represent is at risk. To address this, Coral Vita engages with a variety of stakeholders—ranging from government entities to international development agencies, cruise lines, and hotels—who depend on the services that healthy reefs provide. Gator's approach involves making a compelling case to these stakeholders: by investing in reef restoration, they can prevent further financial losses linked to the decline of coral ecosystems.

This commercial model not only promises to bolster Coral Vita's growth but also aims to secure the necessary funding to make a significant impact on coral restoration efforts globally. This sustainable approach would ensure the financial stability needed to support his family, including covering the costs of diapers for his little one, while also contributing to the preservation of vital marine ecosystems.

Gator stresses that a for-profit model led by entrepreneurs might be able to amplify traditional scientific endeavors to create more environmental impact. That is because, while scientists are doing essential work, they often are unable to translate their research into practical and scalable solutions. In contrast, his entrepreneurial approach is directly focused on addressing real-world problems as quickly and cost-effectively as possible.

Entrepreneurs like himself are positioned to make significant environmental impacts through market-driven solutions. Coral Vita's for-profit structure allows the company to grow and scale, which is essential for addressing the vast global problem of coral reef degradation. The potential for commercial solutions to make a difference lies in their ability to attract investment and generate resources that can be reinvested into restoration efforts. As he sees it, harnessing the power of the market is crucial to addressing environmental challenges on the scale necessary to make lasting change.

Thus, there is a significant role that entrepreneurs play in addressing climate issues with the speed and urgency required. Gator does not view the divide as being between scientists and entrepreneurs but rather points to the challenge posed by policymakers and existing industry players who benefit from maintaining the status quo. Scientists have already provided a deep understanding of environmental problems, and there should be no debate regarding their findings. However, continued investment in research and science is crucial for understanding the finer details of environmental challenges and developing the necessary technologies to combat them.

Eco-entrepreneurs are vital for taking the solutions science provides and scaling them globally. The rapid technological progress needed to address environmental issues is unprecedented, but the tools, technologies, and passionate entrepreneurs already exist within the climate tech movement. Gator is proud to be part of this community and believes that through collaboration with policymakers and local communities, substantial progress can be made for future generations.

He addresses the question about the growing demand for air conditioning and other luxuries in developing countries, such as China and India. While developed countries like the United States have made strides in reducing their environmental footprint, emerging economies continue to build coal plants and increase their energy consumption. Countries like China continue to rely on coal.

Gator rejects the notion that developed countries, such as the United States could continue to enjoy their current standard of living while denying developing countries the opportunity to improve theirs. Wealthier nations have a responsibility to support the technological advancements that would allow countries like India to raise their standard of living without relying on harmful fossil fuels like coal and natural gas.

Instead, he advocates for helping developing nations transition to clean energy by providing the necessary technologies and financial support. He argued that developed countries should not view this as mere charity; it is also a self-interested strategy, as reducing global reliance on fossil fuels benefits everyone in the long run. If countries with large populations, like India, can adopt eco-conscious energy solutions for air conditioning and other luxuries, the entire planet would benefit from a reduced carbon footprint.

This means giving developing nations the "American version" of capitalism without also providing them with the environmentally responsible technologies to manage their growth will hurt everyone. In Gator's view, if this approach isn't adjusted, the entire world would suffer, including the United States. There would be worsening climate catastrophes such as fires, droughts, floods, and hurricanes that are already impacting countries globally, including America. It is crucial for the global community to work together to address these pressing issues as quickly as possible.

Crucial Experiences

Gator is encouraging people to go scuba diving. This experience of nature firsthand is a crucial foundation for acting in a more environmentally conscious manner. For him, going outside, whether through scuba diving, snorkeling, or simply walking in nature, helps people understand and appreciate the value of natural ecosystems.

He had a particular magical dive at the Great Barrier Reef. There's a dive site called "The Gumdrop," a massive coral colony that stands about sixty to seventy feet high and thirty to forty feet around, shaped like a giant gumdrop. Slowly descending down the face of this enormous living creature, teeming with giant clams and fish, was one of the most special moments of his life, one of the most beautiful things he had ever experienced.

Coral Vita is based on Grand Bahama in the city of Freeport, which is a quick trip from Miami or Fort Lauderdale, Florida. While Nassau, the capital of the Bahamas, is home to the well-known Paradise Island resorts, Freeport is where Coral Vita's coral farm and restoration work takes place.

For Gator Halpern, the act of witnessing coral reefs or other natural environments is the first step toward protecting and restoring them. People need to avoid touching coral, but he encourages them to get close to nature in any way they can. Whether it is exploring underwater worlds or walking in the woods, the more we experience nature, the more motivated we will be to live in harmony with it and take action to preserve it.

Top Ten Environmental Hypocrites

#3 Elon Musk

How Much Do They Talk? (0 = not at all to 10 = all day) = 10

Amount of Environmental Action? (0 = plants trees daily to 10 = giving speeches) = 6

Real Environmentalist Score = 16

It's hard to think that the force behind Tesla is actually an environmental hypocrite! Elon Musk, the billionaire entrepreneur behind companies like Tesla, SpaceX, Neuralink, and The Boring Company, is widely regarded as an environmental visionary. The point of Tesla is to kill gas-using cars. Surely that is good. No, it's GREAT!

But remember what a hypocrite is: saying one thing and doing another.

There is a dark side to Tesla's environmental record. Tesla is years behind in releasing their greenhouse gas emissions or setting targets to curb climate pollution.[194] Still missing is an analysis of its supply chain, the company's biggest source of emissions. Mining the lithium and cobalt needed for the Tesla batteries is particularly dirty. Lithium mining has caused mass fish kills, excessive freshwater consumption, and strict, harsh chemical use.[195] Tesla agreed to pay $1.5 million to settle California hazardous waste lawsuit in early 2024.[196] Then three months later, the State sued Tesla for environmental violations claiming its Fremont plant emits harmful pollutants including nitrogen oxides, arsenic, cadmium and other harmful chemicals. Since 2019, 112 instances for as much as 750 pounds of illegal air pollution were discovered.[197] Over in Germany, half a million trees were cut to build their European gigafactory, equivalent to

---

[194] https://www.theverge.com/2023/3/2/23621205/elon-musk-tesla-masterplan-sustainable-energy
[195] https://www.cbc.ca/news/science/ev-electric-vehicle-carbon-footprint-1.5394126
[196] https://www.reuters.com/legal/tesla-agrees-pay-15-million-settle-california-hazardous-waste-lawsuit-2024-02-02/
[197] https://www.reuters.com/legal/tesla-is-sued-over-emissions-california-plant-2024-05-14/

around 13,000 metric tons of CO2 emissions.[198] Tesla's reliance on carbon credits to boost its financial performance has raised questions about the company's true environmental impact.[199] Most importantly, the true environmental impact of a Tesla will not be known for a long time. These lithium batteries are dirty to make and worse to deal with after their short lifespan. Amazingly coincidentally, our hero Wayne Elliott lost a valuable employee from his battery recycling business to Tesla. Wayne was excited to drive cross-country to see the employee and get the gigafactory tour. In the summer of 2024, Tesla abandoned its lithium recycling effort, and the employee was fired. Also in the same summer, a Tesla semi-truck caught fire, demonstrating the inherent problems of the technology it uses. Fire retardant chemicals were spread on the truck but were not effective. Fifty thousand gallons of water were needed to finally stop the fire. Firefighters said that the battery reached temperatures of 1,000 degrees. Amazingly, the highway was closed for fifteen hours as firefighters ensured the batteries were cool enough to move. To make sure the battery did not reignite, fire officials took the truck to an open-air facility and monitored it for 24 hours. Lithium is a problem on so many levels: mining, manufacturing, transport, and disposal.[200]

Another problem with the "Tesla will save the World" argument has appeared recently. EV car sales have greatly disappointed. *Money* Magazine commented in November 2023 that, "interest among buyers has underwhelmed and plans for a rapid transition away from gas-powered cars could be in jeopardy."[201] This sales disappointment has occurred while large tax rebates remain in place. What happens when the incentives go away? In response, Tesla slashed its prices once. Ford decreased production of its electric pickup truck, the F-150 Lightning. Ford also postponed $12 billion of electric car research and spending. It lost about $36,000 for every EV it sold last quarter. How long will a corporate board allow that to happen? Mercedes-Benz continues to discount its electric vehicles. GM delayed three model launches and renounced their public goal of producing 400,000 EVs by the middle of next year. Honda announced it was ending plans with GM to jointly develop affordable EVs. Toyota has prioritized hybrids over EVs. Chairman Akio Toyoda told reporters that "people are finally seeing reality."[202]

---

198 https://www.fastcompany.com/91177603/tesla-cut-down-500000-trees-to-build-its-german-gigafactory
199 https://www.green.earth/news/teslas-record-high-sales-of-carbon-credits-fuel-financial-growth
200 https://www.dailymail.co.uk/wires/ap/article-13845053/It-took-50-000-gallons-water-Tesla-Semi-fire-California-US-agency-says.html
201 https://money.com/why-americans-not-buying-electric-cars/
202 Ibid.

There is a proposal by the US Environmental Protection Agency that requires that 67% of new cars be EVs by 2032.[203] In 2024, EV market share in the U.S. was just 10.2%.[204] What happens to Elon's reputation if the goal is missed and the country in effect says, "We don't want those"?

Moving on to Elon's other big company, SpaceX, its rocket launches generate substantial carbon emissions and environmental impacts. Before they built their launch facility in south Texas, Elon (his friends are allowed to call him that) promised that the launches would have a small eco-friendly footprint. The surrounding area would be "left untouched." He bought a donut hole property, a small piece of land surrounded by state parks and federal wildlife preserves. Right next door to the breeding grounds of the most endangered turtle and important migration habitats. Unfortunately, that is not what happened. In short, government officials of many agencies were left "in disbelief over (the amount of) environmental damage."[205] First, the rockets are the dirtiest ever, largely due to their size.[206] Their new rocket, the Falcon, is four times larger than Texas originally agreed to. He promised $50 million worth of infrastructure and pollution and has already built $3 billion worth. A second launch pad is under construction. Workers commute by hovercraft because the local roads are inadequate. An April 2023 explosion sent sheets of steel, concrete chunks and shrapnel almost a half mile away, much further than the FAA had thought possible. The debris slammed into a bird habitat. The protected areas have been damaged with debris on 19 occasions in the last five years.[207] In 2023, there were record-breaking 223 attempted spaceflights, most by SpaceX.[208] Their goal is over a thousand per year. And, finally, the launch facilities lack a deluge system to flood the pad with water and lack a flame trench to safely channel exhaust away from nesting birds and breeding turtles.[209] All other large rocket launch facilities have these environmentally conscious features. Maybe Elon could not afford them? Is getting to Mars worth destroying Texas? Well, actually, that's a hard one...[210]

---

203 https://www.investopedia.com/epa-emissions-rules-7377417
204 https://www.autosinnovate.org/posts/press-release/2024-q4-get-connected-press-release
205 https://www.bloomberg.com/news/features/2023-08-25/elon-musk-s-spacex-explosion-left-major-debris-after-starship-rocket-launch
206 https://www.space.com/spacex-starship-rocket-launches-environmental-impact
207 https://www.nytimes.com/2024/07/07/us/politics/spacex-boca-chica-takeaways.html
208 https://www.space.com/spacex-starship-rocket-launches-environmental-impact
209 https://www.livescience.com/space/space-exploration/disastrous-spacex-launch-under-federal-investigation-after-raining-potentially-hazardous-debris-on-homes-and-beaches
210 Just kidding.

Musk is obviously very opinionated and strongly defends his opinions, no matter how far out of mainstream science they are. Andrej Karpathy was the Tesla senior director of artificial intelligence. Karpathy had just finished reading Matt Simon's new book called, "A Poison Like No Other: How Microplastics Corrupted Our Planet and Our Bodies."[211] Mr. Simon is a science journalist for *Wired* magazine and his profile on Amazon says that he likes long walks on the beach while trying not to think about the destruction that the microplastics are causing our oceans. Anyway, Karpathy posted about how much he was learning from this book. Musk X-ed (tweeted), "Plastics are not a significant health risk. It's bs."[212] Denying that plastics are scary (remember that big blob in the Pacific Ocean?) is sort of like denying climate change itself.

Musk's personal lifestyle also draws scrutiny. It's hard to discern what real estate he owns personally. Many articles talk about his extensive residential holdings. Just a couple years ago, he had seven mansions in Los Angeles, mostly on one street.[213] He also famously announced he was selling all his stuff[214] and would live in a shack at SpaceX. Or on a cot at Tesla's factory. Very noble. Just a year or so later, he secretly purchased a home in Austin, Texas, for him and his girlfriend Grimes and some of his kids to live in.[215] Very performative of him.

Just like everyone else on this list, his private jet use is interesting, and hypocritical. He owns 4 private jets, having just purchased a new Gulfstream G700.[216] In 2023, his private jets took 441 flights.[217] That would get you halfway to Mars, don't you think? According to *Fortune* magazine, he flies more than any other billionaire on Earth and releases over 2,000 tons of carbon emissions a year.[218]

Most indicative of his commitment to performative environmentalism was his suspension of Jack Sweeney's X account. College student Sweeney runs a site

---

[211] https://www.amazon.com/Poison-Like-Other-Microplastics-Corrupted-ebook/dp/B0BMDFD5YX?ref_=ast_author_mpb
[212] https://www.msn.com/en-us/money/other/tesla-ceo-elon-musk-disputes-former-company-exec-downplays-impact-of-plastic-not-a-significant-health-risk/ar-AA1pfCOv
[213] https://www.admiddleeast.com/story/where-is-elon-musks-home-all-the-properties-the-worlds-richest-man-has-owned
[214] https://finance.yahoo.com/news/elon-musk-reportedly-bought-secret-161511784.html
[215] Ibid.
[216] https://simpleflying.com/elon-musk-private-jet-guide/
[217] https://www.businessinsider.com/elon-musk-private-jet-travel-2023-12?op=1
[218] https://finance.yahoo.com/news/elon-musk-flies-private-jets-202943606.html

that tracks private jet usage by celebrities. He was suspended without any explanation.[219]

While Musk's contributions to promoting electric vehicles, renewable energy, and technological advancement are significant, the inconsistencies in his behavior continue to fuel criticism and cast a shadow over his environmental legacy.

---

[219] https://fortune.com/2022/12/15/elon-musk-private-jet-twitter-account-suspended-free-speech-jack-sweeney/

Chapter 9
Academic Scandals

Who are the players in the environmental debate? Why is there even a debate in the first place?

There is a debate because the players cannot agree on what is happening. One side argues that the environment is in danger, caused by human use of oil, coal, and other pollutant-releasing energy sources. The other side argues that the environment is always changing, and that humans have almost no impact on that change.

The first side, call them Team Alpha, is generally acknowledged to include the academics, some scientists, the Democrat Party, environmental organizations like Greenpeace, and some corporate leaders. The other side, call them Team Omega, includes the oil companies, many industrial companies, most mining and agricultural companies, the Republican Party, some scientists, and conservative think tanks.

Interestingly, if you ask ChatGPT, "Who are on the two sides of the environmental debate?" the answer is "1. Environmental Advocates" and "2. Skeptics and Economic Pragmatists."[220] The need for this book is demonstrated by the rest of the ChatGPT answer. Nowhere does it include the entrepreneur or small businessperson. Only big businesses make it on their list.

The status quo understanding of the environmental players on the field, as represented by ChatGPT, does not include the most important player, the entrepreneur. When activists make their predictions, they exclude the possible incredible advances that new businesses will develop.

The real entrepreneurial environmentalists say, "Hey! I am all of those! I am an environmental advocate. I am devoting my life to it. But I am a pragmatist, too! I must make money to pay the employees and make money for my investors!"

To remind, the thesis of this book is "that the Real Environmentalists are not the scientists, lawyers, activists, academics or politicians who talk about climate change, how horrible climate change is and how humans have caused it, but the capitalist entrepreneurs working to solve the very real environmental problems we face, regardless of who caused them."

---

220 ChatGPT

The goal of this book is to point out that much energy, time and brain power is being wasted on the wrong science. Billions of dollars are being spent guessing about the future climate, arguing about the validity of models, publishing to win grants, and pursuing science with a preformed agenda. That money could be spent on solutions. The real heroes of the environmental fight are the people solving the problem, not the academics or activists.

As hero Dr. Stephen Mayfield said, "It was an enormous epiphany for me! I realized that, oh my God, I'm still doing the same science I was before, but by making a product, people could relate to it."

Since the heroes have been named, it is only right to name the villains. There is an ongoing debate about the basic facts of the environment because the villains are more concerned with their funding than with actually solving the problem. It was pointed out earlier[221] that some environmentalists would suffer greatly if the problem was solved. What would the academics do if carbon capture works, and environmental security is achieved?

In 2020, MIT held a symposium encouraging universities to be more active in finding solutions, as opposed to making more projections of doom. Professor Paula Hammond, head of the Department of Chemical Engineering and a co-chair of the symposium, said, "Higher education has a responsibility, an opportunity to set their sights on being an exemplar organization and community in how to face, respond to, and address the climate change issue."[222] Associate Provost Richard Lester continued, "Research universities must be a source of innovations to address global climate change, because our existing government-led innovation system is falling short, even relative to the inadequate benchmarks set by governments themselves."[223]

Simply said, academics are the problem. They have made many, many wrong predictions and they are acting in a morally questionable way.

---

221 Page 41, first paragraph.
222 https://news.mit.edu/2020/universities-climate-action-1023
223 Ibid.

Blatantly Wrong Predictions

Consider these false projections….

1. In 1968, Dr. Paul Ehrlich published "Population Bomb." Ehrlich predicted that by the 1970s and 1980s, hundreds of millions would starve to death due to overpopulation.[224] Just a year later, Ehrlich said, "We must realize that unless we are extremely lucky, everybody will disappear in a cloud of blue steam in twenty years."[225] Seems like the world got "extremely lucky." 1989 was a good year. Madonna released her first album, the Game Boy was launched, the Exxon Valdez spilled millions of gallons of oil (well, that's bad), and the Berlin Wall and Communism collapsed.

2. Around the first Earth Day celebrations in 1970, doomed predictions were everywhere. One prediction claimed that by 1980, cities would require gas masks due to pollution, nitrogen buildup would block sunlight, and global famine would claim millions of lives.[226] The Boston Globe wrote, "Air pollution may obliterate the sun and cause a new ice age."[227] Denis Hayes, an organizer of the first Earth Day, predicted mass starvation across the US by the 1980s. Peter Gunter, a North Texas State University professor, wrote, "Demographers agree almost unanimously on the following grim timetable: by 1975 widespread famines will begin in India; these will spread by 1990 to include all of India, Pakistan, China, and the Near East, Africa. By the year 2000, or conceivably sooner, South and Central America will exist under famine conditions… By the year 2000, thirty years from now, the entire world, with the exception of Western Europe, North America, and Australia, will be in famine."[228]

3. On October 6, 1970, Dr. Ehrlich from Stanford doubled down and said, "The oceans will be as dead as Lake Erie in less than a decade."[229]

4. In the 1970s, scientists were predicting a great Global Cooling. During this decade, some scientists believed Earth was headed for a

---

224 https://www.smithsonianmag.com/science-nature/why-didnt-first-earth-days-predictions-come-true-its-complicated-180958820/
225 New York Times, August 10, 1969.
226 Ibid.
227 The Boston Globe, April 16, 1970, quoting James Lodge Jr., scientist at the National Center for Atmospheric Research.
228 https://www.aei.org/carpe-diem/18-spectacularly-wrong-predictions-were-made-around-the-time-of-the-first-earth-day-in-1970-expect-more-this-year/
229 Redlands Daily Facts, October 6, 1970.

cooling period or a new Ice Age. Articles and books raised concerns about freezing conditions. In 1971, NASA and Columbia University scientists wrote, "In the next fifty years, the fine dust man constantly puts into the atmosphere by fossil burning could screen out so much sunlight that the average temperature could drop by 6°." [230] In 1974, satellites were first used to study the World's weather. The Guardian wrote, "Worldwide and rapid trends towards a mini–Ice Age are emerging from the first long term analysis of satellite weather pictures."[231] On April 28, 1975, *Newsweek* published a provocative front cover article called "The Cooling World," in which writer and science editor Peter Gwynne described a significant chilling of the world's climate, with evidence accumulating "so massively that meteorologists are hard-pressed to keep up with it."[232]

Amazingly, the entire academic doom community was able to switch to global warming in just a matter of three or four years. Now of course, global warming has given way to climate change with increasingly horrible summers. The media and academics say the heat causes many deaths already. The numbers of heat deaths will only increase. Except, lots of science says otherwise. Bjorn Lomborg is president of the Copenhagen Consensus and a visiting fellow at Stanford University's Hoover Institution. He wrote, "Headlines from around the world tell us of hundreds of deaths caused by recent heat waves. The stories invariably blame climate change and admonish us to tackle it urgently. But they mostly reveal how one-sided climate-alarmist reporting leaves us badly informed. The stories contain a kernel of truth: Global warming is a real, manmade problem that needs addressing. As temperatures increase, so will the frequency and severity of heat waves. But the media fail to report the full story and thus lose focus on the most effective ways to help." He continued, "Each year, more than 100,000 people die from cold in the United States, and 13,000 in Canada — more than 40 cold deaths for every heat death."[233] Oh, forty to one, cold deaths to heat deaths.

This incorrect belief, this media focus on heat deaths, has a huge impact on policy. The assumptions are wrong and shockingly the

---

230 Washington Post, July 9, 1971.
231 The Guardian, January 29, 1974.
232 https://longreads.com/2017/04/13/in-1975-newsweek-predicted-a-new-ice-age-were-still-living-with-the-consequences/
233 https://nypost.com/2021/07/14/more-die-of-cold-medias-heat-death-climate-obsession-leads-to-lousy-fixes/

policy is wrong! Climate policies that drive gas prices up, by design, will mean fewer people can afford to properly heat their homes and more will freeze to death.

5. In 1970, ecologist Kenneth Watt predicted crude oil would run out by the year 2000.[234] Global oil output was 48 million barrels per day (bpd) and there were just over 528 billion barrels of proven world oil reserves.[235] In 2023, after using billions and billions of barrels per year, global oil production was at about 95 million barrels per day (bpd) and there are 1.57 trillion barrels of proven oil reserves.[236]

6. According to Senator Gaylord Nelson, "Dr. S. Dillon Ripley, secretary of the Smithsonian Institute, believes that in 25 years, somewhere between 75 and 80 percent of all the species of living animals will be extinct." This demonstration of Senatorial prowess comes from 1970, too.[237]

7. In 1988, NASA scientist James Hansen's famous testimony predicted significant warming and extreme weather events. While some predictions were accurate, others overstated the degree of warming which assumed higher emissions than occurred.[238] He also predicted decades of droughts. The subsequent years actually enjoyed record levels of rain.[239]

8. Also in 1988, sea level threats became big news, and the predictions have been even more inaccurate. Predictions suggested that the 1196 small islands than the Maldives Islands would completely disappear within 30 years. Even worse, within four years it was predicted that the Maldives would run out of drinking water.[240] In the next year, it was predicted that New York City's West Side Highway would be underwater by 2019.[241] All still dry. Except for the drinking water. Still plentiful and wet. And some islands are actually getting bigger. "A reanalysis of available data, which cover 30 Pacific and Indian Ocean

---

234 https://www.aei.org/carpe-diem/18-spectacularly-wrong-predictions-were-made-around-the-time-of-the-first-earth-day-in-1970-expect-more-this-year/
235 https://jancovici.com/en/energy-transition/oil/what-is-an-oil-reserve/
236 https://www.statista.com/statistics/236657/global-crude-oil-reserves-since-1990/
237 https://www.aei.org/carpe-diem/18-spectacularly-wrong-predictions-were-made-around-the-time-of-the-first-earth-day-in-1970-expect-more-this-year/
238 https://www.pulitzercenter.org/sites/default/files/june_23_1988_senate_hearing_1.pdf
239 The Miami News, June 24, 1988.
240 The Canberra Times, September 26, 1988.
241 Salon.com, October 23, 2001.

atolls including 709 islands, reveals that no atoll lost land area and that 88.6% of islands were either stable or increased in area."[242]

9. In the late 1980s, the UN claimed entire countries would disappear due to rising sea levels by 2000 if global warming was not addressed.[243] Will everyone have to buy a new globe?

10. In 1990, the Intergovernmental Panel on Climate Change (IPCC) Report was published by the UN. The IPCC's initial climate report projected temperature rises that exceeded actual observations. Over the years, the models have improved but early projections were often exaggerated.

11. "Snowfalls are now just a thing of the past" said David Viner in 2000. He is a senior research scientist at the Climatic Research Unit of the University of East Anglia. However, snowfalls have continued regularly.[244]

12. Predictions in 2002 suggested that Mount Kilimanjaro's glaciers would disappear by 2020 due to climate change. Nope. Still there.[245]

13. Many reports from the 1990s and early 2000s claimed that coral reefs worldwide would die due to rising ocean temperatures and acidification. *The Guardian* even published an obituary.[246] While coral reefs are under threat and far too many have died, they have not disappeared, and incredible new reefs are being built like the one mentioned earlier in the Caymans with the USS Kittiwake. Amazingly, the Great Barrier Reef has recently reached unprecedented levels of coral cover, levels not seen since 1986.[247]

14. Everyone accepted Peak Oil in the 1990s-2000s as absolute truth. Repeated predictions of "peak oil" claimed that the world would run out of oil by the early 2000s. However, technological advancements such as fracking have increased oil reserves.

---

242 https://wires.onlinelibrary.wiley.com/doi/abs/10.1002/wcc.557
243 https://www.instituteforenergyresearch.org/climate-change/climate-alarm-failed-prognostications/
244 Ibid.
245 https://www.politifact.com/article/2022/feb/07/kilimanjaros-ice-fields-didnt-disappear-2020-doesn/
246 https://www.theguardian.com/environment/ng-interactive/2014/mar/great-barrier-reef-obituary
247 https://apps.aims.gov.au/reef-monitoring/sector/list and https://x.com/BjornLomborg/status/1808134536854700215

15. Al Gore predicted in his 2006 movie "An Inconvenient Truth" that the Arctic would be ice-free and sea levels could rise twenty feet by 2013. Is a source needed to prove this one was wrong? And most famously, he predicted that polar bears would face extinction due to melting ice. He even used a fake picture of one bear on a small chuck of ice. However, polar bear populations have increased in many areas.[248] Nevertheless, the media still pushes the extinction trope. The New York Post, usually considered a right-wing paper, wrote on September 12, 2024, about new polar bear safaris. From the article, "The fact that polar bears are a dying breed is part of the allure." Why would the safari company continue to push their extinction? Because they "could be extinct by 2100."[249] A new prediction! Wiser this time as it is much further off, presumably after the author is dead and less accountable.

Gore was even rebuked by his side. *The Huffington Post* wrote, "Like many doom-mongers before him, Al Gore's predictions of impending disaster have fallen somewhat short of the mark -- a point to keep in mind as he hits theatres this summer. Take it all with a grain of salt."[250] A UK High Court judge ruled that the movie could only be shown in schools with guidance notes to prevent political indoctrination.

16. A highly publicized study in 2006 predicted that global fish populations would collapse by 2048 due to overfishing.[251] While overfishing is an issue, the catastrophic depletion predicted has not been realized, and many fisheries have implemented more sustainable practices. Red Lobster's Endless Shrimp deal destroyed the restaurant chain, not the shrimp population.[252]

17. In 2009, then-British Prime Minister Gordon Brown warned that the world had only 50 days to save the planet from global warming.[253] He sure blew that one! Not to be outdone, King Charles (he was Prince of Wales at this time) announced we only had eight years to save the

---

248 https://x.com/bjornlomborg/status/1596907524577320960
249 https://nypost.com/2024/09/12/lifestyle/why-polar-bear-safaris-are-booming-across-northern-canada/
250 https://www.huffpost.com/archive/ca/entry/al-gores-predictions-of-doom-scramble-his-message_b_16669842
251 https://www.nytimes.com/2006/11/03/science/03fish.html
252 https://www.independent.co.uk/news/world/americas/red-lobster-bankruptcy-endless-shrimp-b2548417.html
253 http://news.bbc.co.uk/2/hi/uk_news/8313672.stm

World.²⁵⁴ Maybe he should focus on things closer to home, like controlling his younger brother, Prince Andrew. 2008 was the year Jeffrey Epstein was convicted of all his gross stuff.

18. The UN predicted that by 2010, there would be 50 million climate refugees due to sea-level rise and other climate impacts.²⁵⁵ Still waiting…

19. Rajendra Pachauri, former head of the UN's Intergovernmental Panel on Climate Change (IPCC), warned that unless drastic action was taken by 2012, it would be too late to save the planet.²⁵⁶ His "Point of No Return" seems more likely to be a Stallone and Schwarzenegger movie.

20. Peter Wadhams, a climate scientist, predicted that the Arctic would lose all its summer sea ice by 2016, a claim that has not come true.²⁵⁷ He claimed ships would sail over the North Pole, killing Santa! Part of that is true.

21. Multiple reports from 2000 to 2020 predicted dramatic warming of 10 degrees or more by the mid-21st century. Current warming trends, while concerning, have not matched these extreme predictions. Buehler? Buehler?²⁵⁸

Wow, these are lots of mistakes! Simply asked, "Why would anyone believe the latest environmental doom prediction when the academics have such a horrible record?" The Competitive Enterprise Institute wrote, "Modern doomsayers have been predicting climate and environmental disaster since the 1960s. They continue to do so today. None of the apocalyptic predictions with due dates as of today have come true."²⁵⁹

---

254 https://www.independent.co.uk/climate-change/news/just-96-months-to-save-world-says-prince-charles-1738049.html
255 https://www.sciencedirect.com/science/article/abs/pii/S0262407911609524
256 https://www.climateone.org/people/rajendra-k-pachauri
257 https://www.weforum.org/agenda/2016/08/arctic-ice-melt-by-2017-says-peter-wadhams/
258 From Ben Stein in the movie Ferris Buehler. Stein is commentator on political and economic issues and began his career as a speechwriter for US Presidents Richard Nixon and Gerald Ford before entering the entertainment field as an actor, comedian, and game show host.
259 https://cei.org/blog/wrong-again-50-years-of-failed-eco-pocalyptic-predictions/

Morally Questionable Academics

Not only have the worst doomsday forecasts been proven wrong, but the academics have often acted in a morally questionable way. Consider these situations:

1. Climategate (2009)

Climategate is one of the most controversial events in the history of climate science, occurring in November 2009 when thousands of emails and documents from the University of East Anglia's Climatic Research Unit (CRU) were leaked. These documents were immediately seized upon by climate change skeptics, who claimed that they provided evidence that scientists were lying to exaggerate the threat of global warming. The scandal caused a media storm and cast doubt in the public's eye over the credibility of climate science. Despite multiple investigations clearing the scientists of wrongdoing, Climategate remains a key moment in the debate surrounding climate change, as it highlights the contentious intersection of performative science, politics, and public opinion. Here are ten of the most controversial quotes from the leaked emails:

    A. Dr. Phil Jones, Director of CRU, wrote, *"I've just completed Mike's Nature trick of adding in the real temps to each series for the last 20 years (i.e. from 1981 onwards) and from 1961 for Keith's to hide the decline."* The phrases "Mike's Nature trick" and "hide the decline" were widely interpreted as evidence of manipulation.

    B. Phil Jones again: *"I can't see either of these papers being in the next IPCC report. Kevin and I will keep them out somehow—even if we have to redefine what the peer-review literature is!"* This suggested a desire to block papers with contrary views from being included in IPCC reports, even going so far as to change the process to exclude certain ideas.

    C. Dr. Michael Mann, a Penn State climatologist, wrote, *"I think that trying to adopt a timeframe of 2000 years, rather than the usual 1000 years, addresses a good earlier point that Keith made with regard to the regression-based approach and spread, but still allows us to emphasize the unprecedented nature of the recent warming."* This is an attempt to frame data in a way that emphasizes modern warming. Or said another way, "We don't like the look of this, so change it until we do."

D. Climatologist Tom Wigley wrote, *"If you think that [temperature rise] is bad, wait until you see the next [report]. Hansen and his group have gone completely off the rails. They are now defending solar changes as the cause of climate change."* This quote implies that alternative theories were dismissed. The idea that the Sun may impact climate here on Earth is crazed sacrilege! Hansen suggested the Sun may have an Earthly impact. That is considered "off the rails." This is best tested by asking a five-year old. Ask them, "Do you think things that happen on the Sun, like the Sun exploding huge fireballs, impacts things on Earth?" Expect 100% affirmative responses.

E. Kevin Trenberth, a climatologist, wrote, *"The fact is that we can't account for the lack of warming at the moment and it is a travesty that we can't."* Isn't this an admission that the data didn't support his presupposed guesses?

F. Phil Jones wrote, *"The scientific community would come down on me in no uncertain terms if I said the world had cooled since 1998."* Seems like an admission that the data shows a cooling. But an even bigger worry is what his friends would say!

G. Michael Mann wrote, *"It would be nice to try to 'contain' the putative 'Medieval Warm Period' even if we don't yet have a hemispheric mean reconstruction available that far back."* This was seen as an effort to minimize the impact of historical warm periods that might challenge the narrative of unprecedented modern warming.

H. Phil Jones wrote, *"I've been told that IPCC is above national Freedom of Information Acts... One way to cover yourself and all those working in AR5 would be to delete all emails at the end of the process."* This is an attempt to avoid scrutiny by deleting email records.

I. Keith Briffa (Climate scientist): *"I know there is pressure to present a nice tidy story as regards 'apparent unprecedented warming in a thousand years or more in the proxy data,' but in reality, the situation is not quite so simple."* Skeptics used this as evidence that the consensus view on climate change was oversimplified or overstated.

J. Phil Jones: *"I would rather delete the file than send it to anyone."* Seen as a sign of unwillingness to share data with skeptics or critics.

The leaked emails spanned over a decade, covering a variety of topics ranging from data collection to scientific methods and personal communication between scientists. Climate skeptics quickly focused on specific excerpts from the emails, alleging that these communications showed that scientists were intentionally manipulating climate data to fit a preconceived narrative of catastrophic global warming. The timing of the leak was especially notable as it occurred just ahead of the 2009 United Nations Climate Change Conference in Copenhagen, which was intended to be a pivotal moment in addressing global climate policy.

In response to the controversy, multiple independent investigations were launched. They included the UK House of Commons Science and Technology Committee, The University of East Anglia (UEA) Review, Pennsylvania State University Inquiry, and The InterAcademy Council Review.

Amazingly, these unconnected, totally independent, separate reviews found the exact same thing! Everyone was innocent of everything, and the fox would continue to guard the henhouse.

For climate skeptics and those already doubtful about the scientific consensus on global warming, this scandal reinforced their belief that climate science was biased and untrustworthy. In the media, the emails were portrayed as a smoking gun that revealed the supposed corruption of climate science, and the story spread rapidly through both traditional news outlets and blogs.

A 2010 poll conducted in the United States found that belief in climate change had decreased following the scandal. Before Climategate, about 57% of Americans believed that human activities were the main driver of global warming; after the scandal, this number dropped to 47%.[260] Similarly, the number of Americans who thought that climate change was exaggerated in the media increased.

2. Hockey Stick Graph Controversy (1998)

The "Hockey Stick" graph, first introduced by climate scientist Dr. Michael Mann (Penn State) and his colleagues in 1998, represents one of the most widely

---

[260] https://www.researchgate.net/publication/240105870_Climategate_Public_Opinion_and_the_Loss_of_Trust

recognized and debated visual representations in the history of climate science. Mann was mentioned in the section above for perhaps changing data to fit his goals. The "Hockey Stick" graph is the star of Al Gore's movie. Remember the scene with a line that goes through the roof and Al gets in a bucket lift to dramatically ride up into the ceiling with the data line. The graph reconstructed Northern Hemisphere temperature records over the past millennium and looks like a hockey stick with relatively stable temperatures for most of the graph (the shaft) followed by a sudden upward spike in the last century (the blade). Get it?

Climate skeptics challenged both its scientific validity, and the methods used to create it, leading to years of political and scientific debate. Mann and his team used tree rings, ice cores, and historical records as proxies to reconstruct temperatures over the last 1000 years. It was one of the key pieces of evidence in the 2001 IPCC report.

Mathematician Stephen McIntyre and economist Ross McKitrick argued that this proxy methodology was flawed and that it artificially produced the Hockey Stick shape, regardless of the underlying data. Some skeptics argued that these proxies, particularly tree rings, were not accurate enough to provide reliable temperature estimates over such a long-time frame. Also, the tree-ring data does not match instrumental temperature records after 1960. This was known as the "divergence problem." They claimed that if the proxy data were unreliable for the 20th century, they could not be trusted for earlier periods either. That means that the data from 300 AD and 750 and 1134 fit better than the data from 1983 and 1992. Does that make sense?

Mann and his colleagues acknowledged the divergence problem! But, they said, BUT... but maintained that it did not invalidate the overall conclusions of their research. Some thousand-year-old frozen beetle turd or something confirmed the tree-ring data, so it's all good.

The Hockey Stick graph became a political litmus test, topic and tool. The graph's prominence in the 2001 IPCC report made it a target for politicians and organizations that opposed climate change legislation, particularly in the United States. The George W. Bush administration, which was opposed to the Kyoto Protocol and other climate agreements, seized upon the controversy surrounding the Hockey Stick to cast doubt on the scientific consensus around global warming.

The controversy gained further momentum when the US Congress got involved. In 2005, Republican Congressman Joe Barton, chairman of the House Energy and Commerce Committee, launched an investigation into the work of Michael Mann and his colleagues. Barton demanded that Mann provide his raw data, computer codes, and records of correspondence—a move seen by many scientists as an attempt to intimidate climate researchers. The investigation, which was led by a political committee rather than a scientific body, further fueled the narrative that climate science was uncertain or even fraudulent. "Government attacks scientists, details on the Nightly News!"

In 2015, political commentator Mark Steyn wrote a book called, "A Disgrace to the Profession."[261] It includes quotes and commentary from 119 scientists denouncing Mann and the hockey stick science. They said things like,

> "So today, most scientists dismiss the hockey stick. They do not consider the hockey stick graph to be a correct representation of the global mean temperature."[262] – Dr. Madhav Khandekar, Research Scientist with Environment Canada;

> "So, I was very surprised when I saw the first celebrated hockey stick curve, and the Third Assessment Report of the IPCC. I could hardly believe my eyes."[263] – Professor William Happer, Professor of Physics at Princeton University;

> "The blade of the hockey stick could not be reproduced using either the same techniques as Mann and Jones or other common statistical techniques."[264] – Professor David Legates, Professor of Geography and former Director of the Center for Climatic Research at the University of Delaware;

> "The behavior of Michael Mann is a disgrace to the profession."[265] – Doctor Hendrick Tennekess, former Director of Research at the Royal Dutch Meteorological Institute,

> "We now know that the hockey stick graph is fraudulent."[266] – Doctor Michael Fox, Professor of Chemistry at Idaho State University; and

> "Do I expect you to publicly denounce the hockey stick as obvious drivel? Well, yes."[267] – Professor Jonathan Jones, Professor of Physics at Oxford University Department of Atomic and Laser Physics.

---

261 https://www.amazon.com/dp/0986398330?ref=ppx_yo2ov_dt_b_fed_asin_title
262 "A Disgrace to the Profession," Mark Steyn, page 7.
263 Ibid, page 9.
264 Ibid, page 11.
265 Ibid, page 15.
266 Ibid, page 17.
267 Ibid, page 31. Notice these footnotes. The book is as damning an intra-professional takedown as ever published. 119 of his colleagues line up to denounce this Mann guy.

And on it goes. 113 more.

Despite this seemingly total denunciation, Mann continues to win big awards. According to Wikipedia….

> On June 19, 2017, Climate One at the Commonwealth Club of California said that he would be honored with the 7th annual Stephen H. Schneider Award for Outstanding Science Communication.
>
> He received the James H. Shea Award from the National Association of Geoscience Teachers for his "exceptional contribution in writing or editing Earth science materials for the general public or teachers of Earth science."
>
> On February 8, 2018, the Center for Inquiry announced that Mann had been elected as a 2017 Fellow of its Committee for Skeptical Inquiry.
>
> On February 14, 2018, the American Association for the Advancement of Science announced that Mann was chosen to receive the 2018 Public Engagement with Science award.
>
> On September 4, 2018, the American Geophysical Union announced Mann as the 2018 recipient of its Climate Communication Prize.
>
> On February 12, 2019, Mann and Warren Washington were named to receive the 2019 Tyler Prize for Environmental Achievement.
>
> In April 2020, he was elected member of the National Academy of Sciences. Along with Antonella Santuccione Chadha, he also received the World Sustainability Award from the MDPI Sustainability Foundation.
>
> In 2022, the American Physical Society recognized Mann with the Leo Szilard Lectureship Award "for distinguished contributions to the public's understanding of climate science controversies, and to how our individual and collective actions can mitigate climate change."
>
> In 2023, the American Humanist Association gave Mann their 2023 Humanist of the Year award.
>
> In 2024, The British Royal Society named Mann as a Foreign Member.[268]

---

[268] https://en.wikipedia.org/wiki/Michael_E._Mann

Damn! That's lots of awards!

It is so confusing! How is the average person that spends hundreds of hours studying all this supposed to make tails or heads of any of it?!?

The media tells us the end is coming. Leo said so too. So, a smart person would naturally want to read a little and find out what's going on. And what's going on seems to be that the scientists are fighting a lot amongst themselves and doing very little research that's going to make anyone's life safer or better!

As is often true, the media has lagged the science and science reporting. Within the scientific/academic community, the hockey stick seems hotly debated. The media, however, continues to promote this dubious science. Within some of the scientific/academic community, Mann remains a hero.

Mann sued Steyn for his comments during his radio show. Mann won. That is a topic for a free speech book another day.

Here are two takeaways for this book. First, the science all this is based on seems a little less solid. Second, they (and by "they" this book means those PhD having sorts) sure spend a lot of time arguing about the problem instead of fixing the problem. Oh, three takeaways. Al Gore looks, yeah, not so good. He based a whole movie on science questionable enough to have attack books written about.

3. NASA GISS Temperature Revisions (2007)

NASA's Goddard Institute for Space Studies (GISS) maintains one of the most important global temperature records, known as the GISS Surface Temperature Analysis (GISTEMP). This dataset tracks surface temperature changes on Earth. The GISTEMP dataset is built using a combination of land, ocean, and satellite data, some of which goes back to the 19th century.

In 2007, climate blogger Steve McIntyre, known for challenging mainstream climate science, published a post questioning NASA's US temperature dataset. Apparently, NASA modified data. Some more than others. The raw data was "fixed" because NASA created a set of rules that justified that. For example, a new parking lot was built across the road from Station 12. Parking lots trap heat. Do you move the monitoring station? Decades of data from thousands of stations was fixed.

In August 2007, NASA corrected errors in its US temperature dataset. Data from the year 2000 onwards was affected. This led to 1934 being ranked as the hottest year in the US (instead of 1998).[269] The article linked in this footnote is titled, "1934 is new hottest U.S. year after NASA checks records." Did NASA check the records or fix them? "From now on, we will be lying less!"

The media had fun with this and sold some papers. Rightfully so! This stinks.

4. NOAA "Pausebuster" Report (2015)

In 2007, John Christy and Roy Spencer, prominent climate scientists at the University of Alabama in Huntsville, along with others studying satellite data, announced that they were seeing a break in the global heating data. The concept of a global warming "hiatus" or "pause" refers to a period when the observed rate of global surface temperature increase appeared to slow, despite continued rises in greenhouse gas concentrations.

The pause or hiatus was noted by several researchers, but one of the most prominent reports came from the Intergovernmental Panel on Climate Change (IPCC) in its Fifth Assessment Report (AR5), released in 2013. The report acknowledged that global surface temperatures had not risen as quickly from 1998 to 2012 compared to previous decades, which contributed to the public and scientific discourse on a potential hiatus.

In 2015, the National Oceanic and Atmospheric Administration (NOAA) released a report officially titled "Possible Artifacts of Data Biases in the Recent Global Surface Warming Hiatus."

This report addressed claims of a global warming "hiatus" or "pause." The study, led by NOAA scientist Thomas Karl, revised earlier temperature data and concluded that there had been no significant slowdown in global warming. Did you read that last sentence carefully? Throwing out some unneeded phrases, the sentence repeated.... "The study... revised earlier .... data..." *That is an elegant solution! Change the data! Hiatus goes away! I was right all along!*

The "Pausebuster" report sparked significant controversy. US Congressman Lamar Smith, trying to get re-elected, launched investigations. Multiple independent reviews, including one by the American Meteorological Society and several other climate science institutions, were announced.

---

[269] https://www.latimes.com/archives/la-xpm-2007-aug-15-sci-temp15-story.html

Amazingly, these unconnected, totally independent, separate reviews found the exact same thing! Everyone was innocent of everything, and the fox would continue to guard the henhouse.[270]

5. IPCC Himalayan Glacier Melt Controversy (2010)

The Himalayas is a mountain range in Asia, with the plains of the Indian subcontinent to the south and the Tibetan Plateau to the north. The range includes Mount Everest.

The UN IPCC's Fourth Assessment Report (AR4), published in 2007, said the Himalayan glaciers would melt by 2035.[271] They are vital for freshwater supply to millions of people in Asia. The report set off a frenzy. Yeah, and they were wrong. Mind-bogglingly wrong.

Guess how the prediction made its way into the IPCC. Maybe a scientist wrote a... NO! It's so crazy, let's get right to it. Indian glaciologist Dr. Syed Iqbal Hasnain said the glaciers were threatened in a 1999 interview. The interview was cited in the 2005 WWF (World Wide Fund for Nature) report. The WWF report was quoted in the IPCC report in 2007.

The statement was not based on rigorous scientific evidence. Instead, it copied from a rumor during a windstorm. *And then my hairdresser told me the scientists said...*

The IPCC quickly admitted the mistake. They acknowledged that the claim had not been verified and was not derived from peer-reviewed literature, a core requirement for IPCC assessments. The then-chair of the IPCC, Dr. Rajendra Pachauri, issued a formal apology and described the error as "regrettable."

There are more controversies. The polar bear debate was just discussed. There are more bears now than at any time since the 1970's. Overhunting is horrible and stupid. International cries and pressure worked. Protections against hunting worked and the population numbers are back up. Overhunting and environmental catastrophe are not the same thing.

---

[270] That exact sentence was used 3-4 pages earlier. But it works just as well in this instance! Maybe that revels something! No matter the cause or situation, regardless of macro or micro events, the outcome is the same. The scientists are judged by the scientists. Scientists announce the scientists are innocent! The fox will continue to guard the henhouse.
[271] AR4, Working Group II Report, Chapter 10.

Then there is the surface temperature accuracy debate. Satellites vs. ground-based measuring. The damn Yamal trees and their pesky rings![272] Sea-level rise measurement disputes.

These controversies are often used by climate change skeptics to challenge every aspect of climate science.

So what? Why spend so much time beating up on the academics?

Bloomberg reports that the World is spending two trillion dollars per year on clean energy investments.[273] "China leads with $676 billion invested in 2023, or 38% of the global total. Together, the EU, US and UK invested more than China in 2023, which was not the case in 2022."

Bjorn Lomborg of the Copenhagen Consensus and Stanford University's Hoover Institution wrote, "Countless studies show that when societies add more renewable energy, most of it never replaces coal, gas or oil. It simply adds to energy consumption. Recent research shows that for every six units of new green energy, less than one unit displaces any fossil fuel. Analysis in the United States shows that renewable energy subsidies simply lead to more overall energy being used. In other words, policies meant to boost green energy are leading to more emissions." That's not what they wanted.

A recent peer reviewed article in Science Direct stated that during energy transitions, a time when a new energy source is added to the mix, additional sources are added and that its "entirely unprecedented for these additions to cause a sustained decline in the use of established energy sources."[274] Coal supplanted wood during the 1800s but overall wood use actually increased even "while coal took over a greater percentage of energy needs. The same thing happened when we shifted from coal to oil: By 1970, oil, coal, gas and wood *all* delivered more energy than ever."[275]

---

272 The Yamal tree ring data controversy refers to a scientific debate that emerged in the late 2000s, centered around the use and interpretation of tree ring data from the Yamal Peninsula in Siberia. One of the most notable studies using Yamal tree ring data was by Keith Briffa, a prominent paleoclimatologist at the University of East Anglia's Climate Research Unit (CRU). Briffa and his colleagues used this data to support the so-called "hockey stick" graph. In 2008, Steve McIntyre, who runs the Climate Audit blog and had been previously involved in questioning the statistical methods behind the "hockey stick" graph, analyzed the Yamal data and accused Briffa of data cherry-picking. McIntyre argued that Briffa had used a small subset of tree ring data (only 12 trees) from Yamal.
273 https://about.bnef.com/blog/global-clean-energy-investment-jumps-17-hits-1-8-trillion-in-2023-according-to-bloombergnef-report/
274 https://www.sciencedirect.com/science/article/abs/pii/S2214629618312246
275 https://nypost.com/2024/08/11/opinion/we-are-wasting-2-trillion-a-year-chasing-green-fantasies/

The thesis of this book suggests, actually demands, that a much greater academic focus be on finding practical solutions. Trillions of dollars are being wasted or incorrectly spent because academia has failed its primary mission to provide useful, unbiased science based on fact.

Top Ten Environmental Hypocrites

#2 Al Gore

How Much Do They Talk? (0 = not at all to 10 = all day) = 10

Amount of Environmental Action? (0 = plants trees daily to 10 = giving speeches) = 8

Real Environmentalist Score = 18

Al Gore, former Vice President of the United States and Nobel Peace Prize laureate, is widely known for his environmental activism, particularly his efforts to combat climate change. His 2006 documentary, "An Inconvenient Truth," brought global warming to the forefront of public discourse. However, Gore has also been labeled by critics as one of the greatest environmental hypocrites. This perception arises from several factors, including his personal carbon footprint, financial interests in the green economy, and the way he has handled his public and private actions regarding environmental issues. A 2018 peer-reviewed study found that the former vice president faced by far the most accusations of hypocrisy for being a climate activist while living a rich and carbon-intensive lifestyle![276] He was accused more than anyone else! Of course, that data is seven years old now, so other hypocrites have had time to catch up. Maybe he should be higher on this list?!

You cannot discuss the hypocrisy of Al Gore without talking about the hockey stick. A team led by Dr. Michael Mann, the director of the Center for Science, Sustainability & the Media at the University of Pennsylvania, whose name already featured prominently earlier in this chapter, published a paper in 1998 discussing how to isolate climate signals from noisy data. The data shows temperatures exploding in the future. Al Gore made the hockey stick famous in his Academy Award winning documentary. In the movie, Gore shows a graph of world temperatures, and to show how explosive the projections are, Gore rides a

---

[276] https://www.researchgate.net/publication/325702488_Climate_Hypocrisies_A_Comparative_Study_of_News_Discourse

scissor-lift to the top of the screen at the ceiling's lowest edge. It's the denouement of the movie and Gore's ticket to an Academy Award.

Interestingly, when Al Gore won his Nobel Prize, Dr. Mann started claiming that he was a Nobel winner, too. Some articles and sources still list him as a winner. Others use nebulous grammar to make it seem like he did win. For example, this sentence from Scripps New Service: "Mann, along with Vice President Al Gore and colleagues from the Intergovernmental Panel on Climate Change, received the Nobel Peace Prize for establishing a consensus on the link between human activities and global warming."[277] Apparently, the Nobel Prize Committee was forced to contact Mann with some kind of cease-and-desist.[278] Geir Lundestad, Director for The Norwegian Nobel Institute, confirmed that Michael Mann had never been awarded the Nobel Peace Prize.[279]

Unfortunately, not everyone agrees with the hockey stick. ZME Science, a two-decade old science website, wrote that the hockey stick "is quite possibly the most controversial graph in the world."[280] So controversial that a book was written about it. As already emphasized earlier in this chapter, in "A Disgrace to the Profession," a hundred climate scientists denounced the hockey stick, not only in theory, but the practice of the science behind it. Mann has been accused of bending the data aggressively.[281]

The Gore related question: why would you base your movie on the most controversial theory out there? Seems a little reckless, no? Maybe Al didn't care. The theory supported what he wanted to say, so he went with it. Or Al and staff didn't research the theory and accepted it without question. No matter the circumstances, it is clear that the theatrics outweigh the certainty of the data. It was a great performance, Al, an Academy Award winning performance!

---

277 https://www.scrippsnews.com/science-and-tech/climate-change/renowned-climate-scientist-s-12-year-defamation-lawsuit-goes-to-trial
278 https://www.nationalreview.com/corner/michael-manns-false-nobel-claim-charles-c-w-cooke/
279 https://canadafreepress.com/article/nobel-committee-rebukes-michael-mann-for-falsely-claiming-he-was-awarded-th
280 https://www.zmescience.com/science/michael-mann-warren-washington-climate-change-10022019/
281 https://www.amazon.com/dp/0986398330?ref=ppx_yo2ov_dt_b_fed_asin_title The book includes quotes such as: "substantively discredited," Dr. Hamish Campbell of the New Zealand Institute of Geological and Nuclear Science; "not credible anymore," Dr. Eduardo Zurita, Senior Scientist at the Institute for Climate Research in Germany; "obvious drivel," Professor Jonathan Jones, Professor of Physics at Oxford University; "contradicted by the results of more than 100 previous studies" Dr. David Demming, University of Oklahoma, and "at best bad science," Dr. Lee Gerhard, Principal Geologist of Kansas Geological Survey.

During a 2017 interview with Jake Tapper on CNN, Al said, "I live a carbon-free lifestyle."[282] In another interview, he said, "We are going to have to change the way we live our lives."[283] Ah, the hypocrisy!

The National Center for Public Policy Research found that his Tennessee home "guzzles more electricity in one year than the average American family uses in 21 years," and consumed more electricity than the average family uses in 34 months.[284] His swimming pool uses more electricity than six normal houses. After negative media reports, he spent tens of thousands of dollars installing green upgrades. In fact, "Gore's home used *more* electricity last year than it did in 2007, before he installed all those energy-reducing features."[285]

Yet, he claims to live "carbon free"? He claims he buys "carbon offsets" to account for all the CO2 his home and lifestyle produce. For example, he pays $432 a month into a "Green Power Switch" program that helps fund renewable energy projects in Tennessee.[286] Remember what this book highlighted about carbon credits in the Bill Gates hypocrisy section. For Al, a new source confirms the sad truth. Dr. Kevin Anderson, deputy director of the Tyndall Centre for Climate Change Research at the University of Manchester, UK, wrote, "Offsetting is worse than doing nothing. It is without scientific legitimacy, is dangerously misleading and almost certainly contributes to a net increase in the absolute rate of global emissions growth."[287] No worries though, Al is offsetting, so it's okay for him to do any damage he wants! He owns at least two other homes.

Despite this, Al has been involved in even greater hypocrisy. He sold his Current TV network to Al Jazeera for $500 million. Gore reportedly pocketed $100 million and was criticized by the left and the right. Al Jazeera is backed by Qatar and oil money. Even comedian and fellow Democrat Jon Stewart was upset:[288]

---

282 https://www.youtube.com/watch?v=2cKSJ5PCgDM
283 https://www.forbes.com/sites/michaelshellenberger/2019/08/20/the-real-reason-they-behave-hypocritically-on-climate-change-is-because-they-want-to/
284 https://www.investors.com/politics/editorials/al-gores-climate-change-hypocrisy-is-as-big-as-his-energy-sucking-mansion/
285 https://nationalcenter.org/ncppr/2017/08/01/al-gores-inconvenient-reality-the-former-vice-presidents-home-energy-use-surges-up-to-34-times-the-national-average-despite-costly-green-renovations-by-drew-johnso/
286 https://www.investors.com/politics/editorials/al-gores-climate-change-hypocrisy-is-as-big-as-his-energy-sucking-mansion/
287 https://www.nature.com/articles/484007a
288 https://oilprice.com/Energy/Energy-General/Al-Gores-Hipocrisy-The-Climate-Crusader-Profits-from-Fossil-Fuels.html

> *Jon Stewart:* "You had an opportunity to make a statement, probably, about your principles, and some people would feel, and for me as well, I thought it was an odd move. Not because of some of the other things, but because it is backed by fossil fuel money."
>
> *Al Gore:* "I get it. I get it. I get it. But it was an easy choice after doing the diligence on the network itself."
>
> *Jon Stewart:* "Can you see how people at home might think — but he's asking me in my life to make choices about light bulbs and a cost-benefit analysis for the purpose of sustainability when I just want to see my book. That's the issue."
>
> *Al Gore:* "I'm very, very comfortable with it. I completely get the criticism, but this was a good choice and the net benefit for the US is going to be very positive."

Even Jon Stewart gets it! Gore wants us to change our light bulbs while he counts his $100 million! How is the next benefit going to be positive for the US? What BS, but at least Jon Stewart sees it, too. It's a hypocrisy so blatant that even a friend called him on it.

Another area where Gore faces accusations of hypocrisy is his financial interests in the green economy. Gore co-founded Generation Investment Management, a firm that focuses on sustainable investments. While investing in green technologies and sustainable practices aligns with his environmental advocacy, critics argue that it also presents a conflict of interest. They suggest that Gore stands to benefit financially from the policies he promotes, which raises questions about whether his advocacy is driven by genuine concern for the environment or by potential financial gains. This dual role as both an advocate and investor creates a perception of self-interest that detracts from his credibility as an environmental champion.

Gore's involvement in carbon offset markets further complicates his image. Carbon offsets allow individuals and companies to compensate for their emissions by funding projects that reduce carbon dioxide elsewhere. While this mechanism can play a role in mitigating climate change, it has also been criticized for enabling high emitters to continue their activities without making significant changes to reduce their own emissions. Gore's purchase of carbon offsets to counterbalance his personal carbon footprint has been seen by some as an attempt to buy his way out of guilt rather than making meaningful lifestyle changes. This practice can be viewed as a superficial solution that fails to address the root causes of climate change.

Furthermore, Gore's public persona and private actions have often been at odds, leading to further accusations of hypocrisy. While he has been a vocal advocate for renewable energy and reducing fossil fuel dependence, his financial portfolio has included investments in companies linked to the fossil fuel industry. For instance, Gore was reported to have a stake in Occidental Petroleum, an oil and gas company, through his involvement with the venture capital firm Kleiner Perkins. Such investments can be perceived as contradictory to his environmental advocacy, undermining his moral authority on the issue.

In conclusion, the perception of Al Gore as one of the greatest environmental hypocrites stems from several factors, including his substantial personal carbon footprint, use of private jets, financial interests in the green economy, involvement in carbon offset markets, and the dissonance between his public advocacy and private actions. These elements combine to create an image of a leader whose actions do not always align with his words, leading to accusations of hypocrisy. While Gore's contributions to raising awareness about climate change are significant, the inconsistencies in his behavior continue to cast a shadow over his environmental legacy.

Chapter 10 – Conclusion

The Real Environmentalists vs. The Pretenders

So here we are. You've made it through the stories of shipbreaking, battery recycling, health companies, and plastic-eating startups. You've waded through footnotes, endured my digressions, and maybe even rolled your eyes at a joke or two (probably more than two). Thank you for sticking with me. Now let's tie a bow on this whole damn thing.

I promised you two things at the beginning of this book:

1. That I would tell you about the **real environmentalists** – the entrepreneurs who are actually saving the planet.

2. That I would out a bunch of **hypocrites** – the academics, politicians and celebrities who fly around on private jets while lecturing you about reusable grocery bags.

Mission accomplished.

But I don't want to end this book with just a bunch of laughs at Leo's expense or with admiration for Wayne Elliott's unbelievable work ethic (though both are deserved). I want you to leave with a clear understanding of what's going on and what you can do.

First, Let's Get One Thing Straight

You cannot recycle your way to salvation by skipping a straw at Starbucks. You cannot "like" your way there on Instagram. You cannot buy an $8 oat milk latte and call it climate activism.

And no, Al Gore giving another speech does not lower the planet's temperature. It just raises the room's humidity.

But you know what does matter?

- **Ship recycling.**

- **Battery innovation.**

- **Sustainable consumer products that actually last.**

- **Entrepreneurs who are willing to get their hands dirty (sometimes literally covered in asbestos) to solve real problems.**

That's why I spent so much of this book on Wayne Elliott. He didn't hold a press conference. He bought a junked submarine and cut it apart. He didn't post an Instagram reel. He started Canada's largest shipbreaking yard and got it certified to world-class environmental standards. He didn't offset his carbon with a trendy forest in South America. He actually removed toxins from Lake Ontario.

Compare that to the people on the Top Ten Hypocrites list. They're busy planting forests of press releases. Wayne is busy planting actual solutions.

Why the Hypocrites Are Here

Now, some of you might be wondering: Jim, why did you waste so much ink making fun of billionaires and politicians? Why spend all those pages dunking on Elon Musk's space garbage or Harry and Meghan's "two kids to save the planet" award?

Simple: because that's what the media eats up. You think *The Daily Mail* is going to run a front-page story on ballast water management in the Great Lakes? No. But they'll trip over themselves to write, *"ChatGPT Analysis RANKS DiCaprio #1 Environmental Hypocrite."*

And guess what happens then? People who never would have heard of Wayne Elliott will now read about him. People who thought environmentalism was just about politicians wagging their fingers will suddenly discover there are entrepreneurs building real solutions. The hypocrites are the bait. The entrepreneurs are the catch.

You want to hook the public? Sometimes you need chum in the water.

The Real Environmentalist Equation

Let me boil it down for you. Here's the formula I think about:

Capitalism + Grit + Environmental Awareness = Real Change

- **Capitalism** because profit drives scale. You cannot scale a better battery or a cleaner shipbreaking yard with hashtags. You scale it with customers and investors.
- **Grit** because this work is not glamorous. It's hard, dirty, and often thankless. Nobody cheers when you spend ten hours with a blowtorch inside a rusted hull. (Well, maybe I cheer, but I'm weird.)
- **Environmental Awareness** because without it, capitalism just churns out more disposable junk. The difference between a polluter and a real environmentalist is the direction of the energy. Same drive, different target.

That's why Wayne, Larry Wyman, Kevin Gast, Gator Halpern, and Stephen Mayfield are heroes. They are proof that when capitalism and environmentalism meet, we don't get hypocrisy. We get progress.

What You Can Do

This is the part of the book where I'm supposed to give you "10 Easy Tips to Save the Planet" like a BuzzFeed listicle. Don't worry, I won't insult your intelligence.

Here's the real deal:

1. **Support Real Environmentalists.** Buy from the companies solving problems, not greenwashing them. If a sofa company like Lovesac is using 100 million recycled bottles in its fabrics, buy that sofa instead of fast furniture.
2. **Vote With Your Wallet.** Don't fall for performative nonsense. If a celebrity tells you to fly less while they jet to Cannes, don't clap. Roll your eyes and keep moving.
3. **Start Something.** If you've got an entrepreneurial itch, scratch it in the direction of the environment. There are thousands of unsolved problems. You don't need to invent fusion power. Just make one dirty

4. thing cleaner, one waste stream smaller, one process more efficient. That's enough.

5. **Spread the Word.** Share these stories. Tell your kids about Wayne Elliott, not just about Greta on a yacht. Teach them that capitalism isn't the villain. It's the toolbox.

A Final Word on Hypocrisy

The richest 1% emit more carbon than the poorest 66%. That's not a typo. That's why I didn't feel bad at all writing jokes about Nancy Pelosi's refrigerator or DiCaprio's jet habit. The hypocrisy isn't just annoying. It's deadly. It costs lives.

So, no, I won't stop poking fun at them. Somebody has to say it out loud. And maybe, just maybe, the ridicule will sting enough to make a few of them rethink their act.

But honestly? I'm not holding my breath. They'll still be on their yachts. Which is fine, because people like Wayne Elliott will still be in the shipyards. And when the history of this era is written, it won't be the speeches that saved us. It'll be the sparks from the blowtorches.

Oh, and to all you yacht owners whose feelings I hurt I will take it all back for a ~~week~~ month on any 200-foot plus toy that is available. Have your people call my people, please.

Wayne Gets the Last Word

I asked Wayne once what keeps him going after 50 years in shipbreaking. He said, "Jim, ships don't recycle themselves."

That's it. That's the whole philosophy. Problems don't solve themselves. You either complain about them, or you get to work.

So let the hypocrites keep talking. The real environmentalists will keep working. And if you're smart, you'll stand with the workers, the builders, the doers. Because that's the side that wins.

The Call to Action

Here's the big finish:

- Don't be performative.
- Don't be a hypocrite.
- Don't wait for permission.

Be a real environmentalist. Start something. Support something. Share something that actually matters.

And if all else fails, at least stop using plastic straws. Not because it will save the world, it won't, but because paper straws make your enemies miserable, and that's worth a little soggy lip every now and then.

Thank you for reading. Now go do something real. After you write a 5-Star review on Amazon.

Top Ten Environmental Hypocrites

#1 Leonardo DiCaprio

How Much Do They Talk? (0 = not at all to 10 = all day) = 10

Amount of Environmental Action? (0 = plants trees daily to 10 = giving speeches) = 8

Real Environmentalist Score = 18

Leonardo DiCaprio is renowned for his acting prowess and environmental activism. Some of his great movies include The Revenant, Titanic, Inception, The Wolf of Wall Street, and Aviator. He is also famous for his dating. His girlfriends include Bridget Hall, Naomi Campbell, Kristen Zang, Amber Valletta, Helena Christensen, and Eva Herzigová.[289] And that is just the women in the 1990s! Do not worry, they are all still the best of friends.

His most famous environmental activity is speaking at the United Nations in 2017. In addition to Leo, Anne Hathaway, Jason Momoa (Aquaman), Emma Watson, the Korean boy band BTS, Greta Thunberg, and Angelina Jolie have spoken at the UN Based on what? What skill or experience do they have to justify the appearance? Where are the standards published?

Back to Leo's speech, the UN Secretary-General designated him as a Messenger of Peace. The average world temperature went down 1.2 degrees centigrade just from this speech! The speech was very well received, and that is the only thing he has done to help the environment. He has not planted trees, cleaned beaches or de-oiled ducks. Everything else that he gets credit for doing relates back to a thirty-minute speech that an intern at his PR agency probably wrote.

In November 2023, VegNews reported about the ten things Leonardo is doing to "save the Planet every day."[290] Every DAY!! The article reported the ten things as, 1. Producing documentaries, 2. Using his platform, 3. Spreading the message, 4. Investing in vegan businesses, 5. He's UN approved, 6. Starting a foundation, 7. Betting on cell-based meat, 8. He's into solar, 9. Ushering in new ethical fashion, and 10. Revolutionizing fast food. This fawning article could not find

---

[289] https://www.augustman.com/in/entertainment/culture/leonardo-dicaprio-girlfriends-and-dating-history/
[290] https://vegnews.com/leonardo-dicaprio-save-the-planet

one real action he has ever done. Has he ever put a glass bottle in the recycling bin? If he had, he could claim to volunteer at a recycling center. Where is the video of him cleaning beaches for ten hours?

Speaking to the UN is very admirable and impressive. Millions of people gave up straws inspired by the speech. Yet, his advocacy for environmental causes is performative only.

DiCaprio's lifestyle as a Hollywood superstar is often cited as a primary cause for global warming. Despite his vocal support for YOU reducing YOUR carbon footprint, his use of private jets, luxury yachts, and multiple mansions paint a different picture.

Private jets, in particular, are notorious for their high carbon emissions. Private plane use creates ten times as much greenhouse gases as flying commercial.[291] In 2016, DiCaprio faced significant backlash when he flew from Europe to New York and back to accept an environmental award.[292] Not learning from his mistakes, in 2021, he flew from New York to Miami and back for a party.[293]

In 2023, he testified in a court case involving illegal fundraising for the Obama campaigns. DiCaprio is not charged with any crimes but was testifying about indicted Malaysian billionaire Jho Low. Leo is so concerned with the environment and his personal use of resources that the group celebrated a New Year in one time zone and then hopped a plane to get ahead of time so they could celebrate the New Year in another time zone.[294]

The need for extra security is understandable. Commercial travel would limit his ability to multitask. Using private jets, he can make three movies a year, attend eighteen environmental conferences and still have enough time to romance nine supermodels on three yachts!

Let's convert that into normal American. Say you live in Michigan and want to take the family to DisneyWorld in Orlando. It's expensive, so you decide to drive instead of flying. It's 24 hours each way if you drive, so you get less time actually

---

291 https://www.greenmatters.com/p/environmental-impact-private-jet
292 https://qz.com/690321/leonardo-dicaprio-took-an-outrageous-8000-mile-trip-in-a-private-jet-to-pick-up-an-environmental-award
293 https://pagesix.com/2021/12/02/leo-dicaprio-takes-jet-round-trip-to-nyc-to-party-in-miami/
294 https://www.independent.co.uk/news/world/americas/crime/leonardo-dicaprio-jho-low-fugees-trial-las-vegas-b2313596.html

in the parks. For comparison, for Leo, he could take first class on Delta, but then he would only have time to romance eight supermodels. Is that fair?

Another point of contention is DiCaprio's use of luxury yachts. Yachts are known for their extravagant energy consumption and significant environmental impact. Lifestyle social scientist Gregory Salle has categorized superyachts as a form of ecocide, "Ecocide is something that causes deep harm, harm that is lasting over time. You could apply this to what superyachts are doing."[295] Damn! Ecocide! Super Ecocide! "Leo, welcome to my yacht! It's called the Super Yacht Ecocide! How many super models did you bring?" said the billionaire host. The average super-yacht releases more greenhouse gases than 1,500 cars combined.[296] One super-yacht website summed it up best, "Year after year, the women keep changing, but the super-yacht remains."[297]

Finally, Leo owns lots of houses, probably more than he needs. While DiCaprio has made efforts to invest in eco-friendly properties, the sheer number of his residences and their environmental impact cannot be ignored. He owns four homes in California, two in New York, and an island in Belize.[298]

---

295 https://cleantechnica.com/2024/06/19/superyachts-for-the-super-rich-cause-a-whole-lot-of-environmental-damage/
296 https://luxurylaunches.com/celebrities/leonardo-di-caprio-2023-new-year-yacht-party.php
297 Ibid.
298 https://www.elledecor.com/celebrity-style/celebrity-homes/g61113758/leonardo-dicaprio-homes-real-estate/

Appendix 1 – The Methodology Behind the Celebrity Hypocrites

Some of you will want to know: how exactly did I rank the "Top Ten Environmental Hypocrites"? Fair question. This appendix is for you.

First, let's be clear: this isn't a beauty contest, and it isn't scientific peer review. Nobody got extra points for their yacht's paint job. But we did use a repeatable framework to minimize bias (and yes, I asked my AI Friend to help, so it wouldn't just be my personal opinion).

Here's the scoring system:

Category 1: Volume of Talk (0–10)

- How often do they present themselves as environmental champions?
- A "10" is someone who never shuts up about it. A "0" is someone who never mentions the environment at all.

Category 2: Actual Action (0–10)

- How much real environmental action have they taken?
- A "10" is hands-on cleanup, creating technologies, or funding real solutions. A "0" is doing nothing but posting selfies.

Category 3: Lifestyle Contradictions (Penalty Points)

- Private jets, mega-yachts, twenty houses, or other absurd consumption.
- For every major contradiction, we subtract points.

Final Score = Talk Score + Action Score – Hypocrisy Penalty

Why Use This Methodology?

Because without a framework, all we have is "Jim thinks Leo is worse than Gates." By scoring each category and running it through ChatGPT for cross-checking, we eliminated as much human bias as possible.

Yes, there's still subjectivity. But it's consistent subjectivity. You may quibble about whether Musk deserves to be higher than Gates, but the system was applied evenly.

Why Include This List at All?

Because celebrity hypocrisy sucks all the oxygen out of the room. If we don't expose the phonies, they'll keep hogging the spotlight that should go to the real environmentalists. The list is a media magnet — bait for tabloids, headlines, and late-night jokes — but behind the humor is a serious point: **we cannot afford to confuse performance with progress.**

And the entire, original Long Form explanation is on the site www.RealEnvironmentalist.com. Please check it out. After you write a 5-Star review on Amazon.

It is really long, so we reduced it to save trees, and straws.

Appendix 2 –
Directory of Real Environmentalists

(Top 5 companies in each category, out of 265, listed here. See the complete list at www.RealEnvironmentalist.com) Please write a 5-Star review on Amazon.

1. Energy & Fuel *(48 companies identified)*

- **Tesla** – Yes, Elon's a hypocrite sometimes, but Tesla made EVs mainstream.

- **Ørsted** – Danish giant turning away from oil and into offshore wind.

- **Neste** – World leader in renewable diesel made from waste.

- **First Solar** – American solar panel manufacturer cutting costs and scaling clean power.

- **Bloom Energy** – Building fuel cells to replace dirty generators with cleaner alternatives.

2. Recycling & Waste *(52 companies identified)*

- **Marine Recycling Corporation** – Wayne Elliott's shipbreaking company, dismantling hazardous vessels responsibly.

- **TerraCycle** – Finding ways to recycle "unrecyclable" stuff like cigarette butts and chip bags.

- **Rubicon Global** – A tech platform modernizing trash hauling and recycling logistics.

- **AMP Robotics** – AI-powered robots sorting recyclables better than humans.

- **Loop Industries** – Recycling PET plastics back into high-quality plastic endlessly.

3. Consumer Products *(41 companies identified)*

- **Lovesac** – Turning 100+ million plastic bottles into durable furniture fabric.
- **Patagonia** – Outdoor gear company that pioneered recycled polyester and supply chain transparency.
- **Allbirds** – Shoes made from wool, eucalyptus, and sugarcane, not petroleum.
- **Method** – Eco-friendly soaps and cleaners in recyclable, stylish packaging.
- **Seventh Generation** – Household products designed for sustainability and transparency.

4. Food & Agriculture *(39 companies identified)*

- **Beyond Meat** – Plant-based protein company reducing demand for industrial beef.
- **Impossible Foods** – Famous plant-based burger with real meat taste, less carbon.
- **AppHarvest** – High-tech greenhouses bringing efficient, local produce to the US
- **Indigo Agriculture** – Using microbes to help crops grow with less chemical fertilizer.
- **Apeel Sciences** – Natural coating that extends fruit shelf life and cuts food waste.

5. Plastics & Oceans *(36 companies identified)*

- **Parley for the Oceans** – Partnering with Adidas and others to turn ocean plastic into products.
- **The Ocean Cleanup** – Ambitious Dutch project removing plastic from rivers and oceans.

- **Bureo** – Making skateboards, sunglasses, and more from recycled fishing nets.
- **4ocean** – Pulling plastic out of the ocean and funding it through bracelets and merch.
- **Wildplastic** – Collecting wild plastic waste and reusing it in new packaging.

6. Biotech & Science *(34 companies identified)*

- **Ecovative** – Mycelium-based packaging replacing styrofoam and plastics.
- **CarbonCure** – Injecting captured CO2 into concrete to make it stronger and greener.
- **Pivot Bio** – Microbial fertilizer replacing synthetic nitrogen.
- **LanzaTech** – Turning industrial emissions into fuels and chemicals.
- **Novozymes** – Using enzymes to clean up industries from textiles to detergents.

Appendix 3

Wayne's involvement in Strauss Naturals has been the core of his third career. We wanted to introduce you to some of their amazing products.

Strauss Naturals Health Insight 1

Heartdrops®

The Strauss family of herbalists dating back 8 generations has created a world-renowned heart formula that helps support you with every heartbeat. That's around 72 times a minute, 100,000 times a day, and 3.6 million times a year. Your heart is one hard worker!

And so are Strauss Heartdrops®. Doctors, especially Cardiologists maintain that "you are only as old as your arteries." They know that arterial aging wears out your brain, heart, kidneys and other organs as well as causing damage to hearing and eyesight.

Heart disease is the leading cause of death for North American women accounting for 1 in every 4 female deaths, killing more women than all forms of cancer combined. Heart disease is also the leading cause of death among young women. No longer a "man's disease," more women than men now die of heart disease. Only 54% of women recognize that heart disease is their #1 killer. Almost 65% of women who die suddenly of coronary heart disease have no previous symptoms. And over 90% of women have one or more risk factors for developing heart disease.

Clasp your hands together. That's the size of your 9-12 ounce heart. Your heart is like two pumps in one: the right side receives blood and pumps it to the lungs. The left side does the opposite; it receives blood from the lungs and pumps it out to the body.

Strauss' flagship formula for cardiovascular support combines eight synergistic herbs and a proprietary process that remains unduplicated. Trust the original. Aged Garlic Extract (AGE), Hawthorn fruit, and European mistletoe leaf are used to support a healthy cardiovascular system.

Please go to Straussnaturals.com

Strauss Naturals Health Insight 2

Cardio Support Drops™

Cardiovascular health requires good heart rhythm. The master pacemaker in our heart sends electrical signals that stimulate the cardiac muscle and the heart to expand and contract to pump oxygenated blood throughout your body. Don't skip a beat, pick up some today!

When you think of your future, think of your cardiovascular system (heart and brain), because they go together. Just like Cardio Support Drops™ and a healthy lifestyle.

Did You Know? There are several types of irregular rhythms known as arrhythmia or irregular heartbeat, including:

- Bradycardia (less than 60 beats/min)
- Tachycardia (greater than 100 beats/min)
- Atrial Fibrillation (characterized by a disorganized, irregular heartbeat)
- Sometimes intermittent arrhythmias can develop in cases of chronic stress.

How can Cardio Support Drops™ help?
- Skullcap Herb Top used traditionally to help support a strong heart
- Hawthorn Flower, Fruit and Leaf is used traditionally to strengthen and invigorate heart and circulatory function.
- Indian Sarsaparilla Root is used traditionally as an anti-inflammatory and has cardio tonic, diuretic and anti-bacterial properties.
- Peppermint Leaf is used traditionally to relax tension, block inflammation and soothe muscle and nerve pain.
- European Mistletoe Leaf is used traditionally as a vagal nerve tonic to aid in strengthening a weak pulse.

Strauss Naturals Health Insight 3

Kidney Support Drops™

Your kidneys are key organs that help blood maintain healthy pressure levels. When functioning properly, kidneys constantly filter waste and extra fluids from the blood.

Did You Know? Good health depends on maintaining healthy blood pressure levels. The average kidneys filters around 45-50 gallons of blood a day to get rid of wastes, acids, toxins and extra fluid (water weight) in your body.

Kidney Support Drops™ helps support healthy kidneys, so they can help support you. Kidneys that are healthy and function properly can do their part to help maintain already healthy blood pressure. Congested, damaged, or infected kidneys can lead to excess water retention and edema. High blood pressure (HBP), also called hypertension, is often referred to as a "silent killer" because it does not signal any warning signs or symptoms, especially during its early stages of development.

Consequently, many individuals go undiagnosed and become at risk for heart attack or stroke, two leading causes of death. Kidney Support Drops™ contain a synergistic blend of herbs used to help support healthy kidney function and a healthy urinary tract.

- Gravel Root is used Traditionally in Herbal Medicine to help maintain kidney health and function.
- Juniper berry and its essential oil are used Traditionally in Herbal Medicine to help maintain healthy urinary flow.
- Goldenrod is also used Traditionally in Herbal Medicine to help promote urination, drain water, relieve occasional edema, and to also nourish and strengthen the kidneys.
- Uva Ursi leaf is specifically indicated for bladder and kidney health helping to soothe, strengthen and tonify.

Please go to **Straussnaturals.com**

Strauss Naturals Health Insight 4

Bladder Support Drops™

Diuretics are substances that help the body get rid of salts and excess water via increased urine production.

Did You Know? Research shows that Stress Incontinence affects up to 50% of both men and women ages 19-55 and more as the age increases.

Overactive Bladder Syndrome (OAB) is a chronic, challenging condition consisting of urinary storage related symptoms (urinary urgency, urinary frequency, urgency incontinence and nocturia) demonstrated to have an impact on the quality of life for both men and women.

A urinary tract infection (UTI) is an infection in any part of your urinary system — your kidneys, ureters, bladder and urethra. Most infections involve the lower urinary tract — the bladder and the urethra. Many things can affect one's bladder health. However, certain signs may mean a bladder problem.

Some signs and symptoms are:
• weak stream while urinating
• difficulty voiding the bladder
• cloudy urine or blood in urine
• sudden and urgent need to urinate
• frequently waking up at night to urinate
• infection; pain or burning while urinating
• leaking urine (urinary incontinence)
• passing only small amounts of urine after strong urges to urinate

Strauss Naturals Health Insight 5

Prostate Support Drops™

Our synergistic blend of traditional herbal ingredients provides a safe, natural and effective formula to support a healthy prostate.

Did You Know? Benign prostatic hyperplasia affects about 50 percent of men between the ages of 51 and 60 and up to 90 percent of men older than 80.

Men with the following factors are more likely to develop benign prostatic hyperplasia (BPH):

- age 40 years and older
- lack of physical exercise
- erectile dysfunction
- family history of benign prostatic hyperplasia
- having extra fat on your abdomen (abdominal obesity)
- medical conditions such as obesity, heart and circulatory disease and type 2 diabetes

Signs and symptoms of BPH start when the enlarged prostate puts pressure on the urethra and bladder. This can narrow (constrict) or block the urethra, which can cause changes in bladder habits such as the following lower urinary tract symptoms:

- difficulty passing urine
- blood in the urine
- frequent urination (urinary frequency), especially at night
- a strong or sudden urge to urinate (urinary urgency)
- weak or slow urine stream
- being unable to empty the bladder completely, which can lead to urinary tract infections and bladder stones
- difficulty starting the urine stream (straining)
- difficulty controlling the bladder (incontinence), which can cause urine to leak and dribble

Please go to Straussnaturals.com

Strauss Naturals Health Insight 6

Menopause Drops™

Menopause Drops™ are used traditionally in Herbal Medicine to relieve symptoms associated with menopause and post menopause.

Alleviates hot flashes, night sweats, mood swings, sleep disturbances, vaginal dryness and other menopausal symptoms. For women seeking natural alternatives to traditional hormone therapy, prioritizing holistic wellness and healthy aging.

How can Menopause Drops™ help? Helps women regain control of their bodies and improve their overall well-being using a mild and noninvasive approach, suitable for individuals who may be hesitant about traditional medications. Alleviates hot flashes, night sweats, mood swings, sleep disturbances, vaginal dryness and other menopausal symptoms.

Uses high-quality herbal ingredients with a proven track record for addressing menopause symptoms. Contains extracts of 20 different medicinal herbs that all have use as female tonics and as other remedies in support of the female reproductive system and symptoms associated with menopause and/or pre and post-menopause.

Strauss Naturals Health Insight 7

Woman's Wonder™ Drops

Menstrual and Menopausal support.

An effective plant-based formula for women's health:

• supports relief from painful symptoms of PMS, including cramping, bloating, restlessness, and mood changes.
• helps women cope with the natural stresses placed on the body during your period.
• multi symptom hormonal support Woman's Wonder is a liquid combination product containing extracts of 11 different naturally-sourced herbs with a long history of use in supporting a healthy menstrual cycle, balanced energy, mood levels, and hormonal health.

The Woman's Wonder formulation was designed to provide a safe, balanced product for self-use. The Woman's Wonder formulation is safe and effective when taken as recommended for its intended uses/purposes.

Did You Know? Period pain, or dysmenorrhea, is a common experience for many during menstruation. Around 80% of women experience period pain at some stage in their lifetime. You can suffer from period pain from your early teens right up to menopause. Most women experience some discomfort during menstruation, especially on the first day.

In fact, pain is the most common problem that people complain of during their menstrual cycles alongside premenstrual symptoms including bloating, mood swings, tender breasts, swollen stomach, lack of concentration, tiredness, and clumsiness.

Please go to Straussnaturals.com

Strauss Naturals Health Insight 8

ColdStorm® Drops

Helps support a healthy respiratory system. The only bottle you need for the WHOLE FAMILY!

Supports a healthy respiratory system.

Common colds are the main reason that children miss school and adults miss work. While winter and spring are the most common times people get sick, you can get a cold anytime of year. Colds usually last 7-10 days and adults usually catch 2-3 colds per year and children catch even more.

Catarrh is a build-up of mucus in an airway or cavity of the body. It usually affects the back of the nose, the throat or the sinuses and can lead to:
• reduced sense of smell and taste
• constant need to clear your throat
• the feeling that your throat is blocked
• blocked or stuffy nose that you can't clear
• persistent cough
• a headache or facial pain
• crackling sensation in your ear and some temporary hearing loss
• runny nose and the feeling of mucus running down the back of your throat.

These symptoms can be frustrating to live with and may affect your sleep, making you feel tired.

Strauss Naturals Health Insight 9

Immune Support Drops™

Immune Support Drops™ are a blend of naturally sourced herbs including Myrrh Gum, Goldenseal Root, Cayenne Fruit, and Vitamin C used to help support a healthy immune system.

Easy to take, liquid drops in an ideal travel size with a Refreshing Spearmint flavor! Strauss Immune Support Drops™ Used to help support a healthy immune system.

Immune Support Drops™ are a blend of naturally sourced herbs including Myrrh Gum, Goldenseal Root, Cayenne Fruit, and Vitamin C used to help support a healthy immune system. Easy to take, liquid drops in an ideal travel size with a Refreshing Spearmint flavor!

Whether you work in an office, take public transit, or travel for business, coughs, colds, and bronchitis are easy to pick up and can leave you feeling terrible. Immune Support Drops™ support healthy immune function.

Did You Know? The design of our immune system is complex and influenced by an ideal balance of many factors, not just diet, and especially not by any one specific food or nutrient. However, a balanced diet consisting of a range of vitamins and minerals, combined with healthy lifestyle factors like adequate sleep, proper gut health, exercise and low stress, most effectively primes the body to fight infection and disease.

Please go to **Straussnaturals.com**

Strauss Naturals Health Insight 10

Immune Support Drops™

Immune Support Drops™ are a blend of naturally sourced herbs including Myrrh Gum, Goldenseal Root, Cayenne Fruit, and Vitamin C used to help support a healthy immune system. Easy to take, liquid drops in an ideal travel size with a Refreshing Spearmint flavor!

Immune and Respiratory Health Whether you work in an office, take public transit, or travel for business, coughs, colds, and bronchitis are easy to pick up and can leave you feeling terrible. Immune Support Drops™ support healthy immune function.

Consider taking with Strauss Heartdrops® for additional immune support.

Did You Know? The design of our immune system is complex and influenced by an ideal balance of many factors, not just diet, and especially not by any one specific food or nutrient. However, a balanced diet consisting of a range of vitamins and minerals, combined with healthy lifestyle factors like adequate sleep, proper gut health, exercise and low stress, most effectively primes the body to fight infection and disease.

What factors can depress our immune system?
- Older age
- Environmental toxins
- Excess weight
- Poor diet
- Chronic diseases
- Chronic mental stress
- Lack of sleep and rest

8 Steps to Help Support a Healthy Immune System
1. Eat a balanced diet
2. If a balanced diet is not readily accessible, taking herbals and a multivitamin can help
3. Don't smoke or quit if you do
4. Drink alcohol in moderation
5. Perform moderate regular exercise
6. Aim for 7-9 hours of sleep nightly
7. Aim to manage stress
8. Wash hands throughout the day

Please go to Straussnaturals.com

The End

Go write a 5-star review on Amazon.

www.ingramcontent.com/pod-product-compliance
Lightning Source LLC
Chambersburg PA
CBHW060459030426
42337CB00015B/1652